Cozumel

BELIZE
★ Belmopan
Semuc
Champey ● Roatán
GUATEMALA ●
Guatemala City HONDURAS
Atitlán ●●
Antigua ★ ● Tegucigalpa
San Salvador ★ ★
EL SALVADOR Leon ● NICARAGUA
Managua ●
● Corn Islands
San Juan del Sur ● Isla de
Playa Escameca ● Ometepe
● Puerto Viejo
COSTA RICA ● San Blas
Montezuma ● ★ Bocas del Toro Islands ● Cartagena
San José ★ PANAMA ★
Fortuna Panama ● The Darién Gap
Cloud Forest City

Minca ●

Medellin ●● Guatapé

★
Bogotá

COLOMBIA

Iquitos
●

PERU

★ Lima
Machu Picchu
●● Cusco
● Huacachina

TALES
OF THE
MODERN NOMAD

MONKS, MUSHROOMS & OTHER MISADVENTURES

JOHN EARLY

Cover Design: Relish New Brand Experience
Book Layout and Typography: Relish New Brand Experience
Editor: Suzanne Paschall

©2016 by John Early
www.johnearly.ca

Published by EarlyByrd Productions
Saskatoon, SK, Canada
johnearlynomad@gmail.com

Printed in Canada by Friesens Book Division
First edition: November, 2016

Permissions list for all copyrighted work used in this publication are
described on page 296.

Print ISBN 978-0-9952666-0-5
Electronic ISBN 978-0-9952666-1-2

LIBRARY AND ARCHIVES CANADA CATALOGUING IN PUBLICATION

Early, John, 1986-, author
        Tales of a modern nomad : monks, mushrooms & other
misadventures / John Early.

ISBN 978-0-9952666-0-5 (hardback)

        1. Early, John, 1986- --Travel. 2. Backpacking. 3. Voyages around
the world. I. Title.

G465.E27 2016   910.4'1   C2016-905657-0

DEDICATION

This book is dedicated to every person that has been a part of the journey and helped sustain my daily momentum in any way or form. Whether it was letting me sleep on your couch, picking me up on the side of the road, telling me about your secret travel spot, putting a word in for me about a job abroad, or simply sharing a laugh on a spontaneous adventure...I am ever grateful.

ACKNOWLEDGEMENTS

None of this would have been lived or written if it weren't for the support and encouragement from my family. To my parents and sister, Andi, I can't thank you enough for your love and understanding when I leave for months and years at a time. Suzanne Paschall for editing and believing in my crazy project. To Terry, Robyn and the team at Relish New Brand Experience for taking the initiative to forage through all 15 of my travel journals and really bringing this book to life.* To all my friends that have shared their insight when I randomly message them a poem or thought that needs feedback—especially Jayme Acres, Erica Siddall and Candace Fox. And lastly, thank you Norma and Normita— my guitar and ukulele—for always being there for me while I put you through some of the wildest of travel days and risky escapades.

*All the scribblings, sketches and design elements in this book have been scanned directly from the covers and pages of my travel journals.

♪♫ **Throughout the book these notes symbolize song lyrics of original tracks that can be streamed at www.johnearly.ca

All currency comparisons in the book use the US dollar as reference.

LIVE A LIFE WORTH JOURNALING

16 DAYS IN CHIANG MAI — TO LEARN THAI — 2015

me — High Rising tone
re — Middle tone
do — falling tone / Low tone

maa — 'horse'
maa — 'dog'
maa — 'come'
meh — 'mother'

TABLE OF CONTENTS

Introduction

I never intended to write this book. I also never intended to backpack the world for nearly a decade, along the way finding jobs and experiences I never knew existed.

Not planning, but doing, often brings out the truest intentions. I learned that lesson early on in my travels.

Go, adapt, learn, flow, create and smile. Those six verbs have got me nearly everything I've ever wanted out of life.

The keys to my natural evolution and growth as an individual have all been simple ways to approach and apply myself to an action or state of being. That is the essence of who I am and who I have continued to become.

My name is John.

Join me in the journey.

CHAPTER 1

You Are
Here

"Perhaps the most terrible (or wonderful) thing that can happen to an imaginative youth, aside from the curse (or blessing) of imagination itself, is to be exposed without preparation to the life outside his or her sphere—the sudden revelation that there is a there out there."

TOM ROBBINS, *JITTERBUG PERFUME*

NASA's photo of The Milky Way

The KNOWING

Venice, Italy.

Traveling really can change your approach to life.

I've learned more from backpacking
   solo than I ever could in a school
   or textbook.

Perspectives broaden.
     Relationships tighten.
     Gratitude for everything you
      have sinks in.
     You step further into yourself
      with each commitment to the
      potential in front of you.

Something gets ignited from within.
A passion for life.
     An independent spirit.
     A desire to keep moving
     as you discover different ways
      to get completely connected
     with the present moment.

I remember when it initially
   really hit me.
My first big trip:
     Seven months in Europe
      to finish my degree.
I was sitting with my original
   travel journal on a bridge in
   Venice, Italy.
     Radiohead's *Reckoner* started
      playing in my headphones.
     And I looked around.
In that moment, it was like I tapped
   into it
     without even knowing
     what *it* was.
I was suddenly interpreting life
   as if I was in on a secret
     that no one else knew existed.

But it does exist.
And I have been trying to put it
   in words
     while fueling the fire to
      keep it lit
     ever since.

Two full passports in 10 years has become my souvenir of good decisions. (Antigua, Guatemala)

DECISIONS.

~ YOU CAN ONLY GET BETTER AT THEM THE MORE YOU MAKE ~

- j. early

Ogoh-ogoh monsters during Bali's New Year's Eve parades. Photo: Jade Hyde

The Silence of
Nyepi

Balinese NYE, Ogoh-ogoh Monsters & Other Oddities As A Tourist

Just before my departure for Bali, Indonesia, I'm informed of two things:

1. I will be flying into Bali just before midnight on their Hindu New Year's Eve holiday, known as *Nyepi*.
2. This Balinese Hindu tradition means that everything shuts down, electricity is banned and it is punishable to eat or drink, or walk the city streets.

Information like this always feels to me like a sarcastic pat on the back when I'm heading to the airport for a solo trip to a foreign country—let alone for my first experience in Asia.

I'm boarding the last airplane, arriving or departing, to the central Indonesian island of Bali for the next 36 hours. It sounds like I'm the only person just discovering what I'm flying myself into; everyone else has planned a ride or friend to pick them up from the airport. *No taxis at the airport tonight? Lovely.*

As I exit the plane, the heavy humidity hits me like a wet, incense-scented sponge slapping me across the face. Due to the Nyepi holiday, I won't be able to escape staying less than two nights in the nearby town of Kuta—the repressive resort and club-lined residue of Indonesia's first beach to fall to foreign commercialization in the 1970s. With nearly everyone already locked into the darkness of their homes for the next 36 hours, I grudgingly pay four times the advised "max price" for an unofficial taxi from the airport to Kuta Beach. I can't complain however; he's the only transport option available and the rain is starting to pour.

I am dropped off to what I assume is the front of my hostel, but is actually a labyrinth of back alleys lined with Hindu shrine offerings. The passages are far too narrow for a car to fit through. All electricity is cut off and the city is void of life. Nyepi occurs during the first new moon of March, so I don't even have any moonlight to help me comprehend what land I've stepped into. I drag myself through a foot of stagnant water amid heavy rain as I question which wall or turn might be between me and a dry bed. I start cursing my beloved yet heavy guitar, Norma, for being my necessary travel companion. An eerie darkness blankets Norma and me along our lonely first steps within the continent of Asia. *Not the warmest welcome back to backpacking, eh girl?*

After an hour of soaked stumbling and backtracking, I finally hear the most consoling sound: English-speakers conversing behind my sign-less hostel. Ah, English: the comfort of familiarity that we all yearn to leave, yet immediately pine for when we veer too uncomfortably into the deep end of foreign travels. I sit with the group awhile and we enjoy the customary swap of traveler stories—including their experiences amidst the parade of Balinese *Ogoh-ogoh* monsters during the day's New Year's celebrations. I'm intrigued. Apparently, the *Ogoh-ogoh* monsters are the personification of Bali's underworld. These long-nailed, sharp-toothed, grotesque creatures are evil spirits which can never be destroyed, only appeased if people give them enough respect and plenty of offerings in the form of food, flowers, incense and public adoration. In the Nyepi celebration, the idea is almost to give the gargoyle-like creatures an "outing," balancing the distance between good and evil. *It makes waiting for a giant ball to drop in Times Square feel a bit culturally pale in comparison.*

As it turns out, that would be everyone's last conversation. The next day, religious police armed with machetes known as *pecalings* threaten us (politely, but sternly) for speaking or eating and thus not honoring their Nyepi day of silence. Thankfully, the kitchen in my hostel opens for a brief stint for us tourists that did not know or understand the cultural tradition. I hadn't eaten since my plane left Australia (hurray for being an ignorant tourist!). The rest of the day passes in contented (albeit forced) solitude via yoga, meditation—and, of course, the odd clandestine whispers about why Western countries would never be capable of implementing such a peaceful and consumption-free national holiday. The thought of Catholic priests wearing funky hats and carrying machetes whilst marching around monitoring the purchases of Christmas presents doesn't quite capture the same

The locals march their Ogoh-ogoh monsters on the eve of Nyepi.

cultural significance (although there's no doubt it would make an interesting video game)...

The following day, the silence is broken by crowds, congestion and catcalls for taxis and custom-made suits. East Indian and Pakistani street hustlers shout out to me in fake Aussie accents to buy knock-off American products made in China. They think they have a better chance of selling me something if they speak the new local dialect from the onslaught of Australian tourism. *Is this even Indonesia?* It feels like a culturally-appropriated tourist trap that could exist anywhere in the world with tropical weather and too many foreigners. I am fortunate to have had the rare moment to experience a still and silent Kuta Bali—except it won't be quiet again here until next year's Nyepi. *Time to get out of here!*

Waking up while traveling—not knowing where you are—can bring about the most liberating confusion to start a day.

I rent a scooter (for the outstanding daily rate of 30,000 rupiah or $3), and prepare to head north toward the island's two active volcanoes—away from the grime of Kuta Beach. Inhaling the island's rural aromas of wet rice paddies and feral chickens mixed with fried street *tempe* and sweet incense feels more like the Asia I had hoped to find. I fill up my motorbike with petrol from one of the many roadside *warungs* (street stands). I find it ironic that in Indonesia, they store gas in Absolut Vodka bottles—and yet in restaurants, they serve local arak alcohol from what appears to be

The local "gas station" in Kuta, Bali.

4-liter petrol containers. Either way, it helps explain why they both taste the same.

When my alarm goes off at 2 AM my initial reaction is to turn it off and go back to sleep. Then I'm hit by the confusion of this new darkness and bed I'm in. *Where am I and why am I awake in the middle of the night!?* As I wipe the sleep from my eyes I remember that I stopped for the night at a highway guesthouse outside of Ubud and signed up for a sunrise volcano hike. *Right... I'm backpacking Asia!* Waking up while traveling —not knowing where you are—can bring about the most liberating confusion to start a day. Like coming out of a dream to arrive into another dream: I'm thrown into this surreal surrounding with a new vibrancy that slowly sinks into familiar territory, liberating the soul. *Ok, let's climb a volcano!*

The active volcano, Mount Batur, is located four hours north of Kuta, and includes a pitch-black 4-kilometer trek before reaching the summit in time for sunrise. The venture involves several winding trips in the back of a truck and two hours of hiking by flashlight. Our group consists of six Canadians, two Germans and a token New Zealander. Everyone's tired minds and bodies start brightening up after our local guides tell us we've reached the top. Darkness begins to fade, revealing a mass of clouds that blanket our hopes of seeing anything at all, let alone the panoramic sunrise. Our group of Canadians predictably refrain from complaining and switch the topic to hockey.

While our guides serve us our complimentary hard-boiled "volcano eggs" someone shouts out in excitement. Everyone looks out as the clouds part in time to catch an orange ball surging from the ocean. Outlines of the surrounding mountains appear. The island of Lombok takes shape in the far eastern sea. Color spills into the sky. I breathe in deep as if I could inhale the surroundings. I take the moment to be thankful my alarm clock does not have a snooze button.

As day breaks atop Mount Batur, volcanic monkeys emerge from the vapors of the warm crater they live in, well aware when the feeding hands of tourists arrive.

The road from Mount Batur to Ubud—Bali's cultural hotbed and modern yogi Mecca —passes through colorful montages of fruit *warungs*, phenomenal rice terraces chiseled into the mountain and leftover *Ogoh-ogoh* monsters that were not burnt following

Locals vs urbanization outside of Ubud, Bali.

the Nyepi celebration. Following my map is tough since Bali is pretty inefficient at posting street signs. Taking the back roads I pass smiling villagers wearing their bright sarongs. They light their incense and consciously place their daily shrine offerings up to the gods and omens for good luck.

I pull over to the side of the road to watch a local child fly a kite from within his rice paddy playground. Just past the boy I see giant Hollywood lettering stating *Not For Sale*, a haunting theme that sticks with me as I consider the impact of massive tourism that's proliferated over the decades. Foreigners have provided both financial backing and burden to this small island, its people and culture. The sign makes a powerful statement as just further down the expanding sprawl of the city emerges, eating up farmland for resorts, buildings and street stands.

Whichever way you arrive into Ubud, it will be via one of the many bustling roads dense with endless art houses, stone masons or massage shops. Ubud definitely has a different energy and modern bohemian twist amidst remnants of the ancient Indonesian village. There are more yoga studios, fashion boutiques and organic cafes than the trendiest district of any major North American city. As good as the vibe is, it's nice that all it takes to escape the expats and women clinging to their copy of *Eat, Pray, Love* is to slip off the busy main street.

Looking for my homestay, I disappear into a labyrinth of mossy tiles, stonework and sculpture guardians that instantly take me to a

A worker hiking amid the rice terraces outside of Ubud.

different time and place. Behind the inner city walls lies the quiet and original Ubud village: water buffalo and slow farmers tending to open rice paddies by hand. They represent structures and lifestyles that have hardly changed over centuries.

There is a medium class resort visible from my second floor homestay terrace. I see one Westerner using Wi-Fi as he eats breakfast, while another sips a cocktail next to a beautiful pool that juts directly into the area's rice paddy where two local farmers have been harvesting by hand since sunrise. This baffles me. And yet here I am as well, with a digital camera in my hand, documenting this direct cultural barrier of a brick wall separating a rice paddy and a pool of luxury.

We Westerners love experiencing this *culture*—but often from a comfortable distance. And yet the Balinese people still smile at us throughout. Why? If some foreigner came peering into my farm in Canada, margarita in hand, taking pictures of me roto-tilling my garden at home, I would tell him to help out or buzz off. *Maybe I should start lighting more incense as an offering to the gods of happiness and understanding?*

Bali is a lot of things to a lot of people, and has been for decades. Whether you are searching for beaches, surf, eco-tourism, culture, spiritual enlightenment or simply that photo of someone living a different life from your own, Bali is a one-stop island. As I write this (early 2012) plans are underway to rebuild Denpasar, the island's international airport, extending its annual 4.5 million tourists to 20 million. This will make those amazing discoveries a little more difficult to find. Which brings me back to my first impressions on arrival: Whether Bali's infrastructure, people, or culture are ready or not for further masses their Nyepi day of silence will continue to be more important than ever.

MARCH 2012
UBUD, INDONESIA

NYEPI: A Breakdown of the Balinese Hindu New Year

There's more to Nyepi than just being quiet...

Three days before Nyepi:
Melasti aka *Mekiyis* or *Melis*
(The Colorful Ceremonies March)
A cleansing rite, one of the purposes of Melasti is to bathe all the effigies of gods from the temples in natural water (therefore cleansed by the Neptune of the Balinese, God Baruna). The march to the ocean, lake or river is both long and colorful, and once there, the gods are ceremonially bathed before being taken back home to their shrines and temples.

One day before Nyepi:
Tawur Kesanga (New Year's Eve)
This is when most of the action takes place. Also known as the 'Day of Great Sacrifices,' all the villagers dressed in traditional costume come together in the town centers for a kind of mass exorcism rite (with the capital of Bali, Denpasar, staging the grandest procession). This

is a day full of color, excitement, party vibes, and that all-important Balinese carnivalesque atmosphere accompanied by traditional gamelan instruments and music called *Bleganjur*. Handmade monsters made of bamboo called *Ogoh-ogoh* are paraded about in a bid to ward off evil spirits, or *Bhuta Kala*. They are then hoisted up on sticks, offered gifts of food and flowers, and then burnt in a huge and completely riotous bonfire of a ceremony! Curfew alert: Make sure you're back in your hotel by nightfall.

Nyepi Day
(New Year's Day)
Now that all evil has been successfully warded off, Nyepi is the day for the Balinese to demonstrate their newfound self-control. There'll be absolutely no traffic outside—motorized or pedestrian. Stay inside, don't work, talk, drink alcohol, cook or light fires. (And don't let the darkness put you in a romantic mood because *that's* not allowed either!)

The Day After Nyepi
Ngembak Geni
As of 6 am, the Hindus of Bali traditionally forgive each other via an array of activities that form part of the Dharma Canthi. These include reading ancient scripts and singing songs—namely, *Sloka, Kekidung, Kekawin* and others.

CHEERS!

It doesn't matter where you are in the world or what the language, you should at the very least be able to say *cheers* in the country you're traveling in.

Here's my cheat sheet[1]:

Afrikaans	*Gesondheid!*	[ge-sund-hate]	Health!
Arabic	صحتك:	[fe sahetek]	Good luck!
Chinese (Mandarin)	干杯 *gān bēi!*	[gan bay]	Drink a toast!
Croatian	*Živjeli*	[zhee-ve-lee]	Cheers!
Czech	*Na zdravi!*	[naz-dra vi]	To your health!
Danish	*Skål!*	[skoal]	Good health!
Dutch	*Proost!*	[prohst]	Cheers!
Filipino	*Tagay!*	[mah-boo-hay]	Cheers!
Finnish	*Kippis!*	[kip-piss]	Bottoms up!
French	*Santé!*	[sahn-tay]	Health!
German	*Prost!*	[prohst]	Cheers!
Greek	*ΥΓΕΙΑ!*	[yamas]	Health!
Hawaiian	*Åʻkålè maʻluna*	[okole maluna!]	Bottoms up!
Hebrew	לחיים	[l'chaim!]	To life!
Hungarian	*Fenékig*	[fehn-eh-keg]	Until the bottom of the glass
Italian	*Salute!*	[saw-lutay]	Health!
Japanese	乾杯	[kan-pai]	Dry the glass!
Korean	건배	[gun bae]	Toast!
Lao	ສຸງໄຊ	[tam chok]	Cheers!
Norwegian	*Skål*	[skawl]	Good health!
Portuguese	*Saúde!*	[saw-oo-de]	Health!
Russian	На здоровье	[na zdorovje]	To your health!
Spanish	*¡Salud!*	[sah-lud]	Health!
Swedish	*Skål*	[skawl]	Good health!
Thai	โชคดี	[chok dee]	Good luck!
Turkish	*Şerefe!*	[sher-i-feh]	Honor!
Ukrainian	будьмо	[boodmo]	Stay good!
Vietnamese	*Một hai ba, yo!*	[moat hi bah, yo]	1, 2, 3, drink!
Welsh	*Lechyd da!*	[yeh-chid dah]	Good health!
Yiddish	געזונטהייט	[say geh-sund]	Be well!

Songkran celebrations in Nongkhai, Thailand.
© *Thanagon Karaket*

SONGKRAN –
Surviving the World's Biggest Water Fight!

Celebrating Thailand's New Year's Party in Chiang Mai

The brown water lapping in the streets is now creeping up past the curb. Relentless screams and shrieks stifled by ears full of water create a steady background of high-pitched white noise. Traffic has been at a standstill for hours with people fully armored in the backs of trucks like a modern D-Day invasion. I trudge through the water and the crowd with two hands readied on a shotgun, bucket over my shoulder and a smaller pistol strapped to my leg. I ignore the hit from my left because I'm already caught in the crossfire of a dozen people in black bandanas battling for the moat on my right. My body is buzzing the further I march forward. The entire city seems to be caught in an attempt to push towards the epicenter of this energy another 200 meters or so ahead, the main source of this mayhem. I can't stop smiling if I try.

This is Songkran. There's no better way to ring in a new year than with the weeklong craziness that is the world's largest water fight. Thailand's New Year's celebration hits every mid-April with official festivities held over three consecutive days from April 13-15. What started as a tradition of cleansing Buddha statues and images with water and fragrance to bring luck to the new year has exploded into a national holiday based on soaking strangers in the city streets. The timing is right for getting wet, as April is the hottest and driest month of the year in Thailand—even though those managing the strained municipal water reserves might think otherwise.

Songkran
is among the best public forms of joyful chaos you can find.

Songkran is recognized across all of the Buddhist countries of Southeast Asia with the most notorious celebration being held in the northern Thai city of Chiang Mai. Known for its rich culture and abundance of temples, the moat and water that surround the old inner city that provide the perfect battleground and unending fuel for the world's biggest waterfight. Like a wet bucket of shenanigans delivered right to the face, Songkran is among the best public forms of joyful chaos you can find. Just make sure to commit to the full three days of formal water warfare—travel days during Songkran will bring nothing but delays, traffic, soaked luggage and a long trip in wet underwear.

So extend your stay, grab a back-up bucket and embrace the local ways! As you stand in the streets and laugh like an eight-year-old with a water gun, you'll question why the rest of the world doesn't get in on the annual tradition.

APRIL 2013
CHIANG MAI, THAILAND

Photo: Takeaway

TIPS FOR SURVIVING SONGKRAN

Unwritten Rule #1: It is important to continue to respect Thai culture regardless of the debauched nature of the holiday. It is still *their* holiday and not just for drunken tourists, so make sure you wear a shirt in public and refrain from drinking alcohol openly in the streets, for starters.

Unwritten Rule #2: Water throwing only takes place between *sunrise* and *sunset.*

Unwritten Rule #3: It doesn't matter who you are, where you are or what you're wearing…if you are outside of your hotel room and the sun is up… game *on!*

Unwritten Rule #4: Avoid using the dirty street water in your water gun or bucket. Keep it clean!

Unwritten Rule #5: It's okay to pee your pants! With local businesses (and bathrooms) either closed or packed full of soaked bodies, you will never find a more satisfying time to pee your pants with your mates in a downtown city street.

Practical Tips:

1. **Memorize this line:** "*Sah wah dee pee mai kahp!*" It means *Happy New Year* in Thai and you should be shouting it with enthusiasm at all the amazing Thai people who have welcomed you to their celebration!

2. **Don't attempt to ride a bike or motorbike in the streets** during Songkran. Trying to battle traffic in Asia is hard enough without getting a bucket of water directly to the face (car accidents also happen to skyrocket during Songkran).

3. **Use a headband or ear plugs to cover your ears**—a direct hit to the inner ear is NOT fun. On that note, you should probably also buy some $1 sunglasses from a local vendor that wrap around your eyes—getting shot in the eyes is even less enjoyable.

4. **Make sure you're wearing strap-on sandals.** You will likely lose your flip-flops in the street water. If you don't have strap-on sandals, hopefully you've been in Asia long enough that your bare feet can handle the beating.

5. **Buy a decent water gun, but don't bother dropping too much money** as everything will likely break within the day anyway. If you're sticking close to the moat or a main water source, then a bucket and the local homemade one-pump shotguns make the best combination.

6. **Thaepae Gate (or The East Gate)** along the moat of Chiang Mai's inner old city is the heartbeat of Songkran. With stages, DJs, foam parties and more, it is worth getting to if you can battle through the people.

You will read some information that will help you.

SURVIVING THE LINGERING AFTERMATH OF SONGKRAN

After three straight days of pruned toes, trigger finger giddiness and late nights partying along *Backpackers Alley*, I'm ready to dry out and leave behind the madness of Songkran. I'm catching a bus out of Chiang Mai to venture north to Laos for a quick visa run and zip-line some jungle tree houses. What I'm starting to realize, however, is how much the locals like to stretch Songkran into a weeklong event. When you are prepared, a bit buzzed, and ready for a water fight, Songkran is pure joy and exuberant chaos. When you are dry, have all your bags packed and you get caught downtown in an open-air *tuk-tuk* taxi trying to make a bus on time…Songkran is just pure chaos.

Norma (my guitar) and I barely survive our wild *tuk-tuk* to the bus station. Even with my backpack and guitar sealed in garbage bags, the backseat prepped with splashguards and the streets of Chiang Mai slowly returning back to normal, a stop at a red light still makes me a sitting duck for a stranger's water bucket to the face. The aggressive, younger locals might even peel back the splashguard of a *tuk-tuk* to make sure nothing and no one dry is left. *Ok, ha ha…yeah, you got me…dee mak, ya little scoundrel…*

As I arrive to the bus station, weariness is evident on the faces of many—both locals and tourists—getting out of their taxis and in line for tickets. If their faces don't express defeat, their soaked clothes and baggage sure do. My first reaction boarding the beat-up public bus to cross eight hours through Northern Thailand in 104 degree F. heat without AC is to open my window as wide as it goes. Not this week. Sitting down, all the locals immediately close their windows amid the dank humidity of the bus. Fighting the natural urge for fresh air, I close my window like the rest. I start sweating faster than my friend's mom when she accidently ended up at a Bangkok Ping Pong Show (*put that in your scrapbook, Margaret!*). As we pull away, the bus starts reeking of human perspiration. It feels like a steamed can of sardines. *This is why you never wear clean underwear on travel days, John!*

We are not even 10 minutes outside of Chiang Mai and I start to crack... *Air flow. I need air...* I reach up, open my window, and it sucks air in like an open door on an airplane. The breeze welcomingly blows the sweat off my forehead and a grin crosses my face like a dog with its head out the window. I let out a glorious— although slightly guilty—sigh of relief, then catch other people's eyes anxiously glance back as they wonder who cracked the seal. Less than a minute ticks by. Our bus passes a rural village, stops at the only stop sign in sight and a giant bucket of water is thrown directly at my window—the only opening on the bus. My face and everyone around me gets soaked. Besides the initial shrieks on impact, the local Thais exhibit their typical polite temperance by taking the blast in silence, wiping off their mobile screens and sitting contently in wet clothes like nothing happened.

Thailand is a perfect country for a traveler.

It's completely authentic. Wholly and simply Thailand. The country has its own language, alphabet, cuisine, currency, and king! It's the only country in Southeast Asia that was never colonized by a foreign empire, so there is a direct lineage and history that Thai culture draws on that isn't influenced or crossbred by other nations or people—an extremely rare situation. Add in some of the world's most beautiful beaches and it's no wonder Thailand is a top tourist and bustling backpacker destination.

I immediately put the window up, just in time for another wave of water to hit the bus from the buckets of local villagers now lining the street. I raise my dripping hand, admitting guilt. "*Khor to...ah,*" I sputter out an attempt at a public Thai apology. "*Khor thot khappa...* ah shit. My bad amigos!" I shout.

A cute Thai girl across from me hides a quiet laugh with her hand as she brushes water off her seat. For the next eight hours north toward Laos, the two of us share a smile and laugh each time our bus gets hit by a bucket of water. *Oh, Thailand. You and your Songkran...*

Sah wah dee pee mai kahp!

APRIL 2013
CHIANG KHONG, THAILAND

THE TRAVELER'S LUXURY

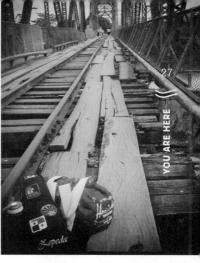

The freedom to float
Such is true luxury though
For the traveler's life
                    is rife
With so many places to go
So skip the plans
                    in your hands
And see how the future can flow
When you show nothing
                    But trusting
Your traveling freedom
                    to float

APRIL 2016

PUERTO VIEJO, COSTA RICA

Traversing the sketchy train bridge
border cross of Sixaola between Costa
Rica and Panama. When neither side
owns the bridge...neither side pays
to maintain it.

MARCH 2010 / SAN FRANCISCO

The glory of traveling solo is that because
you are free of previous judgments you can
become one of two things:
    1) any person you want
    2) yourself

After long enough...they're both the same choice.

Mocean Yoga Retreat, Nicaragua

"I WISH YOU ALL
THE SMILES
YOU CAN FIND
IN THE WORLD"

Thai long-tail boats on an island off Koh Lanta.

My 7 Travel Essentials

Living out of a backpack means what you choose as your *baggage* has to carry its weight—literally. The fewer things you own, the more you connect with them, appreciate them and realize what makes and keeps you, you. This is when material objects become your life and vice versa. Whether it's a musical instrument, a watch from your grandpa, a bracelet from a friend, a little trinket to include in all your photos, or that one postcard you will never mail home, everyone has personal items reminding them of home and keeping them grounded while on the road. Just like the saying, "You become the people you choose to surround yourself with," your journey reflects what you choose to carry on your back.

Outside of personal choices, there are obviously some practical things you need to pack as you cruise through foreign cultures, loud hostels and long travel days. Here are a few of my top must-haves that I've found handy during my past decade on the road.

Ear plugs, also useful so you don't lose your hearing as you lose yourself dancing in front of the bass bins until sunrise. The Lapa Stage at the 2016 Envision Festival, Costa Rica

Custom Ear Plugs

Being able to shut out the external environment for some peace and quiet when it's needed is priceless. Whether it's a flight, bus, loud bar next to your room or simply to save you from throwing a shoe at that one guy who snores in your dorm, they're essential. Regular cheapo earplugs are fine, but I've found it's worth the $80 to invest in sleeper plugs that custom fit your ear, don't fall out and really drop things down a good 30 decibels...*like floating underwater.*

Probiotics

It doesn't matter where you travel in the world, food is made and sourced differently and can take some getting used to. Travelers Trots, Delhi Belly or Montezuma's Revenge are all ways of saying, "You're not from here, your guts are going to have to sort some shit out..." (and there's no better sign that you're a veteran traveler than casual poop talk with a stranger). So be proactive with a daily probiotic and boost that digestive system, ideally with a shelf-stable product since having constant access to a fridge can be a luxury. I take *Renew Life's FloraSmart* daily; grapefruit seed extract if I'm feeling off, and ginseng extract to boost the immune system and for a clean, energizing lift!

Probiotics, because anything that could help prevent getting sick and having to use a local Indonesian squatting toilet is WORTH it. (With only a bucket of water to rinse after...it's a fine art to leave with anything clean and dry.)

A Dry Bag

Some places rain—a lot. A dry bag on travel days (especially during rainy seasons) to keep your passport and electronics dry is crucial. A good dry bag is also key for a beach or day bag, and to seal up food at night so critters don't get at it. Or throw ice in it with some beers and use it as a cooler! *Salud!*

A dry bag, also handy to hide your food away from night critters...until the acrobatic super rat of Gigante, Nicaragua clambers down and chews through the waterproof material and plastic bags to eat your packet of Oreos! My early morning shout of "That motherfucker!" made the other private rooms respond through the paper-thin walls with "Ha ha, that rat get your munchies too?" and "Yeah, Henry's always got a sweet tooth."

A Blank Journal

You should always be open and ready for an experience worth journaling. It gives personal depth to your pictures and stories and much needed time to chill and reflect on your travels. It'll feel like work, and in the moment it will seem like you'll never forget the important things...but it's often the small things that are worth noting and that are often forgotten: names of locals, names of hostels, prices you've paid (it's interesting to see how quickly things inflate in upcoming countries), local slang, quotes from your friends, etc. Other travelers you meet will appreciate your references and your older self will appreciate your personal time capsule.

A blank journal, always a best friend when you are lost in your own oasis. (Huacachina, Peru) Photo by Free & Easy ambassador Brooke Willson.

*Sunday Funday
tight game strong!*

Tights!

And finally, not the most obvious, or sometimes the most practical thing…but hot damn tights feel great! Ok, they also work well for yoga, keep you warm camping and save you from wearing board shorts in those unexpectedly cold mountain towns (Monteverde, Costa Rica…) while also packing up really small in your bag. But most importantly, when the party calls and things start to get a little weird, tights gives you that bright and funky spring in your step so you can dance all night under the full moon light!

So pack light, appreciate your baggage and never take traveling for granted!

MARCH 2016
SAN JUAN DEL SUR, NICARAGUA

Norma, my guitar, the real thing I never travel without— especially when we hitchhike to Sayulita, Mexico.

A Colombian street dancer in Cartagena.

*Getting lost is so **wanderfull**. (Hidden lagoon hike in Railay, Thailand). Photo: Benjamin Neil*

DAILY DILEMMAS OF A TRAVELER

Ok, where am I?
Where am I sleeping tomorrow night?
Have I made that reservation yet?
I should probably buy a ticket early.
Crap, it's full.
How much cash do I have?
I think that guy kept my phone charger...
Dammit, where's my passport??
Hey, who's that?
Oh, she's cool.
Shoot, she leaves tomorrow?
Where's that other crew going?
What's to do there?
How would I get there?
Do I have time for that?

I shouldn't backtrack.
If I stay west, I can't go east.
Would that throw off my plan?
Do I have a plan?
Wait.
Okay.
Deep breath.
Relax.
I can't do it all
—or perfectly.
Let's not try.
Look where I am.
I am.
   Here.

MAY 2015
CARTAGENA, COLOMBIA

37 Minutes in
MYANMAR
A PHOTO JOURNAL OF
MY BORDER RUN TO BURMA

"I can't cook tomorrow…I have to go to Burma!"

"Tomorrow Sunday," Phaiwan says without looking up from her breakfast of spicy rice soup. "Burma closed."

"Oh, right. *Chai chai.*" I answer. There are only a couple days left on my 90-day Thai visa and I am in need of a border run to extend my stay to continue leading adventure travel trips in the amazing country that is Thailand.

"Burma close all border on Sunday. In or out, *same-same*—no open." Phaiwan explains to me. "So *chai*, you make *massaman* with me tomorrow!" She looks up at me, flashes her well-known smile and laughs.

My Thai guard escort to the Burmese border.

Phaiwan is the owner of Smiley's Guesthouse in Khao Sok. She's been the Thai mother to the entire staff of Free & Easy Traveler since we started running backpacker trips there in the early 2000s. "I take you to bus stop Monday, only after you cook!" We both laugh. She knows how much I love the food she makes, especially when I get to help share her secrets in a Thai cooking class. With homemade dishes that include delicacies like *massaman* curry, *tom yum kung* soup and *phad thai*, Myanmar can wait another day.

My knowledge of Myanmar (formerly known as—and frequently still called—Burma), includes the following:

▶ The borders have only recently been open to tourists after many years of civil unrest, making it the new backpacking hotspot for untouched culture and authentic experiences away from the tourist masses that frequent Southeast Asia.

▶ The Canadian government webpage on Myanmar currently advises against "all travel to areas along the borders with Thailand due to clashes between the military and armed groups, ethnic conflict, banditry and unmarked landmines."

▶ A lot of online media posts on Myanmar link to the last Rambo movie. It was filmed along the Burmese border and Sylvestor Stallone called it "hell beyond your wildest dreams" (they filmed in 2007 amid the aftermath of the genocide and protests).

So naturally, I'm going to jump at the chance to do my visa run to Myanmar (instead of the more common Cambodia run from Bangkok). In my experience, governments and media tend to exaggerate reality to either save their butts or create a story. Regardless, reverse psychology works wonders on backpackers seeking a rare experience: Tell us we can't go somewhere? We'll find a way to make it happen. Forbid us to take pictures? We'll only turn off the flash. Show us a secret spot away from tourists? We'll blog it all over the Internet. *Crazy farangs…*

The following morning, I'm up at 6:30 AM to catch a ride with Phaiwan to the local bus stop 40 minutes away. I board a public double-decker bus that has bright '90s carnival graffiti on the outside and an interior color palette that seems to have been selected by pre-school girls. As I sit in my bright pink seat with light blue trim, it becomes evident I am the only white foreigner on the bus (and likely for miles in all directions).

As contradicting as our cultures might be, it proves we're all the same: status prevails and we want what we can't have.

Ah…so Myanmar or Burma?

The ruling military junta changed the country's name from Burma to Myanmar in 1989. The change was accepted by the United Nations and many other countries, but not by the US or the UK. Which name to use is often more a political choice than a linguistic one, but internationally both names are often recognized. As for the local people, they often stick with Burma for talking and Myanmar for formal writing.

The locals all smile at me and point to or remark on my beautiful white skin. To me, I am just a pale Irish descendent unable to tan properly. But here in Thailand, my skin is a pasty luxury that is often sought through the use of skin bleaching and whitening products. To be white in Asia indicates beauty and social ranking; you don't have to earn a living by laboring in the hot sun. Such a contrast to the western view, where a tan and dark skin can signify the luxury of being able to relax outside or vacation during winter months. As contradicting as our cultures might be, it proves we're all the same: status prevails and we want what we can't have.

The three-hour trip to the border town of Ranong is a crowded ride that involves four police patrol stops getting on the bus to look at passports. With Thailand being one of the wealthiest countries in Southeast Asia, its poorer neighbors often seek a better life in *The Land of Smiles*. When my passport is quickly handed back unopened, the officer just smiles as if to say "well I know *you're* not Burmese."

I spend the rest of the ride either holding someone's child (kids in public places are sometimes considered a community responsibility in Asia) or trying to find out the name of the passing town so I can trace my way back tonight. All the locals around me are eager to help the sole tourist while practicing their broken English. I step off the bus with one of the mothers that understands my minimal Thai. She arranges a man on a motorbike to get me the rest of the way to the pier that borders Myanmar. We negotiate a return price—after he promises he'll wait for my arrival back from Burma—and I hop on the back of his motorbike to race across the last street stands of Thailand.

Here are a few pictures of my 37 minutes in Myanmar.

While I'm escorted by the local Thai authorities, this is the first of several immigration checkpoints entering Myanmar's waters.

The Burmese border town of Kawthoung. We arrive at the pier and our young boat driver is insistent that I not spend more than five minutes getting my passport stamped before heading straight back to the boat— probably so I won't find out that my 500 baht ($14) return trip only costs 50 baht from a local Burmese driver.

This young local helps dock our long-tail boat and knows where to find the best local coconut rum. At first I think he's using a skin whitener like in Thailand, but he's wearing Thanaka. Thanaka is made from ground bark and smells fragrant like sandalwood. It has apparently been used in Burma for well over 1000 years to make attractive designs on the face and body and cleanse the skin while protecting from the sun.

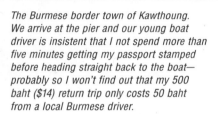

Getting off the long-tail boat I get approached by a few locals that want to talk with me and help me get around town. Many just sit smoking, pointing to the immigration office, familiar with the visa run process. On arrival to the Burmese customs office, a young man named Ali tells me "Oh sorry, closed. Lunchtime. Go walk around. But don't go too far." Welcome to Myanmar border security.

The lady at this street stall isn't finger-painting or making thanaka paste; she's satisfying the local Burmese craving for betel chewing. Betel leaf is an addictive stimulant similar to chewing tobacco. In Myanmar the leaf is commonly smeared with a white slaked-lime paste and various herbs and spices like cloves, cinnamon, aniseed, tobacco, grated coconut or nuts. It is then rolled up and put into one's mouth to suck on while spitting out the juices.

A Thai playground.

After spending a year in Thailand I can finally notice the subtle differences between Thai and Burmese writing. Thai Sanskrit is a series of lines and swirls that often end with a loop at the end resembling a snake like body and head. Burmese is more a series of connected hoops and rings without accents above the symbols. Neither alphabet requires spaces between words.

≡ နို့လွတ်ရည်အအေး
≡ နွားနို့အအေး
≡ သံပုရာရှိတ်
≡ ချောကလက်ရှိတ်
≡ စတော်ဘယ်ရီရှိတ်

It is humbling traveling & living in a country where they don't speak your language ... because you stop talking so much.

A menu in Myanmar.

I have only been in Myanmar for 35 minutes when the young long-tail driver finally finds me and demands I get back on the boat to return to Thailand. I could stay here for 35 *days* and still be fascinated by the difference from Thai culture, just minutes away. It feels wrong to leave a country without the impression that you've truly seen it. But that is the beauty of the snowball effect that becomes the traveler's vortexw: The more you explore, the more you uncover that requires additional travel. The driver hands me his cell phone with his boss on the other end to further prove his need to hurry. *Okay, got it. Time to head back to the Land of Smiles...Burma I'll be back!*

The traveler's vortex: The more you explore, the more you uncover that requires additional travel.

The afternoon is only a brief encounter with a country fresh from decades of civil unrest. With the borders now open to the world, Burmese culture is susceptible to both the opportunity and pillaging that comes with Western tourism and its lifestyle. The boat driver tells me there are already young Burmese women that prefer to wear expensive foreign make-up and skin whiteners than look like a 'villager' wearing their own cultural *thanaka* paste. *There's nothing like First World tourism in a developing country to make a local want what they don't have...*

I land back at the pier in Thailand after only a few hours away, and it already looks like a four-star resort in comparison: paved streets, proper signage, higher prices and a lot more organization of the chaos. My motorbike friend stays true to his word and gets me back just in time to catch the last bus to Khao Sok National Park. My 37 minutes in Myanmar were fun, but I have to get back to work; Phaiwan and I have some more massaman curry to cook...

Chok dee kahp!

OCTOBER 2013
KHAO SOK, THAILAND

TOP 7 COOLEST HOSTELS

Casa En El Agua
Archipiélago de San Bernardo, Colombia

Built on a reef from an old locals fishing post, it's impossible to sleep any closer to the blue Caribbean water. Whether you rent a room or a hammock, your dinner options are chosen from the fresh seafood kept in a coral locker below the floor!

Zephyr Lodge
Lanquin, Guatemala

Perched on a hill with near 360-degree views of the central highlands of Guatemala, Zephyr Lodge has mastered the balance of party and chill out vibes while being close to the must-see natural wonder of Semuc Champey.

Semuc Champey is a limestone bridge and series of turquoise pools that has naturally developed above the Cahabón River which runs underneath.

Green Tortoise Hostel
San Francisco, US

Housed in an old hotel built shortly after the 1906 San Francisco earthquake, the giant ballroom makes for a funky hangout, eating area and jam space with instruments always on stage. Since 1974, Green Tortoise has also offered multi-week road trips (including a trip to Burning Man) and sits in the heart of the city between Little Italy, the Red Light District and Chinatown.

HUMANS OF GREEN TORTOISE:
[Lindsay the Welsh Clown is making balloon animals in the ballroom]
"Lindsay! Are you making balloon animals?"
[He throws a big bag of weed on the table and answers in his thick Welsh accent]
"I'm selling pot, Johnny."
[The next morning, talking to a girl named Sandy Moonbeam over breakfast]
"For the record Johnny, never buy pot off a clown."

Smiley Bungalows & Lakehouse
Khao Sok, Thailand

The floating bungalows on Chiew Lan Lake within Khao Sok National Park are not only the perfect way to escape the crowded tourist trails of Thailand but also the ideal place to eat family-style local meals while listening to the incredible call of the gibbon monkey.

I WONDER IF ANYONE'S EVER SUSTAINED AN ARGUMENT LAYING IN A HAMMOCK..

Naked Tiger Sunset

Naked Tiger Hostel
San Juan del Sur, Nicaragua

Atop the hills overlooking San Juan del Sur is home to the weekly Sunday Funday Poolcrawl (aka *The Biggest Party In Central America*). Whether you stay at the Naked Tiger or not you will end up partying more than you sleep there.

The Arts Factory Lodge
Byron Bay, Australia

The Arts Factory is its own functional community just outside of Byron Bay. With amenities like pool, beach volleyball court, giant sleeper teepees, recording studio, cafe, didgeridoo-making pit, onsite brewery, cow-couch movie cinema and jungle camping... plan to stay longer than intended.
For more about the Arts Factory see page 138

Arts Factory Reception

Casa Elemento
Minca, Colombia

Located over 2000 feet high up in the Sierra Nevada mountains over Colombia's Caribbean coast, Casa Elemento is a perfect escape from the bustle and heat of the tourist towns and also boasts some of the world's largest hammocks to soak in the views.

YOU ARE HERE

BETWEEN WAKING and SLEEPING

The darkness is blacker than normal
  and I haven't even closed my eyes yet.
I lay back.
With a deep breath
  I let the motions of the day
      filter through me:
  Conversations,
    catchy melodies
       and future desires
    get blended,
    rewound
      and processed again.
The flush continues
  from mind through body
  as I feel the stir of earlier
    movements
      like a physical déjà vu.
I must have been in a car for
  a while today.
    I can still feel the wheels
      turning.
Was I swimming in the ocean this
  morning?
    I can still feel the waves
      flowing
It's a full body buzz.
The kind you only get
  when you finally slow down,
      stop,
      and listen.

I lay still
  but begin to swim in my skin.
A deeper breath
  helps further filter the clutter,
    and I'm off on the ride.
I am left alone
  to drift
  between the constellations
    of my thoughts.
Pure thought.
Without resistance
    of the day's countless
      interactions.
The more I give in,
  the more I accept.
  The more I accept,
  The further refined the thought
    rests
    on one
      simple
       breath of content.
The kind of unsolicited fulfillment
  that I wish
    would rise
      with my every morning.

FEBRUARY 2014
LEON, NICARAGUA

The local laundromat and volcano of Nicaragua's Ometepe island.

A Dry Tropical Haiku

*Palm trees and cactus
together on holiday
Nicaragua coast*

WHEN THE SKY BECOMES EXTINCT

Living at Cashew Hill Jungle Lodge in Costa Rica, we are used to hearing all types of comments and questions from new tourists unaccustomed with jungle life. Most often it involves the intense tropical heat, surplus of huge bugs, seeing a sloth for the first time or waking up to the terrifying sounds of howler monkeys. And rightfully so; these are all things that people don't exactly encounter in daily life at home. But nothing prepared me for the most unexpected instance of culture shock I had ever come across. The concept was so foreign—it was actually quite saddening.

"Sorry," I say. "I didn't understand your question."

"S'it normally this bright?" She says again in her thick British accent.

I look around quick. "Sorry, your porch light is too bright?"

Ten minutes earlier I had helped her and her friend with a late night check-in into one of the jungle lodges. They were both in their 20s and had just flown in from the UK for a two-week vacation.

She laughs. "Nah mate, the *sky*! S'it normally this bright out 'ere? I've never seen so many stars!"

I pause for a second then look up from the table outside the Cashew Hill main reception. "Actually," I say trying to break the news gently. "There are barely any stars tonight. The moon is out and you can hardly see the Big Dipper over there."

"Nah, you takin' the piss outta me?" She responds, pointing up to the north. "That up there is the Big Dipper??"

"Yeah, you see those seven stars faintly there and then the North Star up above? I mean it's visible everywhere in the northern hemisphere...sorry, where are you guys from?"

"London, England," her friend responds. "And nah, I've never really seen stars before. We don't really get any of 'em in the big bright haze of the city. But it's really quite somthin', ain't it?"

"Hold on," I say, closing my laptop to focus fully on what she just said. "Neither of you have ever *see the stars before??*"

The notion hit me like a ton of coconuts. *Never seen the stars before.* Wow. What an unexpected luxury it is to grow up in a rural area or spend time in the jungles of Central America.

As the passing weeks go on, the idea keeps recurring: How many people have actually seen the true night sky—unobstructed by the expanding flood of city lights? It turns out to be a difficult question to answer. The more I ask around, the more I start to realize that a lot of people growing up with suburban lives have a skewed idea of what the space above us is *supposed* to look like. There is so much more to it than a couple of stars here and there or a polluted haze that we look at through our phones to be told where planets and constellations allegedly are. The heavens exist! And so do we—right in the middle of our galaxy, the Milky Way, which is visible to our naked eye…or was.

According to *Science Advances*[2], one-third of humanity is no longer able to see the Milky Way—including 60% of Europeans and 80% of Americans. The urban areas where the majority of people now live are simply too dense with light pollution. We have created a permanent "skyglow" above us. Instead of seeing our place in the universe, we have replaced it with streetlights, neon signs and giant billboards. Talk about a shock from culture.

What a sad realization: The biggest thing that exists—our night sky—is becoming extinct. If only we could trap it and put it in a zoo. Or maybe that will be the biggest selling point for buying an expensive ticket for future space tourism: *The chance to see the stars as they once were seen from Earth!*

These are our living heavens, not to be taken for granted. The night sky has been visible to us since the beginning to remind us where and why we exist. Let's not let it die out.

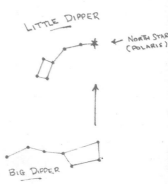

Navigation 101: To find the North Star (Polaris), look for the Big Dipper and line up the front two stars until they reach the bright star on the end of the Little Dipper. You now know which way is North!

*A Coconut is technically not a nut or a fruit…it's a seed.

CHAPTER 2

Lost in Translation

ร้านก๋วยเตี๋ยวปลา

จันทร์–เสาร์ เปิด ๐๙.๐๐–๒๐.๐๐ น.
อาทิตย์ เปิด ๐๙.๐๐–๑๗.๐๐ น.

โทร. 087-8987207

ก๋วยเตี๋ยวปลา   ปลาสำลีมี่มะนาว
ต้มยำปลาปลา   ปลาสำลีแดดเดียว
ข้าวต้มปลา   ปลาสำลีทอดน้ำปลา
แกงส้มปลา   ข้าวหมก
นางหางปลาเค็ม   ก๋วยเตี๋ยว
ต้มยำหัวปลา   ข้าวผัดขึ้น

"A DRIFTER IS ONLY LOST WHEN HE CAN'T RELATE TO THAT WHICH SURROUNDS HIM."

— J. GAREY

Adventures with Japanese Toilets
One-Man Water Fights with Airport Bum Guns

I'm currently sitting in Tokyo's Narita Airport. It's a quick layover as I await my flight to Nicaragua after spending a year in Thailand. I booked my flights through Japan so I could get a taste of a country I've always wanted to visit. Of course, as far as airport experiences go, I could be anywhere in the world. NRT is a typical bland international terminal: long grey corridors, giant duty-free perfume posters hung from high ceilings, and endless automatic walkways that make you feel like a minimal-effort superman heading somewhere important. I'd get the same cultural experiences stuck in a vacuum. I have come to realize, however, one thing that sets this airport apart on the international scene...they have the *best* toilets.

Never have I had so much choice and luxury with a public room of rest. Seat warming, deodorization, waterfall sounds, massaging... *cleansing of the buttocks*?? Why are we North Americans living in the dark ages of toiletry? In Japan airports you can choose from sit toilets, family toilets, bum fountains and even the classic squatter toilets (since after all, I *am* still in Asia). I had done enough squatting after a year in Thailand, so I decide to go with the simple sit

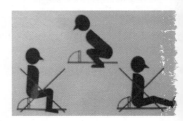

Photo: Yuya Tamai

toilet—except this thing is far from simple. Thank Buddha it comes with instructions.

Upon sitting down, I'm pleased to discover that the seat warmer is already turned on, the "powerful deodorizer" is in full force from the last patron and the armchair toilet remote is telling me that the nozzle is cleaned and ready. *What a considerate crapper!* As I start my *unchi* (see the following list *10 Ways to Say Poop in Japanese*), I busy myself reading the Japanese toilet manual conveniently posted by the airport authority. It's clearly put up for us tourists, who've never had the privilege of such lavatory luxury.

I am not completely certain what is to happen or from where.

When the time comes for the *cleansing of the buttocks*, I make sure the warm water option is on and hit the bum fountain button. I am not completely certain *what* is to happen or from *where*. But within a split second I quickly learn the lesson of checking the water pressure gauge before getting the sneaky Japanese public enema number two. With the water pressure set on *full cleanse*, a 10-year-old might as well have snuck up from underneath me with a fully pumped Super Soaker 2000 and let loose. I jump up from the seat with the bum gun still cleansing my underwear, pants and carry on bags.

With my pants soaked around my ankles, I dance around my personal Japanese water show until I find the *rear washing stop* button to halt the production. I'm completely drenched. I feel like the victim of a Japanese game show where a tourist contestant is set up from the start to be humiliated; the only thing missing is the soundtrack of cheesy sound effects and canned laughter. *There must be a setting for that on this toilet remote here…*

The only thing more pathetic than the spectacle going on inside the stall is the knowledge that there is a lineup of people waiting to use my toilet outside. *Bummer.* They can not only see and hear the entire foot boogie and splashy commotion of my experience, but now need to re-shine their shoes after being on the front line of my one-man water fight.

Photo: Chris 73

Japan must be the only country where you can retain a slight bit of dignity when you leave a public toilet stall soaked, sweaty and kicking water around your ankles. Everyone in the stall lineup stands with quiet politeness as I awkwardly bow with a straight face before quickly dashing out the door. There was only silence, though I did anticipate a slow golf clap to break out in accordance of my bravery and survival...

Maybe this is a reason North Americans should stick to the dark ages of toilets. I didn't think it would take much to make me miss a dingy, public squatter toilet in Thailand, but at least hand flushing a squatter with a bucket won't administer a rude prostate check at the same time.

Kanpai!

DECEMBER 2013
TOKYO, JAPAN

10 Ways to Say *Poop* in Japanese

ben [べん]: Formal term for feces, droppings or excrement.

daiben [だいべん]: The term *ben*, but with the Kanji Japanese word for *big* in front (apparently *Godzillaben* was too long).

ben-pi [べんぴ]: Constipation. The term *ben* is followed by the Kanji Japanese word for *secret* or *hidden*. Think of it as your body's little secret of hiding your poo.

unpi [うんぴ]: Diarrhea stool. The Japanese often connect *unpi* to overeating, being sick, or stress. *Unpi* is usually a yellowish color and it has a very strong smell.

unnyo [うんにょ]: Soft and tender poop, but not diarrhea. It comes out when you feel a little indigestion. *Unnyo* is yellowish or light brown in color.

unchi [うんち]: Nice poop. It comes out when you've been eating healthy balanced meals. *Unchi* has a clean brown color and doesn't smell very much. Hurray for *unchi!*

ungo [うんご]: A poop that comes out a bit on the hard side. Often associated with not eating enough vegetables, or after being constipated. *Ungo* is usually black and really stinky.

kuso [くそ]: Another word that can be exchanged for the formal term *ben*, but more rude. Similar to *shit* in English but with a little less shock value as a swear word.

geri [げり]: Another term for diarrhea, except this one can explain why the Japanese might giggle when they meet a tourist named *Gary*.

tawagoto [たわごと]: Bullshit. You are talking nonsense or silly things. As in "the fact the Japanese have so many more practical and cool poop words than the English language is *tawagoto!*"

Drinking the World's Most Expensive Coffee
Kopi Luwak and the Creature That Creates It

One o'clock in the afternoon. Definitely time for another coffee—especially since I was up at 2 AM to climb a volcano for sunrise. The mountainous region of Bali, Indonesia is not only home to volcanic sunrises but also the source of the world's most expensive coffee—or should I say home to the civet—the defecator, *er*, creator of the world's most expensive coffee. *Wait, what do you mean I'm drinking cat poo coffee?! And people pay how much for this shit back home??*

The civet cat and I having a stare-down

The civet is a Balinese cat, known locally as the *luwak*, and is closely related to the weasel family. Local villagers let the animal roam the coffee plantations to eat the coffee cherries. Then they pick out the partly digested coffee beans from the animal's feces. What you get is *Kopi Luwak*, or cat poo coffee, produced in small amounts that can go for as much as $75 per espresso in downtown London.

I sit down at one of the local plantations south of Mount Batur, the volcano I've just hiked, for a taste test. The farmer serving us happily explains that the whole concept of *Kopi Luwak* came from necessary resourcefulness rather than some gimmicky marketing scheme. The wild animal would eat all the coffee cherries some seasons and leave the farmers with nothing to harvest. Instead of giving up their coffee, the locals picked through the digested, but intact, coffee cherries and noticed a unique taste. *Hmm, you don't say...*

I feel like an equally believable story would have been a farmer's smart-ass son announcing: "Dad, don't throw that away! Let's just roast this shit and sell it to stupid white people for $300 a pound!"

I stare down at the two coffee cups in front of me. There is a lighter hue from the *Kopi Luwak*. I give the cup a swirl, a smell, and take an exaggerated sip as if sampling a fine wine rather than what I'm *actually* doing, which is swallowing the excretions of a weasel.

The first thought that hits me is, "Wow! This *really does* taste like shit."

Well, maybe that is a little too harsh; it mainly tastes like strong coffee. However, *Kopi Luwak* definitely has an essence of being a little predigested. Which is exactly one of the main selling points for the coffee: It is easier on the stomach because it has already been in one. Some brands of Balinese Cat

Regular coffee on the left, the Kopi Luwak is on the right. At a plantation in Bali it costs 30,000 rupiah or about $2.50—a fraction of its global retail price.

It is easier on the stomach because it has already been in one.

Coffee brag that their civet cats pick only the best and ripest coffee cherries. Others promote it saying that the added breakdown through the animal's digestion and the enzymes involved create a smoother taste. Regardless of the claims, the extravagant price or global marketing, *Kopi Luwak* certainly has its own unique flavor.

Before you drop the cash or hike a volcano for this *cuppa kopi* though, I would consider just feeding a few coffee beans to your house cat first.

Lost in Translation:
THE PHOTO JOURNAL

Signs in foreign countries often showcase the best examples of a message not coming across exactly as intended. Here are some of my favorites.

In French it means "between lessons/ school" but I'd still think twice about dropping my kid off at this daycare in Arras, France.

Makes sense. The locals in Venice *can't stand* all the tourists.

This museum in Prague is super *ballin'*.

คำสาปเจ้าพ่อตะรุเตา

ผู้ใดบังอาจเก็บหินจากเกาะนี้ไป ผู้นั้นจะพบ
กับความหายนะนานานับประการ จะประสบอุบัติเหตุ
กลับไม่ถึงบ้าน จะหลุดพ้นจากหน้าที่การงาน
จะพบภัยพิบัติไม่มีที่สิ้นสุด จนถึงแก่ชีวิต

The Curse of the God of Tarutao

ose who take these stones from the island are cursed
to face the following disasters:

1.Fatal accidents. 2.Family life shaltered.
3.Being overthrown from the present position.
4.Loss of property and fortune. 5.Loss of life.

For the love of
God...DON'T TAKE
THE STONES!
(Koh Lipe, Thailand)

Free LSD salsa lesson for
newcomers? That'll definitely put
some interesting *pasión y vida* into
the class. (Antigua, Guatemala)

...you never know whatcha
gon' get. Photo: Maggie Thurmeier.
Vienna, Austria

In Jeju, Korea, not knowing what
animal you're eating is part of
the fun! Photo: Maggie Thurmeier

The insects can make you feel fine.
Also they can make you cry.
This museum displays
the thousand insects of Thailand.
Get to know them
and you will understand.

I don't think anything is
lost in translation here...
the owner of this Chiang
Mai insect sanctuary is
simply best buds with
his best bugs. Get to
know them and you
will understand...

The dapper Parisian Speedo days of yore.
(Photo source unknown)

DAMN FRENCH

Les Folies of Living In La France

"*Hé! Qu'est-ce qué vous faisiez?! C'est interdit!*"
"Hey John, are they screaming at us?"

"I have no idea. The French are crazy." I reply standing ankle deep in Rouen's public swimming pool. The lifeguards on the other side of the pool are all gathered together and shouting as they flap around in their matching red Speedos and sunglasses. A fat middle-aged French man wearing goggles walks by. His large belly hiding his tiny swimsuit making him look like a pasty white nudist. "I mean, just look at all of them wearing those stupid Speedos… I thought the French had high fashion sense."

"More like *thigh* fashion sense," Ryan, my new American friend, shoots back. "Oh god, is that a Speedo *vending machine?*" Ryan points to the other corner of the pool. We both laugh and shake our heads. The two of us are ready to jump in the pool but instead start instinctively tugging down on our board shorts as we take in the scene from our vantage point standing in the shallow end of the kiddie pool.

It's winter, 2008, and I am only two weeks into my semester abroad in Rouen, France (an hour north of Paris) as I finish my last year of university. Ryan lives in the same campus residence as me and it has become obvious to both of us that we'll be learning more about how to adapt to the wacky ways of the French than any type of business studies. We had decided to soak up the French culture of an indoor swimming pool to escape the dreary and cold northern rain that has been falling since we started school.

"*Interdit! Interdit!!*" the lifeguards shout louder, more joining in and blowing whistles as they start running towards the kiddie pool.

"Yeah, they're definitely yelling at us," Ryan says casually.

"Maybe we're not supposed to be in the kiddie pool."

"Sure, but I didn't think you were supposed to run around swimming pools either, crazy French." Ryan and I remain unmoved, standing at the edge of the water as five Speedo-clad lifeguards rush up to us. Pointing and shouting in a mess of convoluted French, their budgie-smuggler bathing suits flap with every word and whistle blow. One of them tugs on Ryan's board shorts and another grabs me by the arm as they pull us out of the pool.

SHORT DE
BAIN
INTERDIT

The French Department of Health seems to believe that anything not clinging tightly to your baguette is unhygienic.

"Dude," I say to Ryan, while we get escorted away by the swarm of lifeguards still shouting in French. "I think they're kicking us out…for *not wearing Speedos*."

What a dignified way to learn that board shorts are illegal to wear in public swimming pools in France. The French Department of Health seems to believe that anything not clinging tightly to your baguette is unhygienic. The logic is that since shorts are worn normally on the street, if you were to then swim in them you would dirty the pristine waters of the French public pools. Apparently the law dates back to a 1903 government decision to ban longer shorts and all subsequent requests to change that ruling have been met with a firm "*non.*"

Ten minutes later, Ryan and I are back standing ankle deep in the kiddie pool.

"You look damn ridiculous."

"I was just going to say the same to you."

We both fidget awkwardly in our matching striped blue speedos—purchased from the swimming pool's convenient onsite Speedo vending machine. *Zut alors!*

Damn French.

French culture is known for its incredible cuisine, beautiful cities, *haute* style, love of fine arts and *laissez-faire* lifestyle. There is a reason why France is the most popular tourist destination in the world[3]. Everyone craves a taste of the French way of life. I fell in love with the country with my first step into a French bakery,

Lazy sunsets at Notre Dame. (Paris, France)

or *boulangerie* (even though it has ruined eating bread elsewhere for the rest of my life). And hey, you can't consider yourself a world traveler until you've taken a cheesy photo in front *la tour Eiffel* (and possibly been scammed by a con artist in the process). But as I soak up the relaxed pace of *la belle vie* with a glass of red Bordeaux, *petit pain au chocolat* and glow of a Parisian sunset, there is also something *extraordinaire* that takes some adjusting to: the strangely stern and smug way the French adhere to being laidback and lazy.

The French *laissez-faire* lifestyle is no joke. They take not being serious seriously. It's like hanging out on a Caribbean beach where you brush off work to talk and smoke all day. Except in France the big surf is replaced with big scarves and an excessive embrace of bureaucracy (a French term) so they can formally pass the workload off to someone else down the chain. If employees ever feel an inkling of being overworked they simply go on strike. In the first month of my residency in France, the government-trained employees had gone on strike over a dozen times. To the French, most *problèmes* seem to be met with a shrug, eye roll, then smoke break (in that order).

It isn't like the French work much anyway. According to the 2014 Report by the Organization for Economic Co-operation and Development, France is near the bottom of the list of average annual hours actually worked per worker with 1,473, or approximately 28 hours a week (not including vacation time)[4]. This became apparent the day I arrived into France. Needing to buy groceries on a Sunday? *Non, ce n'est pas possible.* Nearly every shop is closed on a Sunday as it is loosely considered a national holiday and workers must be paid overtime for working on *dimanche*. Same thing goes during French lunchtime during the week, where shops and restaurants will often close between 12 PM and 2 PM.

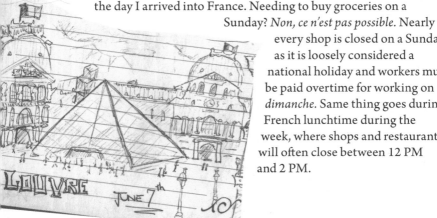

"Wait, what?" I blurt out to Ryan on our first day of school in Rouen. We have an hour break for lunch between classes and just walked to a third restaurant to find it closed like the rest. "Where are we supposed to go for lunch if all the restaurants close *during lunchtime!*?" "The culture of French convenience," Ryan laughs. "I've been trying to talk with the student counselor all week. She has a two and a half hour lunch break every day and the only other times I've had time to visit her office, she's been on smoke break."

"*C'est fou...*"

The craziest part of adjusting to the French lifestyle is that the more I get used to it, the more I appreciate and love it. It's like I finally realized, hey, if *everyone* works less... *everyone* has more time off! Isn't that what a developed society, as a whole, should work toward? Who are we North Americans coming into a foreign culture to demand our constant 24-hour convenience because we can't remember to buy our *baguettes et fromage* before Sunday arrives? In North America, everyone struggles to keep up with the stress of working overtime or multiple jobs, simply so we can afford a consumption-filled lifestyle and exercise it whenever we choose. What would we be willing to give up in exchange for a two-and-a-half hour lunch break? *Hmm, maybe less cheesy products and simply more cheese, non?*

France is definitely a culture based on quality over quantity. And that is something I believe more countries should slow down to achieve. *Bien fait mes amis!* Well done. We might have to get the French to encourage more North Americans to sing Edith Piaf and go on strike for a longer smoke break.

JOHNNY COME LATELY
BY JOHN EARLY

MISCONCEPTION, + ITS AWKWARDNESS WHEN CUDDLING A CLOSE FRIEND ASLEEP:

BONNE NUIT.

DID YOU JUST SAY 'BONE ME'?!

"*Je ne veux pas travailler.*	"*I don't want to work.*
Je ne veux pas déjeuner.	*I don't want to eat lunch.*
Je veux seulement oublier.	*I just want to forget.*
Et puis je fume..."	*And then I smoke...*"

EDITH PIAF (1915–1963)
'JE NE VEUX PAS TRAVAILLER'

"...This Must Be A Monk Thing"

I pull my bicycle into the entrance of the temple grounds. A smiling Buddha shrine sits like a welcome mat in front of a stunning facade of elaborate carvings etched right into centuries-old columns and walls. The entire sanctuary shines so bright with gold I feel the need to keep my sunglasses on. I shrug. *This one seems as good as any for a quick meditation.* There is definitely no shortage of temples to escape into from the bustling roadways of inner city Chiang Mai in Thailand.

The late afternoon sun settles into its perfect perch placing a soft yellow light onto the treetops before it tucks itself away for the night. It gives warmth to the hug of the canopy that encloses the colorfully decorated temple tops. Gentle chanting of prayer resonates behind thick walls. I breathe in a mix of incense and humid air and smile; I can feel the sanctuary of mindful space around me—a needed break from the hustle of rush hour traffic. I prop my bicycle's kickstand in front of the property's spirit house draped in flowers and the day's offerings for good luck: incense, a packet of crackers and an orange Fresca. The little people idols inside look pleased with their snacks and fix of aspartame. I throw a sarong over my back to cover my disrespectful bare shoulders. Good thing sweat isn't insulting in Thai culture.

Today is the halfway mark of my two-week Thai language course in the capital of the northern Chiang Mai province. It is an attempt to communicate better with the locals as I start my second season of leading 40-day adventure travel trips throughout Thailand. Learning to speak Thai is unlike any other language I've come across. I'm still struggling to tell the difference between the words *horse, dog, mother* and *instant noodle*; all pronounced *maa* with slight difference in tone. The first day of class, I accidentally used a rising tone instead of a flat tone when I told my teacher, "I love *muay* Thai". Instead of telling her I love Thai boxing, I told her I love Thai pubic hair. It obviously doesn't take much for intentions to get lost in translation in Thailand.

> **I'm still struggling to tell the difference between the words horse, dog, mother and instant noodle.**

The smile of a young monk greets me as he enthusiastically walks up in his orange robe to say hello. *Ah, the Land of Smiles!*

I take off my sunglasses. *"Sah wah dee kahp,"* I say, as I put my hands together to touch my forehead with a slight bow. (Just earlier, I had learnt the way of the *wei*: the higher up you place your hands and the lower you bow, the more formal respect you show.)

"My name is Pit. What is your name?" He asks in his slow and careful English. Pit's smile and eye contact are so genuine that I can't help but return the endearment.

"Pom chu Johnny," I respond in my limited amount of Thai. Pit starts asking a handful of other English questions that he has clearly been practicing as he gestures a welcome to the temple grounds.

Pit and I quietly remove our shoes at the entrance to the main temple. The doors glimmer with intricate floral engravings and patterned embellishments. Freshly burnt incense perfumes the air, already filled with a glow of positive energy that has been saturating the space for hundreds of years. As new people arrive they separate into two distinct groups: locals flowing into a comfortable practice of bows and meditative sitting, and tourists with their awkward glances and imitated actions. I feel the sense of religious mindfulness sink into everyone who tip-toes carefully around the temple—only interrupted by brisk digital camera clicks and flashes.

Before I get a chance to sit down for my 15 minutes of daily Zen, Pit leans his shoulders in towards me. "More, I show you," he whispers and gestures back outside. His smile concedes his intention to practice his English and show off his Buddhist backyard. I nod, also excited to practice my new Thai phrases from this morning's lesson. *If only I can work in the phrase 'I have a red mango' into our conversation...*

"Okay? I show where I live?" Pit says touching my elbow.

He catches me off guard. "Oh. Yes, thank you." I respond. Of all the times I had visited a monastery or been invited into conversation with a monk, I had rarely had the chance to see where they actually live. *This quick meditation stop is turning into more of a cultural experience than expected. Dee mahk!*

I follow Pit's graceful yet hurried footsteps along a freshly swept dirt path. It proceeds into a hanging canopy of trees that is starting to stifle the last of the day's sunlight. There are several other monks doing various chores, all adorned in their orange robes. The vast majority seems to be young male adults.

We come across a simple two-storey residence of individual rooms that has a slight summer camp feel to it. Pit motions for me to remove my sandals and I follow him up the stairs. I'm not sure what to expect as he opens the unlocked door to his small room. Besides a doubled up mat and pillow on the floor instead of a bed, everything else looks to be pretty normal for a young student in a dorm room on campus: an old computer, books, magazines, discarded flavored soya milk cartons and some posters on the wall (of well known Buddhist monks instead of rock bands). *So this is monk life...*

"It's okay, you lie down," Pit smiles, motioning to the mat on the floor. "Okay, you like massage?"

"Ah, yes. Thai massage is great." I respond as I lay flat on my back. The mat is comfortable but would make a tough bed to sleep on. I try not to act uncomfortable as he quickly starts to massage my feet. He then motions for me to unbutton my shirt.

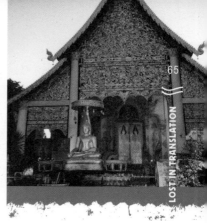

Wow, how lucky am I to get a rare offer for a monk to rub my feet? This must be a monk thing...maybe they have a certain amount of meditative rubbing on strangers feet to reach the next monk level of charitable compassion?

I have had my fair share of Thai massages already. For as little as $8 an hour and located on every corner of any given street in the country, how could you not get a couple of massages a week? It's one of the first unofficial Thai sentences a tourist, or *farang*, hears when they enter the country: *Hello massage kaaaah?* And a Thai masseuse definitely knows how to get up in your business. Whether they are straddling you, standing on you or using any and every body part to flip you around into a pretzel, it's like having a little Asian person manually doing yoga for you. It seems innate that trained or not, everyone in Thailand knows how to give a Thai massage. Don't be surprised if you walk into a busy parlor and all the therapists are occupied so they call you the cook next door to come earn some extra *baht*. Like most things in Asia that don't make sense and wouldn't exactly *feng shui* in western countries, you have to just shrug it off as an added cultural experience.

Pit may only be half my size, but he has strong hands. He is in a squat position on the floor leaning over me and attentively massaging the insoles of my feet. Pit then starts working up my calves with long, circular thumb motions and makes a fairly swift move to massage my inner thigh, then stops.

"Okay? You okay?" Pit says looking up at me with a flat expression for the first time.

I pause. "...ah, everything ok," I answer.

Pit nods and goes back into his diligent massaging, with longer drawn out motions up into the inner thigh.

Those natural, minor alarms start going off in my head. You know those amber alerts from your baby maker zone, that you have to decide to translate as either 'Whoa, back off!' or 'Alright, alright, alright...'

Pit gently grabs my manhood through my loose shorts, shifting it over to my right leg, and starts rubbing my left inner thigh. He quickly looks up at me. "Okay?"

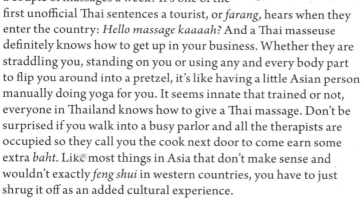

"Ah…okay." I respond with a longer pause this time.

Hmm. He sure is getting thorough with the thighs. This must be a monk thing. Hopefully he gets into the lower back soon.

The silence is getting heavier. I am starting to feel further away from the serenity of the monastery. I try to keep my eyes closed and start to notice Pit's breathing as his massaging gets more meticulous around my crotch.

Did I misuse my tone when speaking in Thai to this guy to get a freaky monk massage? You better not get turned on John!

Once again he grabs my male fortune cookie putting it back to the left side and delves into more right leg rubbing action. My fortune seems to be changing by the minute.

This must be a monk thing. This must be a monk thing.

"Okay?" Pit asks again, becoming aware of my mounting tension.

"…okay."

I lean forward and our eyes briefly meet before he goes back to massaging, this time adding longer massage strokes over the calf. There is absolutely no threat or ill intention in his eyes. His face is calm but starting to give small inclinations of nervousness.

What the hell John! You are in a monk's room with your shirt off, next to an ancient temple grounds in Chiang Mai, getting a creepy Thai massage… How do you end up in these ridiculous situations?

Although I'm undecided on exactly what kind of 'tradition' this may or may not be, I know I will have to get out of this predicament (predicamonk?) sooner than later. My eyes scan the tiled ceiling like it might give me an escape plan. The last thing I want to do is insult a monk in his house.

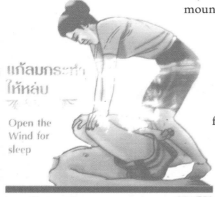

แก้ลมกระทำ
ให้หล่น

Open the
Wind for
sleep

แก้อาเจียน
มืออก

Stretching
for Vomit

"Hello massage kaaaaah? You want open wind for sleep or stretching for vomit?!"

Pit makes another swoop back to my upper left thigh, decisively grabs my udon noodle with both hands and moves it back to the right side—quick massage—then puts it back to the left side.

"Ok, amigo...*no ok!*" I shout, half sitting up.

A light double knock hits the door from outside the room. Pit swiftly pulls my shirt back over my stomach, tries to do up the first button, then awkwardly gets to his feet to open the door just enough to poke his head out and block the view into his room.

Ha! This is NOT a monk thing! I am outta here!

I hear some soft Thai murmuring at the door as I button up my shirt and gather my things.

Let's get out of here John!

I can hear a brief *kahp* being exchanged and Pit makes a quick bow before closing his door again. He sits down and apologizes for the interruption but I am already past the awkward inaction phase and ready to *not* be hit on by a monk anymore.

"I sorry if I make feel you uncomfortable," Pit says in his broken English. We are both sitting cross-legged on the floor. I can see some hurt build in his eyes, which still yield such a compassionate and trusting gaze. I can hardly think of something to say in English let alone in Thai.

Yes, this is the first time I have ever lied to the face of a monk before. But I feel like it is fully warranted.

Has anyone ever used the 'it's not you, it's me' line on a monk before?

He asks if he can email me to practice his English, but I quickly apologize saying that I do not have an email address. Yes, this is the first time I have ever lied to the face of a monk before. But I feel like it is fully warranted. Before I leave, Pit gives me a brief blessing over my head in Thai, touching my forehead with his thumbs. His simple and endearing smile returns to his face.

As I prop up the kickstand to my unlocked bicycle, I start to laugh as I process the events of the last 40 minutes; if I was looking for an authentic cultural experience this afternoon—I think I got it. I push my bicycle off into the busy Chiang Mai streets and narrowly miss being hit by a swarm of swerving *tuk tuk* taxis. Getting back into the bustle of traffic feels strangely welcoming. Each peddle I take on my bike helps shed the awkwardness that still lingers in my overly massaged thighs. Time to head home; it's been a weird day. I've got some studying to do too if I'm to avoid the next instance of being lost in translation. On the plus side, I already feel more confident in knowing what *is* and *is not* a monk thing.

EXPLAINING A MEXICAN CARNIVAL

A Photo Journal Revealing the Flair of the Mexican Fair

Carnivals and fairs around the world all follow the same rulebook for cheap entertainment: greasy junk food, unsafe ways to spin in circles and games designed to rip you off via freaky carnies. In Mexico—where shenanigans are more prevalent, drinking is the national pastime and overall standards are always diminished—the carnival I experienced in Sayulita exemplifies just that. It is a night of drunken laughs, questionable safety and copious head scratching. Come along and discover the wonderful world (and logic) behind the traveling Mexican carnival! *Vamanos amigos!*

Throw a rock, smash a bottle…win a beer! Pay 25 pesos ($1.50) for three rocks. Hit three for three to win a six-pack! This Mexican carnival game standard will eat up your entire night (and pesos) so easily that by the end you'll be convinced it is the smartest thing ever invented.

With beer at hand, take a loaded pellet gun to make the mariachi players, *banda de músicos* or Mexican boy band marionettes play a song. Careful though, if you hit the wrong one, *el Diablo* will snarl at you and spray you with water.

Boliche: it means bowling in Spanish, except the only bowling you do in this family favorite involves throwing a very hard wad of tape at the guy behind the board. to win a beer. This poor carnie's job consists of wearing a rubber devil mask and dodging throws while making the most obnoxious and inaudible noises over a loud speaker. [Note: He was rushed to the hospital later in the night after a direct hit…and after a week of infuriating heckling, those staying in the hostels across the grounds felt little pity.]

Throw Mexican darts for entire bottles of tequila! After you win a bottle of *blanco* or *reposado* be sure to crack it open, slam it back and hit up the dizzy pineapple rides! *Salud!*

After enough beer and tequila, the carnival food might actually start to sound good: mini hotdog burritos, cup of creamed corn with mayonnaise, *tripa* (cow intestine) tacos or *chicharrón* (deep fried pig rinds and skin) with hot sauce… or maybe just stick with the deep fried banana and mango topping.

Land a dart on any star to win…a bucket of groceries! Move over stuffed animals, this game could gift you with corn flakes, crackers, dry pasta, toilet paper, instant noodles *y más!* Funny how it's mainly local mothers and backpackers keen to win the big grand prize…

What happens to an aging mariachi singer? You get to travel with the carnival and sing to the empty bleachers of a small baseball diamond.

Then there are the games that are so cheap and sketchy it's a wonder that someone can actually make a living from it. Try the one where you take a scrunched piece of paper from the carnie's hand after he has simply hand-written whether you won or not—which you know no one has won in 20 years when you see the prizes consist of a couple Disc-mans, the first Nokia cell phone that hit the market, rusty knock off watches and a vintage Casio black and white portable TV. "Amigo, it's like a TV… in your hand, amigo!" He says to me like I've never seen an iPhone, iPad or anything else made since the '90s.

In true Mexican style, the temporary carnival bars outnumber any other stand in a 3-1 ratio in competing for the loudest Mexican banda music. So mathematically speaking you should be downing tres fresa coladas for every game or ride. It's science.

Each country around the world has its own set of adaptations to address our guilt for cheap carnival thrills— even in Lausanne, Switzerland. No censorship on this 'family' ride…"

The Mexican Carnival experience: an exhibition of games and concepts only conceivable…and legal, in Mexico!

MARCH 2011
SAYULITA, MEXICO

Lombok and the Local Truth Telling Potion

The Indonesian Travel Journals

The kids. The first thing I notice leaving Bali and landing on its little brother island to the east are the beautiful local kids. The second is that instead of school bags they're sporting custom bracelet boards slung low over their shoulders. They approach me proffering these beautiful, colorful homemade trinkets—and they don't smile at first. Neither do they ask for much, but as a Westerner I feel they're trying to guilt me into a sale. This is a common experience, and it's never easy to know how to react to kids when you're traveling. But then, suddenly, they're laughing. Especially when they spot that snorkel amidst my things and are now off running into the ocean, stripping down naked, laughing and giggling with their new toy to share in the water before I've even had time to say *yes*.

Kuta, Lombok. Not to be confused with its other, more commercial namesake in Bali, this place is home to incredible surf, simple local food, pockets of unspoiled Indonesian lifestyle—and also, my French Canadian friend, Lys. She convinced me to pay her this visit after meeting up in Australia by endorsing such glories and adding a liberal sprinkling of glowing white sand all over the top. I packed my bags.

My first morning in Kuta begins at 5 AM, when I'm startled awake by the sounds of Old Macdonald's Jungle Farm (you may as well have rolled in a bingo machine next to my head, exchanged the balls for chickens, monkeys and roosters and cranked it to full spin cycle). I step outside to the day's first gray light with the resonance of Muslim chanting over a distant loudspeaker. It reminds me I'm no longer on the Hindu island of Bali but instead, the Muslim island of Lombok. I guess this is the real sound of Indonesia—the most populous Muslim country in the world.

> I step outside to the day's first gray light with the resonance of Muslim chanting over a distant loudspeaker.

What with the chickens and the chanting I realize I'm not getting back to sleep anytime soon, so I eat the hotel's complimentary papaya and pineapple pancakes and set off for a day's surf.

Our new friends and local surf crew, Deo and Tony, are just waking up, yawning and stretching as they lay draped over the wooden tables of the restaurant where they work. They may not have overindulged on their local cheap hooch, arak, the night before (though an 'arak attack' is always likely), but it wouldn't have mattered either way. This, I soon discover, is where they sleep every night. Deo has short black hair, Tony has long sun-bleached surf hair in a pony tail, and they are both as tall as their short surfboards with open smiles to prove they love living and showing people their home of Kuta Lombok. They hook Lys and I up with a couple of surfboards and a motorbike for the combined daily rate of 100,000 rupiah ($7 US). Since they are our friends, I battle

The local kids show off their custom made bracelets.

Deo and Tony lead the way to Seger Beach, the local surf spot.

hard to ignore my new instinct and the Indonesian custom of bargaining every price down. In many parts of Southeast Asia, it's always a fine line between bartering with poverty and trying not to get ripped off. But the demeanor in their smiles is one of simple trust and friendship—their culture abides by a high value of standing behind your word.

We follow them on motorbikes, clutching our surfboards as we pass farm villages, vacant white sand beaches and water buffalo grazing in front of the many roadside *warungs* or convenience stands. Lys and I pull up to Seger Beach where only a couple of other local surfers are in the water. "Good, small waves today. Sometimes too big to surf," Deo reassures me as I look out to see a massive wall of water, five feet off the lip, taking one surfer on a long ride and swallowing the others. *Well, I would hate to see it when there are actual big waves…*

A local man pulls up next to us on his motorbike mobile ice cream stand. He's wearing a fleece and two winter jackets. I look at him in disbelief, standing and sweating in front of him in my board shorts from the intense tropical heat. Today's temperature is pushing 100° F. The man points at his green ice cream cooler and pretends to shiver. We both laugh. *I'm sold! I'm sure the man's never seen snow or been in an environment colder than room temperature but he knows how to market ice cream!*

Three local girls see our transaction and run over to us from under their palmed shade, competing with

He's wearing a fleece and two winter jackets. I look at him in disbelief…

If you're wearing two winter jackets and a fleece sweater in 100° heat…you better be selling some damn cold ice cream!

A traditional Lombok Sasak village hut.

each other to see who will be able to sell their coconut to the new guy first. It's also the first thing I see stepping out from the surf: a fresh green coconut ready in one hand, with a machete in the other, ready to cut it open and give you before you can even get the water out of your ears. It's March, after all—just after the monsoon period and into the start of slow season before the summer tourists arrive. Every extra coconut or ice cream sale provides a good portion of their daily income.

Halfway through my stay at Kuta Lombok, Lys and I go to meet Deo and Tony for breakfast. It is the first time they have not welcomed us with their bright smiles as we walk in to their restaurant home base. The two are absorbed in a heated debate and it's clear something unsettling must have happened overnight. When they translate their solemn conversation to Lys and I, we are so amused with their story it's difficult to not laugh out loud.

Last night, an older man a few *warungs* down from them was

An elderly local woman spins wool.

robbed of over two million rupiah ($150) worth of jewelry, a very substantial amount for the people of Lombok. In order to catch the thief, the man promptly took it upon himself to summon all the locals in the area, where, once assembled, everyone would be asked to ingest a 'magic potion' made of water and special Lombok dirt. This, apparently, is standard practice when it comes to the matter of petty crime.

A confused smile crosses Lys' face. I try to hide my amusement as Deo looks me in the eyes. "You say no to potion," Deo exclaims. "We can call police on you!"

My brow furrows. "Well, what happens if you're guilty, but you still drink the...ah, *potion?*"

Deo and Tony shake their heads. "Oh, no good," Tony replies. "You get big belly full of sick and you have curse on your family and children's family."

Up until now Lys and I have been trying to suppress our entertainment of the situation, but Deo and Tony's pressing urgency wipes the emerging smiles off our faces. They are taking this truth-telling potion summoning very seriously. Lys and I follow them to the meeting place where all the locals have been called. After hours of debate (which for me, largely consists of passing the time by helping a lady shuck raw peanuts for *gado-gado* sauce), they realize that one man still hasn't shown up. *Bingo!* The matter is apparently resolved, and as the rules command, the police are immediately called in. (Later, we find out he had actually confessed before the local authority got involved.) *Wow. If only Canada had such superstition and honesty within our people at home...although that would likely involve a lot of 'magic mud' drinking...*

"Okay, no more work!" Deo shouts standing up. His and Tony's faces have returned to their usual infectious and glowing smiles.

Lys and I at the lookout above the bay of Kuta Lombok.

"Now we surf!"

**MARCH 2012
KUTA LOMBOK, INDONESIA**

#CENTRALAMERICAPROBLEMS
Tourist Anomalies of Adjusting to Life in Central America

What constitutes regular life for the locals between Mexico and Panama does not always come across as *normal* to visiting tourists and expats. Sometimes you have to read between the cultural lines to realize that the oddity you are experiencing might not be so strange to those living there. If you find yourself immersed in the culture of Latin American life, don't forget to embrace the many ridiculous and trivial 'problems' you might encounter.

Here are a few of my own amusing experiences from three years of living and traveling in Central America:

Never really knowing if you're buying limes or oranges.

The oranges are on the left and the limes are on the right—and yes, they might taste the same.

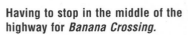

Having to stop in the middle of the highway for *Banana Crossing.*

Road trips in Panama can be bananas, especially when you have to stop for hundreds of them to cross the highway.
Photo: Amy Eyben

Never setting an alarm clock because the roosters or howler monkey will already have you awake by 5 AM.

Howler monkeys sound utterly terrifying and 10 times their size. Imagine the sounds of a hyena battling a T-Rex inside a blender on high speed. That's your new wake up call in paradise.
Photo: Peter Schoen

Instead of paving the streets, the city saves money by dousing the gravel roads in molasses.

The molasses truck sprays the back roads in Tamarindo, Costa Rica. It smells nice but you'll quickly lose your sandals.

Erupting volcanoes become a regular weather forecast

Volcanic ash from Volcan de Fuego after it blankets Antigua in Guatemala. There are even some bars in town that have daily drink specials for when the volcano is erupting.

Bugs are simply bigger and more badass in Central America.

Spiders, moths, cockroaches—or even this crazy ninja warrior-looking grasshopper in Puerto Viejo—all prove that nothing makes insects like the jungle.

Eating *gallo pinto* (rice and beans) for breakfast, lunch and dinner.

A typical Nicaraguan desayuno (breakfast) always complete with gallo pinto. You learn to love the Central American staple, even when you eat it with every local meal.

Taxis will honk when they're: available, occupied, turning a corner, slamming on the brakes, saying hello to a friend, mad at another driver, see a pretty *chica*, playing to the music or simply sitting idle in traffic.

A taxi cab in Panama City. The birthplace of the incessant car honking. Photo: Christopher Powers

Local shopkeepers preferring to not sell you anything because they don't have change and don't want to break your bills.

The Costa Rican currency: colones. It's clearly the coolest currency in the world. Who needs a dead politician on a bill when you can have a shark, sloth or monkey! (...or is that the same thing?)

Being woken up from your daily siesta because the local fruit and vegetable guy drives by shouting Spanish gibberish of the produce he's selling into a homemade loudspeaker strapped to the top of his truck.

Every veggie and food truck announcer in Central America has their own ridiculous way to announce their presence and produce. In San Juan del Sur, Nicaragua, it sounds like a monotone Spanish alien from Mars Attacks speaking one long word of fruit and veggies: "naranja-piña-zanahoria-aguacate-cebolla-tomate-melon-maracuya...

Seeing intestine, tongue or brain on your dinner menu.

A street grill in Sayulita, Mexico. Maybe it was better to not know what was in those tacos...

Whether it's *Island Time*, *Tico Tiempo* or things are running on the *Caribbean Clock*...you never really know how long anything will take in Central America.

Apparently knowing the time in the Bus Terminal in San Jose, Costa Rica isn't that important anyway.

It's often the little differences that are the most amusing and make the biggest impact in proving you are no longer in your home country. Whether they are seen as laughable grievances, minor acculturation or First World problems in developing countries, the contrasts you come across should always remind you to not take traveling for granted. And who *really* needs to know whether they are making orange juice or lemonade in Central America anyway?

¡Pura vida!

MAY 2016
SAN JUAN DEL SUR, NICARAGUA

Getting reverse culture shock by going back home and freaking out that you can flush toilet paper.

The toilet rules in Tranquilo Bar in Nicaragua's Corn Islands.

CHAPTER 3
Manifesting Propitiousness

propitious |prə-pĭsh′əs|
adjective
✦ presenting favorable circumstances or
  showing signs of a beneficial outcome
✦ giving or indicating a probable chance
  of success
  Ex: propitious omens

.CREATE JUST THAT.

If you live a good life
And all you need is the truth
Your self is the proof
For open minds to see what you do
   Believe don't assume
   Break free from taboo
   Create more than take
   And live to be not consume
Stay present and clear
And keep a positive mind
Know when to push forward
And take chance to recline
      In style for a while
      And feel fine direct
      If you ever need to heal
      A deep breath will cause collect
         Regrets, stick the past
         Open today and relax
         If you keep a worried state
         Then you'll create just that

APRIL 2011
SAYULITA, MEXICO

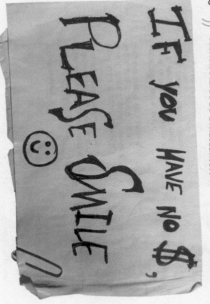

The sign we used on our guitar case when busking Byron Bay for pie money from the 23 Hour Meat Pie Shop (no one ever really knew which hour they closed).

Photo: Amy Garneau

Sleeping Amidst the Monks

Leaving the Tourist Trails for Thailand's Temples

"Oh, no no no...not what we do here," the elder monk says completely rejecting my request while never breaking his full, enlightened smile.

I'm gutted. I have spent the entire day renting a scooter and getting lost through the winding and poorly labeled mountainside that overlooks Chiang Mai in Northern Thailand. The end to my quest: the happiest dismissal possible.

After nearing my second month of backpacking Southeast Asia I am in need of a reset. Too many buckets of local SangSom rum and too much traffic, boat taxis and *tuk-tuks* for day trips with an overload of travelers to meet then say goodbye to. I'm starting to experience the first-world problem of needing a vacation from my vacation. I need to sit in silence for a couple of days—not something that is easy to do in the backpacker scene where the push to have the *best day of your life*, every day, can turn into a burden.

> I'm starting to experience the first-world problem of needing a vacation from my vacation.

Through the grapevine I had heard of a Buddhist *wat* (Thai for temple) near Chiang Mai that allows visitors to stay overnight for several nights, as long as they respect and adhere to the traditional ways. After several years of practicing meditation, a few classes studying Eastern religions and a growing weariness of the beaten tourist trails, I was ready to jump in head first for a few nights. But here I stand: rejected by a monk.

"Not what we do here. No, no," the elder monk continues, "...but...down *there* they may help you." He says, pointing down some weathered stone stairs that lead to a small cluster of houses confined by the surrounding jungle.

This time both of us are smiling contently.

"*Khap koon krup.*" I respond, thanking him with a low bow.

As it turns out there is a small meditation center a short walk below the actual monastery, managed by volunteers and some monks. For a small donation they will feed you, give you a room and supply simple white clothes to wear during your minimum three-night stay. Adherence to the meditation schedule and Buddhist lifestyle is mandatory.

Wat Umong, a 700-year-old Buddhist temple near Chiang Mai that features several ancient tunnels—supposedly built by the king to keep a famous but deranged monk occupied, preventing him from getting lost in the forest.

At first, it sounds like a perfect intake of spirituality and reflection as a needed escape from the backpacking travels. It soon becomes evident how difficult such a drastic lifestyle adjustment will be.

"These are the keys to your room. We will see you tomorrow morning for meditation at 4 AM."

Whoa.

Walking up to my room, I think of the times this month I arrived home at four in the morning, versus the times I had woken up at that time:

My room below Wat Umong.

about 8 – 0. I open the door to reveal my room and bed for the duration of my stay. It is the equivalent of a welcome mat in an empty closet.

The vacation feels over before it starts.

The following days involve early mornings, quiet reflection and the constant attempts to turn off my busy Western mind. There are four other "students" from around the world in residence practicing meditation. One middle-aged man from Eastern Europe has been here for over two months.

We wake by 4 AM and have scheduled meditation throughout the day from 5 AM to 9 PM. A different monk accompanies us at the end of each day to give us a lesson to reflect on for the next morning. Sometimes it is an open discussion. Other times just one or two spoken words to consider for the rest of the day. Once I get into my inner-monk groove, it is incredibly liberating and a refreshing reset to my life's hard-wired circuitry. Challenging, yes, but worth every quiet reflection, intention and daily plate of plain white rice.

> **Once I get into my inner-monk groove, it is incredibly liberating and a refreshing reset to my life's hard-wired circuitry.**

Here are few things I learned from my time with the monks and students of mindfulness:

- ▸ When meditating, it is considered rude to point your feet in the direction of a monk (and *no one* wants to insult and interrupt a monk mid-meditation).

- ▸ If you are having trouble staying focused during your fifth hour of meditation, you might be allotted to walk from one tree to another that is 20 feet away—with a minimum 30-minute interval to do so.

- ▸ Do not eat your rice before the monks at the front of the room have started.

- ▸ You are not to eat anything after your last meal of rice at noon.

- ▸ Always sit and keep silence when eating or drinking*.

    *During our daily hour of spare time, I planned to explore the jungle monastery with a cup of tea and a book. A monk saw me and remarked: "Why you walk AND drink? If you need to drink…sit, drink. Enjoy the tea. Why make yourself so busy?"

My favorite lesson came from a young monk who knew very little English. One morning he held up a piece of paper and a pencil:

"This…me…before meditation." He says, motioning to the pencil in front of the paper.

"I see." [He points to the front of the paper] "Here, no see." [He points to the back]

"After…meditation…I see AND I see." He smiles, pointing to both sides of the paper.

The monks and those that choose to don the orange robe offer such easy and accessible lessons for a simplified life. We often forget how applicable and needed such simplicity is to our modern life. Western society often strives for more by doing more: multitasking, extended work hours, keeping busy…it is all taken as an affirmative that you are achieving abundance and being productive. But clutter doesn't bring clarity. In my short few days adhering to meditation and a simple life, I've become aware of how you can bring more into your life by doing less. Even for a traveler you need balance. After withdrawing from the hectic Western lifestyle to backpack Asia, I discovered the backpacker's need to *experience it all* and *cram it all in* can get more frantic than the daily life I left behind.

My time sleeping amidst the monks has been another step to find the stillness to appreciate the motion of travel.

SEPTEMBER 2012
CHIANG MAI, THAILAND

Enlightening reminders of non-permanence are scattered along the trees of Wat Umong.

INSIGHT ON MEDITATION

Meditation in its most basic sense is simply *awareness of breath*. There is no right or wrong way as long as the basis is mindful reflection of your breath.

But for newcomers or those looking for more insight and techniques to apply during their practice, here are a few simple tips I've picked up over the years:

Sit Comfortably

► Sit cross-legged or find a comfortable chair where you can keep a straight spine

► Sitting on a cushion can help your posture as it elevates the hips above the knees

► Let your right hand rest in your left palm on your lap or place both hands on your knees—open palms to receive energy or down-facing to retain energy

Relax Yourself

► Slow your breath

► Fall comfortably into a slight smile (this is the most naturally relaxed and neutral state when your face utilizes the fewest muscles)

► Experience gratitude for all you have

► Sense your heartbeat as a sound or sensation

Breathe

► Breathe in from your nose and let it expand your diaphragm (lower belly)

► Say to yourself *In* on the inhale and *Out* on the exhale

► Let your breath root your energy down into the ground

► Feel it lift you up and into a straight posture

► Allow each breath to pull you into a deeper sense of soft awareness

Be Aware.

► Bring awareness to all the sensations in your body

► Feel the blood bring energy throughout your physical self

► Ask yourself Who Am I? What Is My Purpose? But do not answer, just live the questions

► Perceive the energy around you as white light

► Breathe in the white light

► Exhale any darkness, negativity or sickness inside you

► Once you are full of white light, breathe in the dark you might sense around you and exhale and share your inner light

► Grasp the sensation that you "have no want." There is no desire to fill any type of cravings: eating, talking, scratching, deciding...

► You have no want—simply be content

When your concentration is challenged, bring it back to your awareness of breath: In...Out...In...

If you are having trouble with random thoughts flooding your mind don't get upset or try to avoid them. Acknowledge they are there and sense them into a bubble and let them float away.

"...feel the warmth of when someone did something of gratitude for you. Let it ring from the heart and feel it reach across your entire body..."

"Draw consciousness away from mind activity and create a gap of no-mind in which you are highly alert and aware but not thinking. This is the essence of meditation."

ECKHART TOLLE,
THE POWER OF NOW

Gili Trawangan, Indonesia

I really only meditate when I need it.

Whether I'm run down, missing sleep, needing a deep breath or simply wanting to give the mind a time out, it's always sought for a restorative boost—a quick pick-me-up.

But meditating when you feel great is where you can really reap benefits. You're already on that lift but now fueling the fire. A pick-me-up to stay picked up. Soaking the intention down into your bones. Letting breath saturate your contentment. Being able to rid the mind that interferes with simply feeling good.

"You should sit in meditation for 20 minutes every day...unless you are too busy, then you should sit for *an hour.*"
OLD ZEN PROVERB

Being mindful of your breath when needing to recover shouldn't overtake the sensibility to also breathe to stoke your existence. This is my new motive to meditate—and something I can definitely pick up.

wisdom |'wizdəm|

noun
+ the quality of having experience, knowledge and good judgment
+ the soundness of an action or decision with regard to the application of experience

The more I meditate, the more I interpret wisdom through the achievement of understanding and controlling your internal dialogue. Being able to quiet, turn off, then turn on that little voice in your head—at will—might be one of the most difficult accomplishments, but perhaps the optimum way to harness wise decisions from experience.

Land of Living Skies. Photo: Mark Tiu.
(Saskatoon, Saskatchewan)

SLOW RIVER

HAVE YOU EVER WATCHED
    THE RIVER MOVE SLOW?
SEARCHED STATUE RIPPLES
    SITTING STILL BELOW?

COULDN'T EVEN MOVE A TWIG
    WITH NO WIND TO BLOW

BUT STEADY YOUR EYES
    BECAUSE THERE STILL IS FLOW

IT DRIFTS QUIET CORNERS CONTENTLY
TAKING TIME
    TO SAY HELLO

AND IT CALMS THE MIND
TO FIND THAT RIVERS SOUL
THAT SIMPLE SLOW
    THAT OPENS UP TO SHOW

THAT THE MIND SHARES
    SIMILIAR SPACE
    WHEN HAVING
    NO BETTER PLACE TO GO.

        john.e

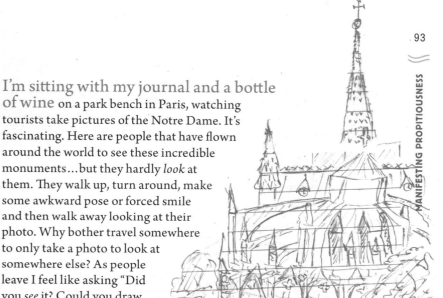

MANIFESTING PROPITIOUSNESS

I'm sitting with my journal and a bottle of wine on a park bench in Paris, watching tourists take pictures of the Notre Dame. It's fascinating. Here are people that have flown around the world to see these incredible monuments...but they hardly *look* at them. They walk up, turn around, make some awkward pose or forced smile and then walk away looking at their photo. Why bother travel somewhere to only take a photo to look at somewhere else? As people leave I feel like asking "Did you *see* it? Could you draw it?" It really changes how you observe something if you have to recreate or describe it. You often notice things that you otherwise would not have noticed at a superficial glance. It's why I've been turned on to sketching things (albeit often poorly) to further soak up and manifest my attendance somewhere. Of course, drinking a bottle of wine to yourself in a park in Paris is also a rewarding motive.

APRIL 2008
PARIS, FRANCE

"People travel to faraway places to watch, in fascination, the kind of people they ignore at home."
DAGOBERT D. RUNES

Watching   VS   Observing

Watching	Observing
► to look and wait expectantly	► examining to gain information
► inaction while stimulated	► ability to notice things/ question the subject matter
► a viewer in the background Ex: a tourist	► involves participating/processing Ex: a traveler

When you look up at the sky,
do you look as if it's always been there?
... or as if you've yet to see it?

Gili Trawangan, Indonesia

In Lak'ech Ala K'in [ein-lah-kesh hal-a-ken]

+ Mayan greeting said with hands cupped over one's heart
+ directly translates as 'I am another yourself' or traditionally interpreted as 'I am you and you are me'
+ it is the statement for the Mayan law of oneness and unity

"Happiness never decreases when being shared." BUDDHA

*The Temple at sunrise.
(Burning Man, Nevada)*

LIFE'S LITTLE OBSTACLES

What is holding you back from
   turning today into the best day
   of your life?

Too average?
All routine?
Shitty news came your way
   or too much stress
                with life today?
Well, which of your best days
   already lived,
             your favorite days,
   did not start with one or all of
   the above?

Actually, to qualify for the *best
days* category
you normally have to overcome
   some sort of obstacle.

You finished a marathon?
       That shit ain't easy.
You jumped out of an airplane?
       Fear is a freak-out.
Landed that dream job?
       That's a stressful application.
You finally won the big game?
       Failure has followed
          previous attempts.
The epic event you planned totally
   backfired…but worked?
       Perfection isn't good
         for anyone.

Life's little obstacles carry
   accomplishment waiting
   to happen.
That is their purpose.
Their true hidden potential.

You can't reach peak satisfying
   moments of achievement
without a challenge to overcome.

So embrace those obstacles.

Conquer them.

Breathe because they'll pass.

When they do,
you might find yourself having
   the best day of your life.

SEPTEMBER 2015
SASKATOON, SASKATCHEWAN

(Koh Lao Liang, Thailand)

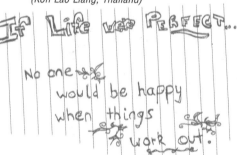

satori |sə'tôrē|
(noun)
✦ sudden enlightenment
✦ Japanese Buddhism term, literally translates as 'awakening'
✦ Zen masters use the word to describe a flash of insight, a moment of no mind and total presence, not a lasting transformation but a brief taste of enlightenment

Playa Escameca, Nicaragua

The calling of your fate can sometimes loom impossibly far away... until it SMACKS you right in the face.

"There is a part of every living thing that wants to become itself—the tadpole into the frog, the chrysalis into the butterfly, the damaged human being into a whole one. That is spirituality."
ELLEN BASS

Reprinted with permission © 2010 Zits Partnership Distributed by King Features Syndicate, Inc.

THE FLOW
OF CERTAINTY

Thank God
    for decisive moments.
The few times
    when you don't question
    or barter options between
      yourself.
You stumble on a moment
    and the choice seems
      already made
        and you say *Yes*.

You're *all in*.
A gut fully trusted.
Your intuition feels the depth
    and dives in headfirst.
No toe dips
    sample sips
      travel tips
        or prewritten scripts.
        Just *Yes*.

It is not a matter of assumption
    either.
    No leap of blind faith.
      No hunch to crunch.
        No information for
        speculation.
Just a continuation in the flow
    of certainty
    like already being on the
      right path
    before realizing
there *are* other options to choose.

Don't question it.
Indecision after committing
    to the wave
      will only cause it to crash
      over you.
You're already on one long ride,
        on the surge of *Yes*.

The only thing that lingers
    is how open-ended the answer
    will be
    of where it goes from here.
Keep it open.
You've already jumped.
Can't close the parachute now.
You have an idea of where things
    might land,
    but you never really know
      how long you can stay certain
      in the moment.

And there lies the paradox
    in the flow of certainty
As it loops back
    into the glorious opportunity
      of *uncertainty*.
Waiting on your next decision
    to commit to the moment.
        with a decisive *Yes*.

MARCH 2016
MONTEZUMA, COSTA RICA

DEAR FUTURE:

A worn worry came to light
And I felt I lost my way
　　So I asked out in the night
　　When I felt the need to say

Oh Future
What will you hold
For my Present moment
　　　　　To please?
What will you bring
To end
　　My current state
　　　　　　Of unease?

Oh Future
Come sooner
And help push this Present
　　　　　To the Past
I'm not sure
I can continue
　　A stupor of life
　　　　This vast

But the Future never replied
Maybe
　　She was shy
　　Or I didn't inquire right
So I kept asking
　　Everyday
Until I got an answer
　　　　One night

Oh Human
I will answer
As my friend
　　Is not quite there
For I am
　　The Present
And yes
　　At times a lot to bear

Oh Human
Stop assuming
　　That a state you cannot live
　　Will forgive you from ruin
Live your life now today
And don't push me away
You can't be content
　　Without the Present
　　And I'm sure here to stay

I smiled
For a while
And felt
　　I now held the key
Talk not
To the Future
　　And start living
　　　　　To be

Simply hold the moment present
When seeking
A present moment
　　　　　To please
And I'll shed this
　　Life's stupor
　　　　And break free
　　　　　　To be me

stupor /ˈst(y)oopər/

-noun
✦ a state of near-unconsciousness or insensibility
✦ a lack of critical mental function and a level
　of consciousness wherein a sufferer is almost
　entirely unresponsive and only responds to
　base stimuli such as pain

APRIL 2016
PUERTO VIEJO, COSTA RICA

Good places keep
good people. San Juan
del Sur, Nicaragua.
Photo: Jesse Jay Levesque

I WAS CONTENT WITH TODAY'S QUESTION OF
*"What is holding you back from being the happiest
person in the world?"*

Until I realized that question is set up for failure and one long list.
The better question is
"What isn't holding you back?"

What in the world is making you a happy person?

Finding Real Paradise
The Plight of the Expat State of Mind

I'm fortunate to have lived in many places that cause friends
and strangers to say "Wow man, you are living in paradise."
Sometimes (especially when I've been in one place for a
length of time) it catches me off guard and I think to myself:
Oh, right! Well then why did I have such a shitty day?

Every incredible beach town has an expat that has been living
there too long. They've gotten salty—too accustomed to being in
a place others only wish they could be and taking it for granted.
They've simply become unhappy. I don't know if it's the sand
everywhere, the identical pictures they see visitors take daily or
the constant travel advice that gets sought from them—it doesn't
matter. First-World paradise problems won't fetch you much pity
from your ex-coworkers still stuck in an office cubicle, rush hour
traffic or a blizzard (or all three). I wish I could tell all salty expats
to *go home!* Go back to where you came from and don't come back
until you're ready to not take this place, and your life, for granted.

I know because I've been that salty expat. It's terrible. I've felt life get sucked out of me from a place that used to drive it into me. It's like continuing to live with a girlfriend knowing you should have left months ago. (*cough* *I'll show myself the door...*) I learned early on in my travels how important it is to make a timely exit from a provisional home base. I need to pack up while things are still fresh and leave before I ruin a good thing. Just as important as finding your paradise is knowing when to leave it behind. Things change. People come and go. Vibes evolve. If I'm not changing with it, *I* become the grump that depresses the new tourists talking about how it *used* to be.

> Just as important as finding your paradise is knowing when to leave it behind.

The one thing that doesn't change is the postcard picture many have in their minds of paradise: a sandy beach on a deserted island with nothing but the shade of a palm tree to keep you company. Thinking of it or just stepping foot on it, many often gasp, "Oh, I could live here forever!" But could you? How long until you can't stand the sandflies, eating rice and beans every day or just get bored of the view? The postcard is just the physical representation of a vision of bliss. Every place has its downfalls and life anywhere can eventually sink into dreadful repetition. Too many of us chase a false ideal that can only ever be a temporary state.

A day's trek is worth it to catch a Cabo San Juan sunset in Colombia's Tayrona National Park.
Photo: Jonathan N. Ellis

That is why I see paradise as a state of mind, rather a place to visit—an *intangible* paradise. I don't want to live in a place where I turn into a lazy, gluttonous tourist being waited on because of the dollars that brought me there. Money shouldn't buy my happy place. Nor do I want it to. If I overwork myself to the point I'm too stressed or broke to enjoy my surroundings, it's time to reconsider what brought me there to begin with.

My utopia is a subjective state where I am living the fullest life I can, fueled by a balanced environment of creative expression, healthy diet and physical recreation in a close-knit community. Paradise shouldn't just be there for the taking—in my paradise, we give back. Being able to add value to the community and its environment strengthens the reason to call it paradise in the first place.

If I am living in a state of paradise, I should be living the dream—my dream.

That's something you can achieve anywhere in the world.
The truth is,
    the less I take for granted,
        the closer I get to the only paradise
            that will *stay* paradise.
        Hold the salt please.

FEBRUARY 2016
PLAYA ESCAMECA, NICARAGUA

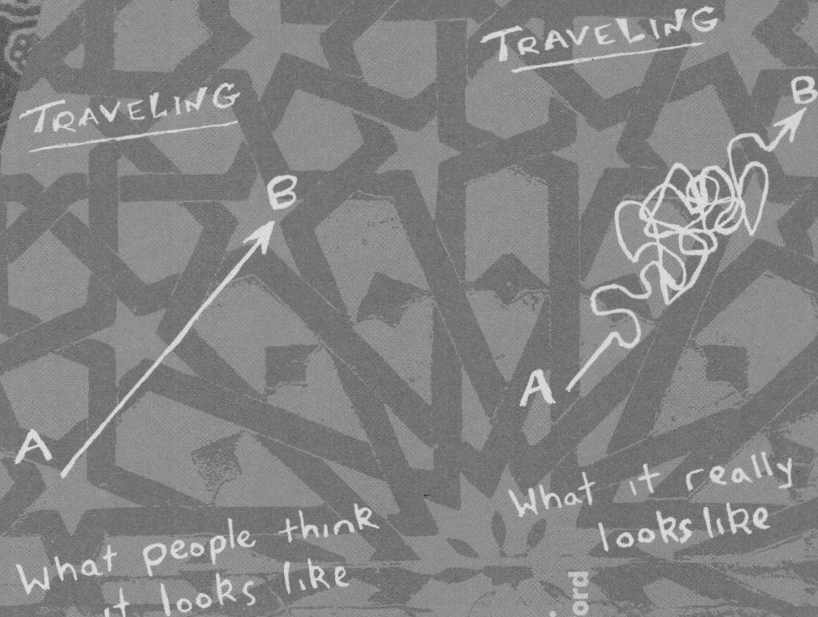
TRAVELING
A
B
What people think it looks like
TRAVELING
A
B
What it really looks like

CHAPTER 4

This Wasn't In The Brochure

EXPECTATION. The dirtiest word in a traveler's vocabulary.

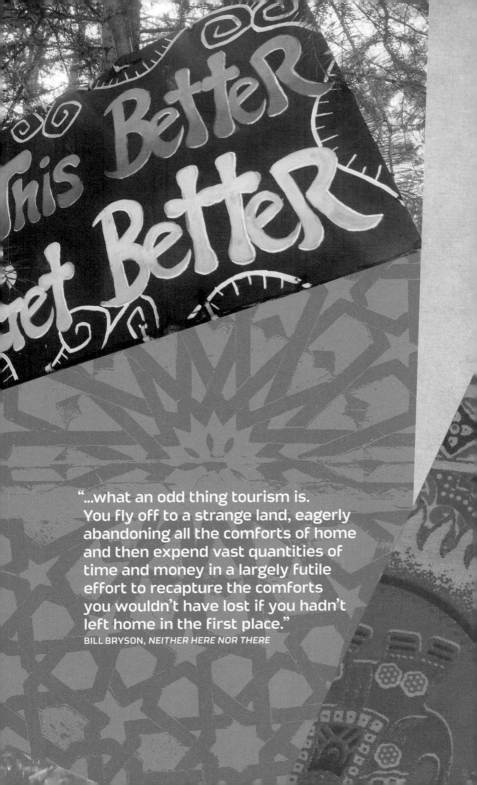

"...what an odd thing tourism is.
You fly off to a strange land, eagerly
abandoning all the comforts of home
and then expend vast quantities of
time and money in a largely futile
effort to recapture the comforts
you wouldn't have lost if you hadn't
left home in the first place."
BILL BRYSON, *NEITHER HERE NOR THERE*

The view of Guanajuato from the El Pipila lookout. *Photo by Kyle Brock*

How To Get Robbed In Mexico

Just Another Cultural Experience in Guanajuato

Will he use a knife? A definite possibility.
How about a gun? No, I've been with him for hours and he can't be hiding that.
Does he have a gang waiting up ahead for an ambush? Hmm, that would make for an exciting afternoon.

I have already accepted the fact that I am about to be robbed. That is a given. As soon as Felipe and I turned that last corner and I realized we were no longer within the beautiful, colonial downtown reach of Guanajuato, I knew the clock was ticking on our day-long friendship.

But what will he use? The question keeps repeating itself in my head. A nervous chuckle escapes my mouth like an unintended burp. Felipe looks over his shoulder with a smile. We start mustering our way up the dusty rocks of the mountain opposite from where we had started.

"*Un poco más arriba ahora.*" Felipe assures me as he gasps for breath. Just a bit more until the top with the 'best view of the city'.

"*Si, si.*" I oblige, offering no resistance.

I have never felt so calm and content walking into such a certain bad situation. I'm not sure if it was all the Eckart Tolle I had been reading (who preaches new age mindfulness and absolution), or the fact that I had been hanging out with Felipe for the whole day—and actually really like the guy.

I had spent the prior months living and surfing around the funky town of Sayulita on the West Coast of Mexico. After getting the pull to keep traveling, I decided to grab my backpack and guitar and head inland to the heart of the country—one of the main destinations being Guanajuato. I had heard about its thriving culture, art and live music scene supported by its large student population and receptive citizens. On arrival, the locals kept welcoming me with a "*Bienvenidos* to the safest city in Mexico!"

I was cursed from the beginning.

Comfortable being
uncomfortable.
—THE UNSOUGHT
ACHIEVEMENT OF THE
SEASONED TRAVELER

I met Felipe during the long climb up to the El Pipila Statue that overlooks the city. I got into conversation with him and an older local couple at one of the lookouts halfway up. Breaking from the midday desert heat, I was excited to practice my Spanish and learn about the history of the city as the locals happily pointed out their

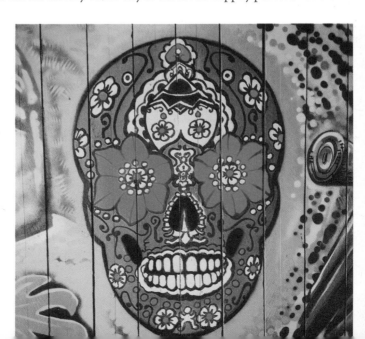

A local mural of Mexico's Day of the Dead skull.

important churches and favorite monuments to a foreigner. Felipe motioned to a distant silver mine where he said he worked, that had been in operation for over a century. He said he loves to share his local knowledge with the tourists on his weekly hike up El Pipila. Two hours later, after I followed him through the city and to the other side of town, I started suspecting why he loves talking and spending time with tourists so much…

Now here I am: entering rural Mexico, climbing up a dusty mountainside, on the wrong side of town, and alone with a stranger—who I am certain is about to rob me.

Estúpido gringo.

Does he have a weapon? He must.

He is a pretty small guy to simply try and take me down.

My mind is calm but starts filling itself with ways to reverse what feels inevitable. *How can I somehow get back to a more public place?* We are now far from it. The two of us have been scaling these dry mountain trails for a lot longer than I should have allowed to happen.

Just keep your distance and don't turn your back to him. You sure know how to get yourself into some fun situations, Mr. Early.

I muster out a few *"si amigo"* type phrases in auto response to Felipe's quickening Spanish. It's getting harder to understand him the higher we climb. I sense Felipe getting nervous as he realizes the grasp I am finally taking on the situation. *Let's get this over with Felipe, rob me already.* We continue in silence, our heavy breathing the only sound to overtake the imaginary ticking of the clock.

Guanajuato

The colonial downtown twists and turns, sandwiched in a narrow canyon that used to be rich in silver and gold. At the height of the area's mining in the 1700s, Guanajuato accounted for over two thirds of the world's silver production—its historic riches still on display via the opulent churches, grand theatres and public plazas hiding around each corner. The underground river that flowed through the hills is long dried up and is now used as a maze of tunnels for cars that can't traverse the tight alleyways above ground. The result is an incredibly colorful and funky pedestrian-friendly inner core. Think of a Mexican impression of an old European town designed by Diego Rivera and Dr. Seuss after a tequila binge. This is Guanajuato.

My calmness is eerily satisfying. *Why does it feel like I'm supposed to get robbed today?* It's like I hit the expiry date of my years of robbery-free backpacking and today is my reissue appointment.

We reach a small plateau and Felipe is still concentrated on going up farther. I finally find the courage to call it quits. "Okay

You will travel to many exotic places

amigo...*necesito agua*," I say, telling him I'm going to head back down to the city and get water. Felipe fires back in Spanish that there is a water fountain if we go up higher into the obviously barren mountain.

Oh man, he's desperate. He really is going to rob me.

Felipe eventually gives in, and passes in front of me to start back down to the city. Before I can turn around, Felipe grabs two grapefruit sized rocks from the ground, holds them up to my head and shouts "*¡Todo el dinero rápido!*"

Ahh...two rocks! Impressive. Of all the weapons I had imagined, handfuls of rocks weren't among them. Buen trabajo, Mr. Felipe, well played.

Then it hits me that I'm actually getting robbed. My stomach drops. I now have to deal with this situation—*quickly*. My heartbeat starts racing faster. *He's small. Is this the moment I'm supposed to punch him in the face? I've never punched anyone in the face...*

Felipe continues to shout unintelligible profane Spanish at me. He raises the rocks higher and closer to my face. Sweat drops off his forehead. His brown eyes have a beady concentration of hatred—a hate I have never felt so close or had directed so intensely at me before. A strange rush of calm passes through me. The Eckart Tolle I had been reading kicks in with a fleeting message of the hopelessness of using violence to solve a problem. I take a breath. A moment lingers while I simply stare back at Felipe. At that instant, I sense him crack and I feel his nervousness is much beyond my own. It is clear he is either uncomfortable with how new he is at personal theft or he is just embarrassed by what he is committing against his new '*amigo*'.

> **At that instant, I sense him crack and I feel his nervousness is much beyond my own.**

"Life will give you whatever experience is most helpful for the evolution of your consciousness. How do you know this is the experience you need? Because this is the experience you are having at this moment.

The primary cause of unhappiness is never the situation but your thoughts about it."

ECKHART TOLLE, *A NEW EARTH: AWAKENING TO YOUR LIFE'S PURPOSE*

"*¡Ahora!*" Felipe shouts, trying to raise his intensity and hide the cracks appearing in his poker face of hostility.

"*Si, amigo. Tranquilo...*" I grab my wallet from my back pocket, open it up to show him everything inside, take all the cash (maybe $100 worth of pesos and dollars) and pass it to his slightly shaking hand. As he inspects his payday, I stay still. My hope is this move will prevent me from losing my entire wallet with credit cards and passport. Felipe looks content and I stick my wallet back into my pocket.

Felipe shouts more rapid Spanish at me. Without grasping the words it's clear he wants my watch, camera and sunglasses too. "Oh, amigo...*todo mis fotos?*" I plead. I attempt to get my memory card from my camera. Felipe isn't allowing it. Rightly so, there are pictures of us both hanging out at El Pipila and around town on there. He makes some twitchy violent gestures towards me and I hand over my camera.

My heart sinks a bit more. *All my pictures!* Who cares about cash and random accessories? When traveling on your own, your camera is your best friend. The one material item you carry that seems human, based solely on the fact you can reminisce with your moments captured together on its memory drive.

Mierda.

After our brief exchanges finish, Felipe shouts something that translates clearly—no matter what language is used: "Now, get the FUCK out FAST!" I start the long, rocky climb back down towards the general direction of downtown Guanajuato. As I grapple down on all fours, I thank myself for not being a macho man and trying to fight an angry local on a deserted, mountain side of a foreign country (had I been reading a Tom Clancy action thriller instead of Eckart Tolle's spiritual mindfulness…it might have been a different walk home). I make it to the closest road along the valley floor without even looking back. It is all already behind me, both literally and mentally. I hope his kids take some cool pictures and he sells some of my belongings to make them a good meal.

> Thank you
> ⌐threat of death
> ... always followed
> by a swift reminder
> of what's worth
> living for.

I smile slightly, not really sure if the family he spoke about earlier that day even exists or if our conversations actually meant anything to him. I prefer to assume they do, and leave it at that.

As I finally make my way back to my hostel (where I have my backpack and backup money locked under my bed), my heart is still racing—except this time from the physical exertion in the midday desert heat. The lady at front desk greets me happily.

"¡Beunas Tardes! How are you today?"

"Todo bien, all good," I say cheerfully. I feel lighter having accepted my fate of theft head-on, somehow gaining more than I lost.

The lady smiles at me. "I hope you enjoy our beautiful city. Did you know Guanajuato is the safest place in Mexico?"

"...oh, good to know." I laugh.

I kick off my shoes and lean back on the bottom bunk of my empty dorm room. My fingers flip through the copy of Eckart Tolle's *A New Earth* still lying on my bed; although, I have no intention of reading it. Its insight has already influenced my actions enough for today.

I wish Felipe were here so I could shake his hand.

Two rocks, eh? Never would have guessed, amigo.

MAY 2011
GUANAJUATO,
MEXICO

A HONDURAS BORDER BRIBE HAIKU:

I have no yellow fever
Nor do I have proof
but this twenty bill

El Tunco, El Salvador

The Taste of Cobra Whiskey 130 Feet Above the Jungle

The longest zip-line stretches almost 2000 feet—over half a kilometer—across the jungle.

Zip-lining Laos' Tropical Rain Forest Treehouses

"Ok, we see you tomorrow," the young Laotian guide says, readying his gear to abandon us and zip-line back into the jungle. It's 4 PM and our group of four backpackers have only just arrived at our new home: a treehouse more than 13 stories above the forest floor. We are officially in the middle of nowhere after a two-hour drive, four-hour trek and series of long zip-lines through the treetops.

"You're leaving us? What do we do for food? Are there lights in this treehouse? What if we have an issue?" We ask questions in rapid succession, amazed and disturbed that both of our paid tour guides would desert us in the middle of the jungle, hours from any form of civilization and with night fast approaching.

"We stay over there," the other guide responds in his minimal English, motioning vaguely off into the jungle. "Food on table in pots. We go now."

Neither of the guides care to hear about our slight survival concerns, but they show us how to twist the wires to light the three small LED lights in the treehouse. They warn us that zip-lining alone at night in the jungle "maybe no safe" and then they zip off into the thick, green canopy.

Mid zip-line commute leaving our jungle treehouse.

Welcome to Laos.

Specifically, the Gibbon Experience Project in the Bokeo Nature Reserve located just north of the tip of Thailand. It is a true one-of-a-kind experience in all of Asia. Word of mouth has caused a lot of hype around the project — both good and bad. Most marvel at the experience, however, those with tight travel funds find the exorbitant prices hard to swallow in the otherwise cheap, developing economy of Laos.

The project is led by the company Animo. They justify their high prices* for their tours by playing up their role as eco-ambassadors and preserving the gibbon monkey population. Their website states that many of their guides would otherwise be working in the logging and monkey poaching industry, which they are trying to halt.

Regardless, how else can a backpacker sleep 130 feet above the jungle in what are supposedly the world's highest treehouses?

Our guides are gone.

Everyone's eyes in our group meet in silence like a prelude to an awkward conversation about the weather. The sound of distant whizzing from our guides' zip-lining fades further away into the jungle's murmur, then silence.

"So… let's see what's for dinner!" one of the girls in our group says, breaking the *We're here, now what?* moment.

Our young Laotian guide. Just because he looks casual doing the four-hour hike and zip-lining in sandals holding two-dozen eggs…doesn't mean you should attempt it.

---

*Approximately $100 per day for a two or three day trip, which is about five to eight times that of the same time backpacking Laos on a moderate budget.

Our group consists of a middle-aged man from Toronto, two girls traveling together and myself—all of us happen to be Canadian—and we are on the *Express* version of the Experience Gibbon tour (only two days and one night). We had hardly spoken to one another on the hike up, besides a few jokes about how the longer three-day tours were sold out because all of the German backpackers were too damn efficient and prepared with their advance bookings and hiking gear.

We drop our bags and zip-line gear and walk to the other side of our new home, which is separated by a giant jungle alatus tree sprawling up from the middle and lifting us above the jungle canopy. There is a small table, barely off the ground, with aluminum camping pots stacked together, several plates and a blue thermos on top.

"Mystery menu is fine by me," the man from Toronto says with a shrug. "I could eat anything after that hike."

"Especially with a panoramic view like this," the tall blonde girl states while taking a picture of the vista. We squat around the table and un-stack the pots to find an interesting Laotian jungle style buffet: steamed greens in soy, curried mystery vegetables, chewy beef stew and a thermos full of white rice.

"I'd say this is the right time to crack a hot beer." I laugh while digging into my backpack. Each of us was given an extra large BeerLao at the base to hike up with, which at the time felt like a 'Here's a welcome present… now *you* carry it!' type of gesture. But now, after a four-hour jungle hike in sweaty tropical humidity, warm beer had never tasted so refreshing.

As dusk sets in and we finish our meal and beers amid the serene setting, everyone's thoughts merge into one as I blurt: "We should have brought more booze."

"Oh, I have this big bottle of Laos cobra whiskey," the guy from Toronto says, casually pulling out a bottle

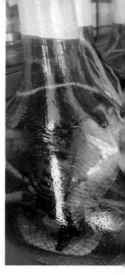

the size of his small backpack. The clear glass magnifies a large spotted snake, perfectly coiled and submerged in a brownish liquid. Its white eyes stare out with a blank aggression paired with impressive fangs and a hood of scales.

"You didn't…" The shorter girl says, putting a hand to her gaping mouth.

"Son of a bitch," I blurt.

We all look around at each other in stunned silence, squatting around our dinner table. No one wanted to admit it, but we all knew there was no way we were *not* finishing that cursedly vile looking bottle.

"Honor is yours," he says, uncorking the bottle and passing it to me. "You wanted some jungle booze."

The cobra whiskey of Laos.

"Son of a bitch," I say again and take a slight whiff of the bottle.

"Oh god, I can smell it from here," the tall blond girl says, covering her nose.

"Don't worry," Mr. Toronto chips in, "the venom in the snake is neutralized by the alcohol."

Tips for the Gibbon Experience:

▸ It is called the Gibbon Experience but don't expect to see any gibbon monkeys; sightings can be rare to none.

▸ Bring gloves. The zip-lines are a self-braking system with rubber from used tires that you pull down to slow down on the wire. You'll want gloves.

▸ Don't expect much from the 'guides': You are lucky if they know any English to answer basic questions let alone help you put on your zip-line gear.

▸ Don't get hurt. There are horror stories posted online of people getting hurt, having to walk back on a twisted ankle or not getting any type of medical attention—it *is* a jungle out there.

▸ Be in physically good shape. The jungle is hot and the trek can be up to five hours depending on conditions.

▸ Be careful booking during the rainy season: Heavy rain and bad weather can make parts of the trail inaccessible which can double the time in getting to the park in the trucks and the hike itself.

▸ Don't rely on the website. The staff can also be difficult to get a hold of for bookings. For the hike duration, online it states a mere hour and half, the office said two hours, at the base the guides said three and it ended up being a four-hour hike with stops.

▸ The guides might do the hike in sandals and tight jeans without sweating but pack smart: bring hikers, a flashlight, lots of water and snacks, gloves for the zip-lines and pack light—but don't forget your cobra whiskey!

"Thanks, you're really selling this." I shake my head. "Cheerssssss!" I hiss and throw back the bottle. I feel the weight of the cobra fall towards me, hitting the top and sending the taste of cheap, gritty alcohol into my mouth. I instantly shudder from the after burn, then get a second shudder as I put down the bottle and unintentionally lock eyes with the dead, bottled creature. The two girls applaud and laugh uneasily.

"Part of the cultural experience, right guys?" I twitch. "The booze tastes like booze, but the scaly floaties don't make for the smoothest shot." A silent moment of disgust passes.

"Screw it, pass me that bottle!" shouts the tall blond girl, "We're in the jungle dammit, let's get weird!" With that we all erupt in laughter and start to pass the bottle around. "By the way, my name's Laura...what are your names?"

And so started the best way to break the ice with four strangers and a dead cobra, stranded atop a tree house, 13 stories above the jungle in Laos. Needless to say the night rattled off in a slithering splendor of laughs, nose-pinched snake shots, and drunken nighttime canopy tours on the zip-lines. The next day's hung-over hike down was slow and painful (good thing we didn't have any overly efficient German backpackers with us...). But hey, why else backpack the world if not to open yourself up to getting a little weird in a beautifully random place?

Tam Chok!

APRIL 2013
BOKEO NATURE RESERVE, LAOS

You know you're addicted to coffee when you're zip-lining a giant boiling kettle to make it.

Random Global Conundrums

Where: Panama City, Panama

The San Blas Islands

Objective: Backpack from Central America to South America.

Obstacle: The Darién Gap. It's impossible to travel by land to South America since the entire land border between Panama and Colombia is thick, off the grid jungle inhabited only by indigenous tribes and narco-traffickers. It's a giant no-man's land and the only missing section of road within the Pan-America Highway that extends the two continents. *Mierda.*

Outcome: Jump on a sailboat from Panama City to Cartagena, Colombia for five incredible days via the stunning San Blas Islands. *WIN.*

Where: Kutna Horá, Czech Republic

Obstacle: Following the onslaught of death from the bubonic plague in the 14th Century, the Sedlec Ossuary and its cemetery outside of Prague are overburdened with bodies to be buried.

Objective: A blind (and slightly crazy) monk is set to the task of exhuming many of the bodies to stack the bones inside the ossuary. Later on in the 1800s, a woodcarver is also employed to put order to the bones.

Outcome: Welcome to 'The Bone Church' and the creepiest tourist attraction, which contains the bones of over 40,000 people now decorated into chandeliers, candelabras and coats of arms.

Ossuary employee: "Oh, I don't mind the bones...it's the living that scare me."

House of Schwarzenberg's coat of arms...literally.

Where: Guatapé, Colombia

View atop the 740-step climb of Colombia's 'G.I. Rock'

Obstacle: La Piedra del Peñol is one of the world's largest monoliths, rising over 650 feet out of the flat ground east of Medellin. Once worshipped by the Tahamies Indians, its ownership has been long disputed. It's named after the town of El Peñol, but the million-year-old rock is much closer to the town of Guatapé.

Objective: The people of Guatapé tried to settle the matter by painting their town name on the rock in the middle of the night but only finished the G and part of the U when a mob of people from El Peñol stopped them.

Outcome: Both towns are now nearby residents of 'G.I. Rock' as it has been nicknamed since.

Where: Surat Thani, Thailand

Objective: Find a late night snack before embarking on our overnight ferryboat to Koh Phangan island.

Obstacle: The only food stand open nearby is a fried insect cart of bamboo worms, crickets, silk larvae and cockroaches.

Outcome: While the worms are overly chewy and cockroaches a little too meaty, the crickets have a delightful crunch and make a tasty snack with the salty soy spray. *A-ròi mahk! Delicious!*

Where: San Marcos, Lake Atitlán, Guatemala

Objective: Have three beautiful Mayan ladies hand make a new strap for Normita, my ukulele.

Obstacle: They also throw in a free "spay cayk" cookie—which I only realize they were saying space cake *after* I had eaten half of the damn strong weed cookie.

Outcome: I spend the rest of the day attempting to get groceries across the lake but too high to get off the water taxi, which I delightedly take back and forth listening to Romeo Santos on repeat between the dozen villages along the lakeshore, almost getting stuck in San Pedro overnight. *No wonder those three ladies never stop giggling.*

Where: Playa Escameca, Nicaragua

Obstacle: Tyson, my friend and owner of Costa Dulce Beach Bungalows comes up to me and says "So, ready to kill your dinner?"

Objective: Catch, behead and de-feather several chickens for family dinner. Although, after a lifetime of eating chickens (a thousand or so?) it would mark the first time I actually kill what I eat—what a sad imbalance.

Outcome: The locals can't stop laughing at the gringo scrambling to catch and kill his day's meal but I finally feel like I complete the circle of eating local.

Where: Medellin, Colombia

Obstacle: The sprawling metropolis of Medellin is unable to provide public transportation to its underdeveloped and poorer *barrio* neighborhoods within the steep Aburra Valley.

Objective: Inspired by ski resorts, the city installs a giant gondola in 2004 to maintain its adherence to cheap and efficient public transit.

View from the Metrocable overlooking Medellin.

The outer barrios *are also incredible places to meet the local kids—some who've never met a gringo before. They excitedly asked me how to pronounce their names in English...but quickly realized English doesn't sound NEARLY as cool as Spanish. Young Alejandra (ah-lay-han-drra with a sexy roll of the R) tried to pronounce her name in English with an attempted twang "AL-EX-HAND-ra" and just wrinkled her face in disgust quickly repeating it in her suave Spanish and nodding her preference.*

Outcome: The Medellin Metrocable, the first of its kind, carries 30,000 people daily and makes for a cheap ($1) and beautiful way to explore the big city's hidden gems and local disctricts.

Where: Southern Thailand

Objective: It's nearly Christmas. Before boarding our 12-hour night train to Bangkok, everyone in our group of 20 buys Santa Claus outfits for a fun holiday photo in the capital city.

Obstacle: We also buy *way* too much SangSom Thai rum.

Outcome: We get completely loaded and end up bringing an overdose of festive spirit to a long and sweaty night train.

Where: Bangkok > Tokyo > Houston > Managua, Nicaragua

Objective: Take 200 custom T-shirts (an 80-pound rainbow-colored bag) from Thailand to Nicaragua as free giveaways for people on a New Year's Eve trip I'm managing.

Obstacle: Forty hours and four countries later, the Nicaraguan customs official thinks I'm an *esptúpido gringo* for thinking I can "smuggle goods into his country" and waves me over to the interrogation room. With no Nicaraguan cordobas or US currency on me to pay for the import tax or bribe the official, I strategize a master escape plan...

Outcome: Pretending to walk into the office, I quickly run outside and flag down a taxi when the guard turns the other way. With no storage options available in the city to keep the shirts (until a coworker can pick them up), I convince my hostel receptionist to let me keep the 80-pound bag in their tiny staff storage for the month by telling them it's for Nicaraguan orphans.

It's my first hour of ever being in Central America... and I'm already going to hell.

San Juan Surf Shop.

SO YOU WANT TO WORK ON A CRUISE SHIP?

The Unexpected Reality of Life and Working at Sea

First things first: Being on a cruise ship is not traveling, it's *vacationing*. You are completely catered to; there are buffet meals three times a day; you don't have to worry about where you'll wake up next or how you'll get there, and every drink comes with a fun little umbrella. It's worry-free. It's entertaining. It's a *vacation*.

For someone that loves to travel—and I mean real nitty-gritty, get amongst it, a-monkey-just-shit-on-my-backpack style traveling—going on a cruise ship is like paying to be stuck on a fake floating hell that marches you through its own gift shops every 10 minutes. From forged photo ops and cookie cutter tour excursions to over-priced drinks and Americanized attempts at international cuisine, a *cruiser* marks the definition of tourist—the antithesis for travelers vying for authentic world culture and experience. Of course, this isn't a surprise to anyone in the travel industry. Booking a vacation either involves going on a cruise, or attempts to avoid the people that 'go on a cruise'.

So how did I find myself—especially after years of traveling like a backpacker—living and working on an American cruise ship for six-months? Well, I'm *not* quite sure. The short version is that I applied for a cool international gig my sister told me about, except I apparently sent my resume to the wrong hiring agency. They liked my resume anyway and in turn offered me a job as Entertainment Host on a large cruise ship in the Caribbean. I responded with "Never been on one, but hey, sounds like fun." Who in their early 20s would turn down getting paid to spend half a year on a boat in the tropics?

The first thing I notice and have to adapt to working on a cruise ship (besides long work hours, cramped living quarters, strict

> A *cruiser* marks the definition of tourist—the antithesis for travelers vying for authentic world culture and experience.

lifestyle guidelines and low quality staff food…while waking up in a beautiful tropical port every day) is the immense international staff. Nearly half of 2,100 capacity of our vessel are ship employees. While the majority of our passengers are from the American South, the workers are from around the world. And we definitely have our own way of life and protocol as we live below decks, under the water line.

The most interesting part is the racial hierarchy seemingly ingrained in the ship culture and recruitment of employees. Our typical cruise ship staff could be stereotyped into the following: The ship captains and engineers are Italian, the kitchen chefs and ship security are Indian, the cabin stewards are Thai or Indonesian, the bartenders and shop keepers are either South African or Eastern European, and the entertainment staff (hosts, dancers, musicians, etc.) are generally Canadian, American, Australian or from the UK (I guess English speakers entertaining English speakers sounds better than white people entertaining white people).

It's an employee melting pot of culture, except instead of one big staff stew, you're often left with an unmixed mass of specific ethnicities sticking to the sides—likely because we have three separate eating quarters and are not allowed to mingle: Captains and engineers (*aka* Italians), entertainment staff (*aka* English speakers) and working class (*aka* non-English speakers). At least the entertainment staff (of which I am one) have the privilege of being able to hang out freely throughout the ship

The most interesting part is the racial hierarchy seemingly ingrained in the ship culture and recruitment of employees.

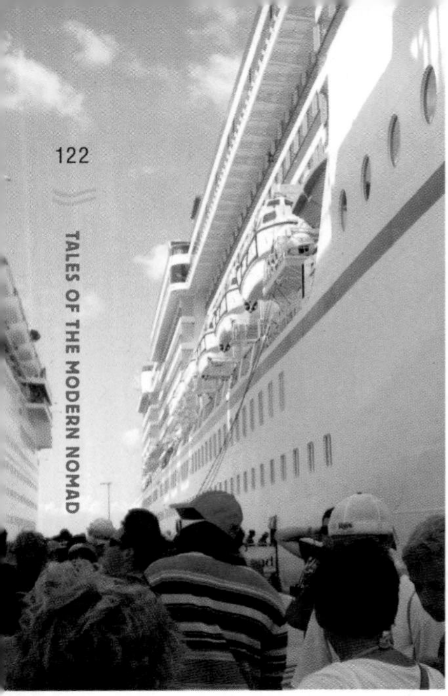

(if we are wearing a suit and tie after hours) and are not banished below the waterline when off duty. *Oh that's where they all go*... So things are structured a little differently below decks than above decks—or, sadly, parallel to life in a First World country. *How do I not have Disney's* It's A Small World *theme song stuck in my head all day?*

The second thing I realize I'll have to adapt to is how to cater to Southern Americans on vacation. With our homeport based in Florida, and the majority of our passengers being from the southern states, I quickly notice: I'm dealing with a different type of mentality. But I get it. People book a cruise to leave any worries behind...unfortunately most check their brain and sobriety at the door as well (cruise ships do have a built in designated driver). Regardless, I try my best to be professional when dealing with the following daily questions:

- "When's the midnight buffet?"
- "Y'all, do these stairs go *up*?"
- "Now I need a refund. The sun hardly came out at all yesterday!"
- "You sound *funny* boy, where y'all from?"
  "Saskatoon, Saskatchewan."
  "Oh my, I'm sahrry. I thought y'all spoke English."
- "Will this elevator take me to the front of the boat?"
- "What do you do with these ice sculptures after they melt?"
- "Does the crew sleep onboard?"
  "Ah, no. We all jet-ski in every morning from Florida."
  "Oh, that's where y'all go..."

The entertainment staff also has this running classic: A man calls down to reception absolutely infuriated: "Now listen, I paid big money to have an ocean view cabin but all I can see is the damn *parking lot*!"

"Sir, we haven't left port yet..."

There is no stupid question left unasked after each of our weeklong cruises. And each week is a busy one. Our ship's run is the Western Caribbean: Grand Cayman Island; Roatán, Honduras; Cozumel, Mexico; and Belize City, Belize. We have a day at sea to start and end the week between Sunday stops at our Tampa Bay homeport. Days at sea are the busiest for us entertainment staff as we deal with amusing more than 1,000 people—all day, all night.

Each week we plan and execute 300+ weekly activities, shows and games. From hosting the big galas in the main theatre to managing the onboard comedy club or MC'ing the Hairy Chest Competition at the top deck pool, there is always something to keep you busy and on your toes. Especially when the karaoke host gets fired and left in Mexico for not making it back on the ship in time or the DJ gets canned because he slept with a guest (big no-

Will this elevator take me to the front of the boat?
PASSENGER

no). It's always exciting to suddenly add to your growing list of duties to entertain, but hey, the show must go on (or at least the night's 20th rendition of *Friends in Low Places*).

Also, if you think proposing drunk to your girlfriend in a dismal karaoke bar on a cruise ship in front of a few sparse seniors while she sings *Crocodile Rock* in a fake feather boa with a random kid in giant Elton John sunglasses will be the epitome of romance—it isn't.

After one month on board and five left in my contract, I finally hit a wall. And not just because our last cruise had to spend two days navigating around a hurricane which gave everyone the simultaneous sensation of dropping in an elevator propelling through outer space. Our opening night theatre production normally draws over 1,200 people. Instead we decided to play bingo with the 20 or so people that weren't locked in their rooms hugging their toilet bowls. It took four of us to hold the bingo machine on stage and call the numbers while clutching our barf bags. *You said you wanted a memorable honeymoon?*

No, I finally had the realization I have to make a perspective shift to get through this next half year. Sure, being on a cruise ship isn't quite my thing. I'm also not making much money. It pays about $40-45 a day, but we run events off and on for 16 hours a day, every day (welcome to international waters and the lack of labor regulation). But at least I've got accommodation and meals covered, including extended breaks in some pretty fun resort towns. *Hey, I'm here, and I'm stuck. So might as well glass-half-full this job, right?*

The universal pick-me-up for any expat or traveler working abroad is "Well, I *could* be working a nine-to-five office job in the dead cold of winter"—always an appropriate reminder. But once you've accomplished the satisfaction beyond the tourist traps, it's hard to let yourself get sucked back in. The pleasure in the lifestyle of a cruiser versus the lifestyle of a backpacker is simply a completely different experience in the world of travel. It's like comparing entertainment to art. The former involves cheap laughs, plenty of diversion and doesn't make you work to get the thrill. The latter—the art of the traveler lifestyle—comprises a deeper level of involvement and analysis within a stimulating framework. Backpacking might not always be a positive experience but you have more likelihood of walking away changed for the better.

We all need a lazy vacation from time to time; a hassle-free escape from the busy workload of home. But if you're looking for an authentic travel (or work-abroad) experience from a cruise ship, set your standards accordingly. It isn't until my second month aboard that I get a legitimate travel question from a young British couple. It's apparent they also feel a little out of place from the style and mentality of the cruiser crowd.

"So," they ask me. "What would be something actually *cultural* to do on this cruise?"

"Wow, no one's ever asked me that before…" I respond, struggling to think of a genuine answer. "Ok, get in a taxi at the next stop and get *as far away* from the port and gift shops as you can. Otherwise, you can just try and sneak into the staff cafeteria and hang out with the stewards."

NOVEMBER 2010
ROATÁN, HONDURAS

Shutting Down The Nicaraguan Border Crossing

...Will Make You Buy a Ukulele

"*Boletos? Boletos? Cambio? Cambio amigo??*"

"*No gracias!*" I shout back at the mob of Nicaraguans waving border forms and wads of *cordobas* in my face. We were sitting ducks too, stuck standing in an hour-long lineup for customs to enter Nicaragua from Costa Rica, easy prey for the *coyote* paper pushers.

"Wow, they're really getting more aggressive this year," I say trying to look over my shoulder at Shaye, my travel coworker, as she gets pushed into my backpack from the billowing mass of people trying to shove into the customs office behind us. I try and tuck Norma, my traveling guitar, even closer to my side.

"Sneaky *coyotes*," Shaye laughs, followed by "eh, *tranqulio!*" and a push behind her with her backpack. Being the umpteenth time we had done this *loco* border crossing over the last few months, we were both well aware that the worse you spoke Spanish, the worse of an exchange rate the *coyotes* would give you for Costa Rican *colones* to Nicaraguan *cordobas*. And the "important tickets" they try to sell you for $1 are just the border forms that are free once you make it into the office. Sneaky *coyotes* indeed.

Shaye and I just finished leading a 40-day trip for Free & Easy Traveler across Nicaragua, Costa Rica and Panama. A company built by backpackers for backpackers and adventure travelers in their mid-20s almost always results in a party trip. The two of us are also nearing the end of our six-month trip leading stint, and it is definitely starting to wear us down. We're almost home free to San Juan Del Sur (our unofficial home base in Central America) where we will collapse for one day off before we start our last 20-day Nicaragua trip of booze cruises, volcano boarding, Sunday Fundaying and jungle hikes. Who knew our dream job would be so damn exhausting?

There are seven other group members with Shaye and I that are extending from our Costa Rica portion of the trip. Since the trips are broken up into four 10-day sections, we are responsible for getting them to Nicaragua for the next series of adventures—if we can only get through this last customs checkpoint. I look around to see all of us wearing an expressionless mix of sunburn and travel-lag across our faces as we absorb the jostle of people and backpacks being squished together. I move to the next step in the lineup, picking up my guitar, a full-sized acoustic in a hard case that weighs more than 20 pounds. It gets heavier as the travel day wanes. A cold shower and a *Toña cerveça*—preferably together—is all I focus on as I get pushed back and forth.

> I look around to see all of us wearing an expressionless mix of sunburn and travel-lag across our faces

"Taxi! Taxi!" shouts another man in my face with a tug on my sweaty tank top. I instinctively put my hand up to say no, before it registers that, hey, we *do* need a taxi.

"Es possible por un minivan amigo?" I ask, thinking it will be ideal to take one vehicle instead of three smaller taxis for our nine-person crew.

"Maybe, yes! *Me llamo* Jorge. I be back for you!" He says excitedly in his broken English before he runs off, shouting on his cellphone. Jorge's wearing tight black jeans and a dark, full button dress shirt with a large sweat stain down the back. How Latin Americans can wear so many clothes in this intense heat continues to baffle me.

Almost an hour later, Shaye and I are gathering our freshly passport-stamped travel family outside the customs complex when Jorge runs up to us. *"Amigos!"* he shouts waving his hands. "I have van for you!"

"Alright guys, time to *vamanos!*" I call out as everyone throws on their backpacks – nearly all adorned by the Canadian flag patch that has become the unwritten clichéd protocol for backpacking Canucks. *We're not American, we swear!*

I turn to Shaye. "Hey, that worked out pretty easy," I say as I put on my backpack and pickup Norma in her worn, heavy case. "I didn't know you could get a taxi-van at the border here."

Shaye nods. "Yeah you're right. Every other time we've come through we've only been able to find regular four-person taxis. Our lucky day I guess."

We march after our new taxi friend, passing the makeshift market that stands as the food court hangout of the Nicaraguan border. Two girls in our group stop to take pictures and soak up the first taste of Nicaraguan culture and cuisine: avocados, plantains, plastic cups of freshly cut watermelon, giant pots of *gallo pinto* (aka rice and beans or "spotted rooster" for the confusing direct translation) and orange Fanta sodas in glass bottles. An elderly lady in a blue-flower patterned apron calls out, "*Quesillo, quesillo, quesillo!*" as she sells Nica-cheese and onion tacos from the basket over her head. If you've never had the privilege of eating Nica-cheese, picture a bland and salty white cheese that always gets you're hopes up because it can look exactly like feta cheese. It isn't. Nor does it taste it. But everything is worth a try when it can be bought for 20 *cordobas*— less than $1.

A Nicaraguan woman selling quesillos in Leon. Photo: Anry Rodriguez

Prices and the cost of living are the first noticeable difference once you leave Costa Rica (or as we write it Co$t-a-Rica) for Nicaragua. Costa Rica is the most expensive country in Central America and it's hard to be living on a backpacker's budget when food and alcohol can sometimes cost more than back in North America. The country has been decades ahead with tourism development and foreign investment even before Nicaragua got out of their civil war in 1990. The local *Ticos* of Costa Rica even have a boastful and *business as usual* stride in their step to display how they've accustomed to the inflow of tourists, foreign investment and money it brings in. Tourism is still fresh in Nicaragua; but things are changing—*quickly.*

A dry wind blows dust into our faces as we cross the dirty gravel lots that make up the Nicaraguan side of the border. Dirt clings to our sweaty skin like dried paint. Shaye and I share a quick smile. We both know we're happy to get back to the dirty Nicaraguan streets, leaving behind the resorts and familiar chain-restaurants that dot many Costa Rican cities and highways. The first thing I see as we approach our minivan taxi is the bold, white letters on the back windshield that spell *En Dios Confiamos,* In God We Trust. Jesus decals and gold stickers cover the rest of the windows to show off the Catholic bling-bling that often decorates Latin-American public transport. *Pimp my ride? More like Messiah my ride.*

Before I reach the idling taxi-van, another Nicaraguan man aggressively approaches me declaring *"Este hombre… no es bueno. No estamos de acuerdo!"* his finger shaking at me and the driver. *They don't approve of him? He's no good? Why, because he got our business and not theirs?*

"Todo bien," I say, waving him off with a smile and a slight drop in my stomach at his threatening words. The man gives me a darting stare under his sweating brow as he walks back to the shade of a nearby tin shanty.

A local lottery vendor on the streets of Grenada, Nicaragua.

Trust is always a toss up getting in a taxi in a foreign country. Official protocol is minimal and transport is often just a guy with a car. It can be easier to not question uncertainty. We load up the taxi-van, with Norma stacked on top of all of our backpacks, and our crew gets inside. Jorge is sitting in the passenger seat next to the driver he's found that owns a larger vehicle. Jorge turns back to face us. "I find you a big van. Very good, *si*?" he shouts a bit overexcited. Shaye and I nod tiredly, ready to get the long travel day over.

As we pull out from the Nicaraguan customs office, I notice several other taxis follow us—without any passengers. I look ahead to see more taxis driving towards us in our lane. Before I can say anything to Shaye—we are completely boxed in. Our driver slams on the brakes as more cars swarm around us in all directions. Over a dozen local taxis surround our taxi-van completely cutting off the incoming and outgoing traffic to the Nicaragua and Costa Rica border crossing. Horns start blaring from all sides.

Jorge jumps out of the passenger door in a panic and takes off running. Several of the taxi drivers run after him as the rest rush out of their cars and start to surround us still in the van. They all look irate as they slap on our windows and shout Spanish threats and obscenities.

"What the *hell* is happening?!" one of my friends in the backseat blurts out.

Another girl grabs my arm, "Ah, I'm starting to freak out John…"

"*Qué esta pasando*??" I shout at our driver as he sits helpless and sweating like a nervous wreck behind the wheel.

More honking and shouting escalates as a line of buses and semi trucks, trying to get across the border, start lining up on both sides of our kamikaze blockade of taxis. The large Nicaraguan man that warned me of Jorge, is up against the front window, yelling furiously at our driver. His brown eyes are beadily focused and burning with hate. *Don't tell me these men are going to beat this poor man to pieces, right in front of us…*

Shaye looks around nervously. "John, I can't make out what they're saying?"

"I think it's something about not being a part of their taxi collective," I shout over the noise. "I don't think our driver is allowed to work in their border territory!"

More shouting ensues before all the doors get pulled open from the mob outside. Our driver gets yanked out of his driver seat and someone starts shouting at all of us to get out of the van. "*¡Afuera! ¡Afuera!*"

"What is happening?!" Someone yells out.

Our group gets split apart as we get pushed into separate taxis that have the border '*frontera*' decal on the windshield. The Nicaraguan drivers throw open the back hatch of the van and start hurling our bags around and into the new taxis. My guitar comes flying out of its case and crashes on the ground— snapping the neck from the body. I lose it. "*Puta madre amigos! Tranquilo con mi guitarra!*" I yell out trying to find someone to explain this madness. *I'll keep calm through some chaotic situations, but if I see my Norma get smashed…I'm throwing in the towel.*

My guitar comes flying out of its case and crashes on the ground— snapping the neck from the body…

I start getting in one of the drivers faces; he insists I just get in one of the taxis and they'll quickly get us to San Juan del Sur. Car horns blast in all directions. The lineup on both sides of the border is starting to escalate.

"John, just get in a taxi. Let's get out of here!" Shaye calls out from one of the cars. I quickly double check that we have our whole crew, now between three different taxis. Everyone looks distraught and confused. I jump in the taxi in the front and we peel out as the rest of the blockade of cars breaks off into different directions.

"Ah…welcome to Nicaragua guys," I say tiredly with a bit of tongue in cheek to the three others in my taxi. "…and *no* that doesn't normally happen here."

"What just happened?" a guy asks in the back seat.

"We kick-started our next adventure!" Shaye shouts. "We're traveling in Central America; weird shit happens."

"What did they do with our driver and that other guy?" another girl asks.

I shake my head. "Couldn't tell you…" An awkward silence lingers after my response. I quickly follow it with a more comforting half-truth. "But, the driver's fine. They would have just scared him a bit, you know, to not run his business around here without paying into their taxi collective. Just local shenanigans…" I force a laugh.

"Aren't there police? How come the police didn't get involved?"

Shaye shrugs. "I'm not sure the police want to even get involved with the local politics. Often times things are simply self-enforced in these areas."

As we drive off, my thoughts turn to my poor broken guitar. *Norma! We need to fix you!* On the way to San Juan, we stop at the well-known artisan markets of Masaya; Nicaragua's most popular stop

> When they tell me they can fix Norma, but they'll need two weeks for the repair, I decide to buy a ukulele to fill the void.

for trinkets and gifts located outside of Granada and its nearby volcanos. It is also home to Zepeda, a family business that has been manufacturing guitars since 1934. When they tell me they can fix Norma, but they'll need two weeks for the repair, I decide to buy a ukulele to fill the void. *Gotta have something to pluck while on the road!*

"What are you going to name the new uke?" Shaye asks me.

"*Normita*," I respond. "She's the new Norma…only smaller."

From that moment on, I realized how much easier it is to travel* with a ukulele instead of a 20-pound, full-size acoustic guitar in a hard case. I love my guitar, but since I'm in transit every other day, it's a game-changer in efficiency. And as a backpacker, sometimes you need all the effectiveness you can get when getting from one place to another.

Travel days are often the best ways to soak up the culture and perspectives of a country. You experience the places between destinations like being able to read between the lines of a country's untold story. As long and brutal as they can be, some travel days have unexpected plot twists which result in serendipitous endings and unexpected souvenirs. Normita, to this day, continues to be my indispensable travel companion—all thanks to some irate territorial taxi drivers that barricaded us into temporarily shutting down the Nicaraguan border crossing.

¡Gracias por el recuerdo amigos!

MAY 2014
SAN JUAN DEL SUR, NICARAGUA

* You can also bust out a ukulele in a bus station or public place a lot more leisurely. It casually sinks into the background, unlike breaking out a full acoustic guitar—which can project the impression to others that they have to stop what they're doing because some hippie wants to play *Kumbaya*.

THIS WASN'T IN THE BROCHURE

*Downtown Zurich
during Street Parade*

The Top 10 Reasons Zürich is a Perfect European City

There's a lot more to Switzerland's biggest city than fondue, chocolate and a financial/banking district. It's not often a prime travel destination like so many other places in Europe and rarely mentioned in the backpacking circuit...but here are 10 reasons why Zürich should top your travel list and what makes it a perfect European city.

The tallest buildings are churches, cathedrals and clock towers
Unlike the other financial centers of the world (New York, London and Hong Kong) Zürich isn't congested with skyscrapers and looming high rises. It maintains all the charm you want in a European city with beautiful and historical architecture.

The public transportation is incredible
Even though the entire city is pedestrian friendly, the city's trains, trams, buses and incredible networks and pathways for bicycling will easily get you anywhere in a snap.

You can swim and tube down all the city's rivers and canals
It doesn't matter if it's a weekend or after a workday, the people of Zürich don't need much reason in the summer to strip down to swim or float in a tube down the city's many different river channels of super clean water. (The locals even have their own system to surf in the canals!)

There are countless parks to hang out, barbeque and drink in
The Swiss love being outside and Zürich showcases that perfectly with its abundance of public parks, gardens, open grassy areas, communal gas barbeques and free drinking fountains with their continuous flow of fresh water from the Alps. (Let's not forget the glorious European custom to openly consume alcohol in public. Not being able to drink a bottle of wine in a park at sunset might be the greatest human leisure we are denied in North America.)

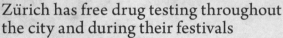

Zürich hosts the world's biggest party and rave parade
The locals in Zürich are known to work hard and party harder. The nightlife and DJ scene in the city is ready to rival Berlin, Paris or London. And in August, the city hosts the Zürich Street Parade aka the biggest party and rave parade in the world with over 100 stages and a million partiers taking over downtown and the financial district.

Zürich has free drug testing throughout the city and during their festivals

Having a prominent party scene is always correlated with one of its obvious attributes—drugs. Kudos to the Swiss government for embracing the 21st Century by providing open information, education and ways to help its people party safe.

The four-hour hike up to the Aescher cabin near Appenzell.

It's only an hour drive or train away to the Alps

It doesn't matter what time of year, there is all-season skiing, hiking, biking and sightseeing in some of the most famous and beautiful mountains in the world...right in Zürich's backyard.

Swiss women are beautiful

There must be something in that fresh air and clean water...

(And as beautiful a welcome and tradition as it is, the Swiss custom to kiss *three* times on the cheeks is a tad overkill—especially when it takes 20 minutes of introductions and imposed cheek smacking with a big group)

Zürich is modern, hip and full of hidden gems

Whether you want to go shopping in boutiques built under a train bridge, eat out on a patio made of old cargo containers or hit up a nightly rave in a castle...there is no shortage of creative ways the people of Zürich like to have fun.

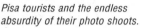

Pisa tourists and the endless absurdity of their photo shoots.

Zürich isn't crowded by hordes of tourists

It might not be on the bucket list for backpackers like Paris, Rome or Prague…but then Zürich doesn't make you feel stuck in a tourist trap or someone's stupid selfie, or make it difficult to actually find locals to talk with.

Zürich is in the heart of Europe

Surrounded by four countries (Germany, France, Italy and Austria) and with four official national languages (German, French, Italian and Romansh) means Zürich has ample culture to tap into and makes visiting another country as simple as taking a short trip by train or plane in any direction.

Photo: Wikimedia Commons

Of course you can't compile a list like this without noting Zürich's one big problem for travellers: The city is expensive. Like, *really* expensive. According to Mercer International,[5] Zürich is the third most expensive city in the world for expats after Hong Kong and Luanda, Angola.

When a rum and coke in a bar is $20 and a standard dorm bed at a hostel starts at $50 (a cheap hotel room is under $350)...you have to be crafty with your spending to enjoy one of Europe's coolest cities. But hey, perfection has a price.

Tschüss!

* *"See you later" in Swiss German*

**AUGUST 2016
ZÜRICH, SWITZERLAND**

Photo: Josh Fink

CORN ISLAND LIFE
Things operate differently in the Caribbean...

The **Corn Islands** consist of Big Corn and Little Corn Island off the Caribbean coast of Nicaragua.

When your local coconut man, Albert, sneaks up behind you:
   "*Jah mon* you need coconuts?"
   "Sure Albie, we'll take a couple..." And he's already gone.
   But hours later he'll find you—somewhere on the island—and pop up behind you with a fresh, cold coconut.

Albert, Little Corn Island's coconut man

When you see that guy with the giant Afro and an even bigger smile... and a bug crawls out of his hair, across his forehead, and back into his hair— and he doesn't even flinch or break his smile...

When you get served your breakfast order of 'fruit bowl with granola':
"Um...sorry, this is just a bowl of oats. I ordered the fruit bowl."
"*Da* island today got no fruit *mon*, maybe on *da* next boat *tomorra*."
"Oh, ok. Can I change my order?"
"But I just bring *ya yer orda*."

When the only flight off the island is delayed 8 hours but no one tells you why and the plane is sitting ready on the runway:
"Sorry, why is there such a long delay?"
"Every *'ting* be *irie* brudda*," the attendant says inhaling a cigarette while sitting outside under a palm tree. "Parts of *da* plane be broken, but all good now...we're just waiting for *da* glue to dry, mon."

*irie is Rastafarian Patois for "all good" or "powerful and pleasing"

When you'd rather not spend the $8 for the incredible Nicaraguan Flor de Caña rum, just drink what the locals drink...*aguardiente* aka Horse Drank*!

*Also recommended to remove nail polish, clear blockages from your drain and disinfect your bowls of any possible parasites.

When local fisherman Ozzie invites you over for the local seafood soup specialty *rondón,* you better be hungry because he cooked enough for 30 people.

Swamp Stuck At The Arts Factory

Hostel Life Gets In-Tents On Australia's East Coast

I am currently living in a tent by the swamp.

If you have encountered this situation, your life decisions have either gone completely amiss or perfectly as planned. The reason I fall into the latter category is because I am not just talking about any ordinary tent/swamp combination, but the grounds of the infamous Arts Factory Lodge outside of beautiful Byron Bay, Australia.

Byron Bay is one of the world's most notorious backpacker havens. It is a constant party with great surf, an incredible music scene and more hostels and hippies than Europe times a drum circle. So when arriving with your backpack into Byron Bay, the options are to choose a hostel downtown, a hostel by the beach, or, like me, check in straight away to the Arts Factory and scrap the next month (or two or three) of travel plans.

The amenities of the Arts Factory are immense. They include a pool, beach volleyball court, giant sleeper teepees, recording studio, café, didgeridoo-making pit, onsite brewery, bar and cow-couch movie cinema. This list alone can make most small towns jealous. However, the true charm and lure of the Factory comes from the jungle camping and the many characters that inhibit the *other side* of the swamp. It's a place where true gypsies and traveling souls seek to sink their roots into; a jungle community created by

It's a place where true gypsies and traveling souls seek to sink their roots into; a jungle community created by those that feel more found when lost.

those that feel more found when lost. The vibe is dense and always shifting by what (and who) gets stuck in it—just like the marsh that confines it. Think of the atmosphere that you get from the camp zone of a major music festival, but on a permanent basis: *The Factory Festival.*

Within four days, I land a gig as the event coordinator for the hostel (which lets me camp for free and use all the amenities). While looking for a tent and space in the jungle campground to call home, everyone points me to *Freddie le Frenchman*—the unofficial swamp real estate agent. Our interaction goes something like this:

"*Oui,* I '*ere* you are looking for *zee* tente, hmm?" Freddie asks me between puffs on his cigarette as I approach the communal table out back. The morning sunlight cuts through the trees to illuminate the smoke hanging overhead. A young man with dreads is playing a melodica while a bowl of cereal and bag of *goon* (cheap Aussie boxed wine) is passed around the table.

"Ah, yeah," I respond. "I'm moving in and not exactly wanting to bus to Brisbane to buy a new tent."

Freddie has short dark hair and a well-kept goatee and mustache. He sits in front of a can of cigarette butts playing with the feather in his hat. "*Non,* no one '*ere* likes busy Brizzy." He says between another long drag. "But you found *zee* right person. I '*ave* a six-person tente that gets some sun near *zee* back—cheap. But for you," Freddie nubs his cigarette out and starts rolling another. "I '*ave* saved an eight-person tente, with queen mattress and nice sofa inside. Swamp-front…very '*igh* demand. *Zee* last person lived *z'er* for a year. It's *magnifique.*"

Two hundred dollars later I officially moved into swamp life and became the newest member of the ongoing festival that is the Factory Family.

Just like any good festival the Arts Factory campground gets all the strange personalities, conversations, jam sessions and shared substance and space that makes you never want to return to traditional civilization. Who would want to depart after finding

The 2012 Arts Factory Fam in the jungle hut.

a functioning jungle community? (And who needs an alarm clock when you have wild bush turkeys dive bombing your tent at dawn?) But that seems to be the only issue when you find that perfect hostel that pulls you in like a vortex: knowing when to leave. It's a tough balance. The lifestyle of volunteering at The Factory can lift your creative spirits and give you a home away from home while dwindling your resources and limiting other travel opportunities.

I guess it *is* a swamp here: Things grow and flourish as much as they get bogged down and stuck. I'll have to see how long I can tell the difference.

> "Be careful who you make memories with. Those things can last a lifetime."
> UGO EZE

MARCH 2012
BYRON BAY, AUSTRALIA

Cockatoo Paul

Typical Factory Family Roster

Cockatoo Paul – Local bush tucker expert, Arts Factory open mic host and didgeridoo master. Just don't pat him on the shoulder where Mr. Pickles has been shitting all day.

Carlos the Spanish Chef - Travels around with pans and grills bigger than your backpack. Be fortunate if you are invited to one of his abundant meals of Spanish *paella* but be warned you might not eat dinner until after midnight.

The Typical Tourist Backpacker – Only has a few weeks to work his way north from Sydney up to the Great Barrier Reef. Will ask you the same questions every day and explain to you how cool the party at Cheeky Monkeys (young backpacker bar) was the night before because everyone was dancing on tables.

The Canadians – Are everywhere and will get mad if you put tobacco in their joints.

Hank the Token Old Dude – Has been on one too many *Acid Wednesdays* but can play a mean *Aqua Lung* on his wooden flute.

Can't Cook Guy – Broke, only eats instant noodles, and will likely show up for conversation right when you have cooked your much more delicious meal.

Albert rafts his drums across the swamp to the Factory for his drum sessions from his pimped out camp setup that includes a swamp-chic living room complete with fish aquarium.

Albert the Drum Instructor – Don't go offbeat during his free lesson or he will frantically explain that it isn't *'tikah da da tikah dip da'* but *'kahta kahta ti dip da tikah'*!

Craigu – Every functioning family needs a good papa bear…and someone that is capable of fixing practically everything. He spends his free time teaching guests how to make didgeridoos in the Arts Factory Didge Pit.

Freddie Le Frenchman – The Arts Factory jungle tent real estate guy. The only time he's seen not smoking is when he is eating a crêpe.

The German Twins – You'll find them by their matching neon Full Moon Thailand shirts, flashing Christmas lights around their necks and loud Euro techno music. Actually they'll find you.

Wonderwall Guy – Please never pick up the guitar until you learn another song.

Ashley the Yoga Instructor – You know you have been partying late when you get home and her morning yoga class is already in session.

'The Jungle Mafia' – Gypsy buskers that will sneak up quick and start a jam if they hear a good reggae beat or that you have free goon.

The Party Starter – No one knows when he sleeps or how he gets his money but he has a constant flow of booze and drugs and is always ready to fire it up (normally sucking in the rest of the hostel with him).

Surfer Dude – He's either completely stoked on the day's surf or depressed from the lack thereof. Always up early, he often gets the wave report from the Party Starter guy as he stumbles back from his all-nighter on the beach.

The Italian Bus Driver – Make sure you're around when he's sharing his infamous espresso coffee (but not when he's forced to drink—and complain about—about other "swamp water" that backpackers call coffee). You can also tell how much coffee he's consumed by how animatedly he yells his "Bus to Toooooown!"

That Danish Guy – After partying with him for two weeks straight it's probably too late to ask his name.

Kangaroo James – He loves to tell everyone about his 100-foot tree swing and fake snake…just don't ask him to sing his *10,000 Dead Flies on the Esky* song.

The Salty Camper – He's been working at the hostel too long, can't stand backpackers anymore and is too reminiscent of that "epic crew" that was around years ago. He would have been kicked out ages ago if he didn't make such a damn fine sandwich.

The Goon Guy – Doesn't matter where or what time of day, the guy has a giant silver bladder of goon ready to pass or pour down your throat. In the rare chance he's finished it, he's probably blown up the bag and passed out on it as a pillow.

The Quiet and Shy American Traveler – Does not exist.

CHAPTER 5

¿Por Qué No?

TOMORROW CAN STAY WHERE IT IS.

My guitar, Norma, on a random island outside of Railay, Thailand.

"The only way to deal with an unfree world is to become so absolutely free that your very existence is an act of rebellion."

ALBERT CAMUS

How to Look Crazy in the Ditch of a Costa Rican Highway
& the Art of Spider Web Bracelets

It wasn't the first guy that honked and yelled some Spanish obscenity, mocking me as he drove down the highway, but the second guy that hooted and hollered... That made me realize:

I must look insane right now.

Here I am, in a ditch, collecting webs from the Golden Orb spider and wrapping them around my wrist... except how could anyone see the webs or realize what I'm doing? It must look like I'm engaging in some sort of strange tai chi: reaching my hands up to the sky, intensely focused and twirling my hands in upward circles. Not that tai chi is weird, but who would want to do it under a power line on the side of a highway, six kilometers outside of Puerto Viejo, in the middle of the Costa Rican jungle?

Locos gringos...

Adding new golden threads to my already three-month old spider web bracelet.

Ready for some *neat*ure? Golden Silk Orb-Weaver Spiders are badass. They are found in tropical regions around the world and are the oldest known genera of spiders (nephila genus), and also the oldest species of web-weaving spiders. Fossilized specimens of nephila spiders date back over 165 million years. The females normally range between 1.5–2 inches long with leg span reaching 4-5 inches (the males are only a fraction of the size) with the larger varieties known to catch and feed on small birds, bats and even snakes.

Golden orb spiders spin intricate meter-wide webs and get their name from the yellow hue of their anchor lines that shine gold in the sunlight. These golden anchor lines not only harness the stickier and thinner inner web that catches their prey, but can also be used to make a web bracelet! All it takes is a brave hand (spider bites are rare and not venomous to humans) and a lot of web hunting of anchor lines to continuously wrap the silk around your wrist. Make sure to twist the bracelet between your fingers as you go and to make it extra wide as it will shrink over time (and expand again when wet). Your web bracelet can last up to a year and prove that not only are you a Bear Grylls of the jungle, but you also know how to look crazy in a ditch in Costa Rica!

> **Golden orb spiders spin intricate meter-wide webs and get their name from the yellow hue of their anchor lines that shine gold in the sunlight.**

¡Pura Vida!

MARCH 2015
PUERTO VIEJO, COSTA RICA

You aren't doing it wrong ...if no one knows what you're doing

I wasn't going to let a good swell ruin my shot at being #DeathByOnesie champion. It also made for quite the added workout—I might as well have been surfing in a giant ShamWow because I soaked up an extra 80 lbs. of ocean.

#DEATHBYONESIE

It's still a bit of a mystery why half of our travel group flew into Nicaragua with animal onesies. None of us had even met yet. The only indicator was a pre-trip Facebook thread that was running on a surplus of terrible animal puns (which was toadally irrelephant to Nicaragua—I'm not lion). Kyle Stephens and I pick up 14 backpackers from the airport ready to lead a 20-day Nicaragua trip for Free & Easy Traveler. Fast-forward six hours and everyone's already loaded on local Flor de Caña rum laughing hysterically wearing full body onesies in the jungle. After the third bottle, we thought it would be a smart idea to sign a contract that we wear them until 'Last Onesie Standing Wins'. This was the birth of #DeathByOnesie ...*and the five sweatiest days of my life.*

You have to be an animal to go volcano boarding on Nicaragua's active Cerro Negro outside Leon. Photo: Justine 'The Bear' Toews

Onesies seem to be a recurring theme in the Free & Easy family. Josh Fink smuggled three bags of them down to Central America so we could deck out our trip leaders and throw a surprise kick into our infamous New Year's Day party at the Surf Ranch to kick start the year.

Free & Easy Traveler and San Juan del Sur's Surf Ranch welcomed in 2016 with a bang and a smattering of onesies.

Drunken Sleepwalking in Abandoned Castles

The Art of Being Lost in Europe

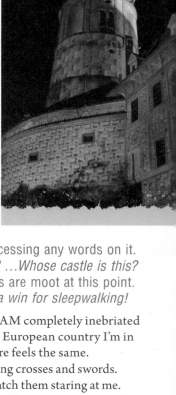

*W*hoa...where am I?
        I've never sleepwalked before. It's a bit weird. As I snap out of my dream state, confusion hits me like reaching the bottom of a long page in a novel without processing any words on it. *Where is everyone? Why am I drunk? ...Whose castle is this?* As I look around I realize all questions are moot at this point. *Who cares, I'm in a castle! Chalk up a win for sleepwalking!*

Well, not to say that waking up at 3 AM completely inebriated and stumbling around unsure which European country I'm in classifies as sleepwalking—but it sure feels the same.

I walk past a row of statues holding crosses and swords. The moonlight hits their eyes and I catch them staring at me. *Sorry, is this your castle? Don' mind me, I'm just passing through...* The only sounds in the night are my fumbled steps over the cobblestones and the steady stream of a distant water fountain. Electric lanterns are scattered throughout the halls and open plazas bringing texture to the brick walls and old arches over the doorways. On the other side of curved windows a small town sleeps quietly below.

This isn't Berlin... Aren't I supposed to be in Germany right now? To my right there is a large wooden board jutting out from the decaying brickwork. *Hey, a map! That should tell me where I am!* I stagger over to a strange chart of the castle in which I happen to be the sole guest.

There aren't even any real words on it, just multi-colored circles with triangles pointing in different directions and some strange lines zigzagging around a little man standing with arrows pointing all over him. "Oh right, that's where I am!" I say aloud, nodding my head. "I'm in the hidden level of the *SHAPES* castle! Clearly."

I pass through a large gate onto a stone bridge. Looking over my shoulder I catch my shadow darting across the coat of arms above the archway. I let out a malty burp that smells like an egg got drunk in a *schnitzel* house. I almost keel over walking into it. "Whoa!" I shout wafting the air and bracing myself on the side of the bridge. I look over to my right and into a dried-up moat that circles the castle. It's full of trees, shrubs and…*a bear!* A large brown bear saunters over and looks up at me with a scowl like the smell just woke him up from hibernation. "Aha! I remember where I am now!" I laugh aloud. "I'm in the Czech Republic!"

Česky Krumlov to be precise. It's all coming back now (possibly because I'm finally sobering up). I came here the day before and scrapped my plans to go to Berlin because of a comment a British guy made to me about "a cool medieval castle town" while I was checking out of my hostel in Prague.

"…just don't feed the moat bears when you're beer rafting those Czech Castles."

"Oh, yeah. Of course," I remember saying like I knew what he was talking about. An American came up to me after overhearing our conversation and within an hour the two of us were on a train

WHEN YOU DRINK ALCOHOL, YOU ARE JUST BORROWING HAPPINESS FROM TOMORROW

The view of Česky Krumlov (UNESCO World Heritage Site) from atop its castle.

to the southern Czech Republic without even knowing each other's names.

And *that's* why I'm so drunk! The American and I spent all yesterday in a raft full of beer, floating down the river that wraps around this castle I'm in! The local who rented us the raft simply kicked our dingy down the river without life jackets or any instruction besides: "Buy beer on river. I find you later." We turned every little beer shack along the river into a contest to see how many locals we could break from their iron-like inability to smile (pretty easy when you get to know them, they just don't like to "smile in public"—it means you're a foreigner). I remember passing out before the sun went down but not quite sure how I ended up in my current predicament: alone in a castle, staring at a bear.

The bear continues to stare back at me as I laugh to myself. He then wrinkles his nose, lets out a grunt and waddles back into the dark bushes inside the moat. I should do the same. Time to retreat back to my fortress and enjoy it before the sun rises and brings the day's tourists with it—European castles are definitely best experienced while drunken sleep walking.

¡POR QUÉ NO!

Česky Krumlov

Tuy 29th 2020

The chaos of Khao San Road.

THE FILIPINO RUM JOURNALS OF BANGKOK

It is December 9, 2013.
I am sitting, sweating in my hotel room in Bangkok.
I leave for Nicaragua in seven hours.

It's a 27-hour series of flights.
> *(Bangkok > Tokyo > Houston > Managua)*

I have just finished a year of leading 40-day adventure backpacker trips in Thailand.

Tomorrow, I'll be on the other side of the world, training to lead 40-day Central America trips.
> *(Nicaragua > Costa Rica > Panama)*

My whole Thailand staff and last group members are waiting for me to come party with them on Khao San Road.

I can't do it.

As much as I love them, and want to see everyone and throw back one last *SangSom* Thai whiskey bucket at our local Bucket Bar street stand for memory's sake (or lack thereof)…

I can't do it.

I need solo time.

Well, just me and my beloved travel companion Norma.

And it looks like a third member is about to join our group for the night: Mr. Tanduay. He's a half-finished bottle of cheap Filipino rum I found cleaning out Shaye Brianne's Bangkok storage bin she must have left in there after her last year of leading trips in the Philippines. I meet Shaye in a few days as we train to lead Central America together for the next year.

Hmm, maybe I'll write her a song.

What better way to say:

"Hey, I don't really know you, but we're going to be sharing a bed, taking a bunch of strangers throughout developing countries, spending 24 hours a day together, partying like a bunch of dirty pirates and trying not to get sick of each other as we attempt to recreate the best day of our lives together – every day – for six months…so, I wrote you a cheeky song about your shitty bottle of rum you left in your storage. You like tacos?'

Shaye and I in our office of shenanigans on a beach in Costa Rica.

And thus the following song was born:

The Tanduay Song

I came in late as only fate could say
It was a one bar town and the night had sunk away
And the bartender shrugged and said the people drank me dry
I looked around to see the people mope
'We just need some drinks to go with our smoke!'
And that's when I pulled out from my back pocket
                My Tanduay

*The night's not done but the beach is dry
I've got a bottle of rum with some fun inside
So who wants to party with me
                And my Tanduay?
                My Tanduay*

The people cheered and threw back the bottle
Someone yelled from the back 'It's a race to the bottom!'
but the bottom never came and neither did that morning sun
So we drank and we laughed and we danced all night
The party seemed to last our entire lives

And all thanks to one magic bottle
of Tanduay

Like a spell the rum flow could not be severed
One drink, and you'd live Free and Easy forever!
And so we drank our youth on the beaches of the Philippines
A young girl kissed me and held me tight
saying 'Let me keep that bottle and I'm yours tonight'
but a man sooner sleep alone
than give up his Tanduay.

The night's not done but the beach is dry
I've got a bottle of rum with some fun inside
So who wants to party with me
And my Tanduay?
My Tanduay

The ladies of the San Juan del Sur fruit and vegetable market in Nicaragua.

After getting food poisoning from undercooked meat twice in a month, it's enough for you to only feast on veggie tacos or a good…

Veggie wRap
Here's the scene
We'll toss your mind to cuisine
I could be a scary vegetarian
And find it serene
Just as long's I got my cereal
Cause I need my bowl of Cheerios
There's no meat in wheat
So nothing to really fear ya know

Work my fruit and veggies
Just like 9 to 5
Keeps me loose and juiced up
Just to keep it alive
I eat my lettuce a cappella
No sauce or Nutella
If steamed greens is your theme
Then I think your pretty stellar

So, no need to fight
But if I needed the rights
I'd give ya the trash talk taken
From my kitchen delight

First I'll smack ya with a liverwurst
Screech ya in with tuna first
Crack an egg and beat your face
With time for another verse
Rope ya like a rodeo
Eat ya like an oreo
Split the middle lick the icing
Like a funky little four year old

Now break it down for the broccoli
But none raw for me
Shh, that's too hard on my teeth
And what's worse is
Your breath's left messed for weeks
So put it under some heat
Never ingest what smells like feet
Its obscene
So keep your carrots cut clean
It's all tricks when you mix thick celery sticks
It's all tricks
And now I thank you for your business

DECEMBER 9, 2013
BANGKOK, THAILAND

THE STREET ART OF BERLIN A Photo Journal of the Graffiti from Germany's Capital

Berlin has long been known for its counter-culture which includes music, art and the freedom of expression that comes with it. When the Berlin Wall fell in 1989, there was an exodus of people from East Berlin to West Berlin that left abandoned many buildings, warehouses and homes. These spaces attracted squatters and low-income artists who made use of the countless fresh canvases for street art and graffiti.

As Berlin continues to grow into a booming metropolitan city in the international spotlight, the gentrification of past counter-culture hubs continues to increase as well. The Mitte district is now the center of the tourist zone. Kreuzberg is no longer just home to alternatives, underground raves and punks. The neighborhood of Prenzlauerberg is now most known for modern design, hip cafés and wine bars. But one thing continues to unite all of Berlin and the artists from around the world who continue to flock there: They *love* their street art.

Here are some of my favorite images of an incredible city and its unquenchable desire to express itself within its own walls.

The gentrification of Mitte: A renowned squatter's hub and its street art gets set for a major face lift

¡POR QUÉ NO?

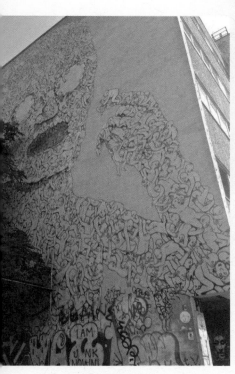

Impermanence is a beautiful thing—especially with street art that might get covered up or painted over the next day. An incredible thank you to all the talented artists who put their passion into art that is free for the public to appreciate and enjoy while momentarily lifting our perspectives during a day of routine.

Stay weird Berlin.

SEPTEMBER 2016
BERLIN, GERMANY

The Puerto Viejo Familia Sunday BBQ on Cocles Beach.

The Differences Between a Traveler, Hippie and Freeloader

Lessons from Hitchhiking with a Gypsy Caravan in Central America

"Don't hitch a ride with them, they're dirty hippies!"

"Easy Sean," I laugh, well accustomed to my friend's lack of a verbal filter. "It's the cheapest way to cross Costa Rica in a day and get to Nicaragua…and they're not *that* dirty." Sean is at the top of a ladder. I re-adjust my grip at the bottom of it while he turns and swings his machete, trimming the leaves of the palm tree above us.

"John, there's no way a homemade gypsy caravan is making it to San Juan del Sur from the Caribbean side of Costa in one day. You're going to end up on a bus or a taxi for sure." Sean grunts between machete swings, dropping palms by my feet. "Even if it doesn't break down, you'll still be pulling over every hour to light incense, make bracelets and break into a drum circle, singing a shitty cover of *Redemption Song*!"

"Hey, that's a classic."

"Yeah, classic *hippie*."

Sean and I share another chuckle and finish trimming the last palm tree of the day. We have both turned into resident helpers at Cashew Hill Jungle Lodge and daily upkeep is essential as the jungle is keen to devour things and turn them back into wilderness. Cashew Hill is in Puerto Viejo, Costa Rica and operated by our good friend Andrew Denley who is turning the focus into a yoga retreat center. Essentially, Sean and Andrew are two Americans living the expat's American Dream—*not* living in the United States.

Nothing passes the time better while working and sweating in the Caribbean sun than shooting the shit with Sean. Sean is what you get if you take the machismo of a male jock and confidence of a local surfer and stuff it into a short and wiry body that loves yoga.

"You know what?" I say, collecting the palms from the ground, "*You're* the one with long blond hair, living in the jungle and teaching yoga…I think *you're* a dirty hippie."

"I might smell like a Rasta's wet dreads right now," Sean says sweating

Mr. Sean 'One-chop' Panora.

profusely. He throws a palm leaf up and cuts it in half with his machete. "But, if you call me anything, call me *One Chop*." He throws another palm up and slices it in two.

"*Pff*," I snark as I pick up an orange that had fallen from a nearby tree. "Half this and I'll call you whatever you want." I throw the orange right at Sean's face. He turns quick, swings his machete, and a loud ding rings through the air. Two chunks of orange—perfectly halved—spin lightly on the ground. We both stare down, wide-mouthed in disbelief. Slowly leaning in, neither of us can tell which side is bigger.

"My name is *One Chop*, and you're a dirty hippie," Sean deadpans as he goes back to cleaning up the palms.

I shake my head. "I can live with being a hippie, but not sure how I'll live without your lame commentary I've put up with all month." I respond, full of sarcasm but knowing I'm going to miss the damn goofball. "Speaking of which, I better go pack up my *hippie* things for the trip tomorrow; if I want to fit in I'll need to refine my killer hacky sack moves and practice a didgeridoo cover of Grateful Dead." We both laugh.

There is a part of me always needing to stand up for hippies, or at least the absurdity of its overly-used and broad designation. Just by being a traveler I'm often automatically labeled vaguely within the spectrum of *hippie* since I currently live carefree without a fixed address. Sure, I also have long hair right now, play guitar, am always barefoot, wear beads, smoke weed… Ok, I've got a *lot* of *hippie* dialed into my personality, but it's the negative connotations that give us hippies and travelers a bad name. The labels of lazy, unaccomplished or moocher don't feel like descriptions of my travels or me. Backpacking can be a lot of work—especially on a budget. Is there not a difference between a traveler, a hippie, and a freeloader?

> **There is a part of me always needing to stand up for hippies, or at least the absurdity of its overly-used and broad designation.**

The next morning I wake early and walk into town to meet with the caravan crew. My friend Dave, the owner of La Ruka Hostel, was the one who tipped me off about the ride to Nicaragua. He said some travelers rolled through his place putting up a handmade notice looking for a few more people to chip in toward gas for their trip up north. "If you don't have money for gas," Dave explained, "they will take any handmade offering or trade capable of opening the heart chakra." Dave then looked me in the eye, "I mean people call me a hippie cause I have dreads…but I couldn't make that shit up if I tried." I couldn't help but laugh. Now, as I trudge down the street with my backpack and guitar, I snicker as I think about the chance to save some money by just playing a poor rendition of Elton John's *Tiny Dancer. Pulls the heartstrings every time.*

Walking through Puerto Viejo this morning makes me miss the Caribbean already: palm trees lazily hanging over the streets, houses on stilts, the smell of street vendors selling their meat patties and fresh coconut bread and hearing the passing whir of bicycles cruising by. It's 8 AM and I still hear multiple Rastas holler at me, "*Ganja*? Need *ganja* boy?" *Ah, the memories.*

Dave told me to meet them down the street from The Lazy Mon beach bar. Their plan is to leave at 8 AM in order to make the border before it closes at 10 PM. I start walking quickly as it is already five minutes past eight. *I hope I didn't miss these guys…* I turn the corner to see an '89 Dodge Grand Caravan with the doors wide open, feet sticking out the back, a half eaten papaya on the roof, bags and clothes sprawled across the grass, a person sleeping in a broken hammock with only one side attached to a nearby tree and a dark haired girl smoking a joint, sitting in the passenger seat with her feet through the window as she puts beads on a necklace. *Ah, I think I found my ride.*

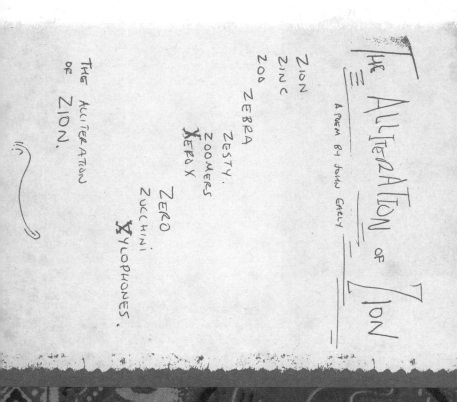

THE ALLITERATION OF ZION

A POEM BY JOHN EARLY

ZION
ZINC
ZOO
ZEBRA
ZESTY.
ZOOMERS
XEROX
ZERO
ZUCCHINI
XYLOPHONES.

THE ALLITERATION
OF ZION.

As I make my way over to the caravan, I step over a dog halfway in the street with its belly up to the sun.

"Don't step on Chico!" A voice calls out from behind me with a laugh, "He's the only one with a real sense of direction." I look over my shoulder to see a tall man in his late twenties with partially dreaded brown hair under a worn, green fedora. He is carrying a giant cylinder of water as he points across the street. "That guy let me fill up this whole thing for *one dollar*! Those bottled water companies can bite me!" He says, putting the container down and holding his hand out to me. "My name's Rain but my friends call me Goat."

"Oh, ah, cool. My name's just Johnny."

"Right on Just Johnny, you wanna go to Nicaragua?" Goat asks as he picks up clothes from the ground and throws them into the back of the caravan. "Hey wake up! Let's go!" he shouts, slapping the mystery feet hanging out.

"Yeah," I say, following Goat around as he picks up more clothes. "Dave told me about your crew heading north."

"Ol' Dave Rickshaw at *La Ruka*? Totally righteous." Goat replies. He smells a dirty shirt, shrugs, then throws it with the rest into the back of the van. "Well, welcome aboard amigo. Can you chip in for gas or you doing *tradesies*?"

"Yeah, I can throw in some cash."

"Perfect. Yeah, seashell necklaces don't exactly put gas in the tank," Goat says (like he's tried it).

"Right, only *Shell* does that." I quip with a cheap grin.

Goat stands straight up and looks me in the eyes. "I hate oil corporations."

A short moment lingers awkwardly. *Ok John, time to turn on your hippie 'politically correct' switch...* Goat turns and walks away flipping back into his cheery self. "Ok amigos!" he shouts openly at the mess around him, "*Vamanos!*"

Two joints, half a papaya and over an hour later we finally hit the road. I'm sitting in the backseat—which is actually an old couch

Highway signs in Costa Rica.

cut in half with the bottom sawed off to fit inside the caravan. The other half of the couch is along the left side of the van, creating a custom L-shaped sofa. The middle seat has been replaced with a shag rug and ample open space. Goat explained how he chopped off the roof of the van, added another two feet of siding, then welded the roof back on to make room for his bookshelves along the top. The result is one comfy and pimped out living room on wheels.

The caravan crew consists of Goat, from northern Oregon; his girlfriend Dancing Water, from Montreal; Blas, a dreadlocked backpacker from Argentina; Max, a Californian non-conformist Goat met while at a Rainbow Gathering in Panama; and Chico, Goat's loyal dog he picked up in Mexico. I have never felt the need to step up my hippie game as much as today.

"I've heard about a few Rainbow Gatherings around Central America," I ask Max, "what was it like?"

Max looks up at me assertively behind his glasses and well-trimmed black beard. "Are you asking what a month live-in amongst the Rainbow Family of Living Light comprises?" he questions. I nod with a slight shrug, knowing that I was about

In Puerto Viejo, even when you set up roots... they still wander.

to be told either way. "Well," Max continues, "it is simply the largest, best coordinated nonpolitical nondenominational non-organization of like-minded individuals on the planet."

I stare blankly at Max.

"I was naked the whole month," he smiles. "It was heaven."

"Oh," I respond. "Sounds splendid amigo. Kind of like a longer, weirder Burning Man?"

"No," Max answers bluntly. "Burning Man is now for the wealthy and corporately indoctrinated elite. Rainbow Gatherings never authorize an entrance ticket or have private luxury campsites run for profit. It's an all-free free-for-all." He starts weaving a necklace from a ball of hemp that's sitting next to Chico on the floor. "When I heard this year's gathering was going to be in Panama, I knew I had to escape the failed nation known as *America*—even though I've come south with only $170 to my name."

"Wow, man," I say while giving Chico a pat on the head. "You've been traveling in Central America with only $170 in your pocket?! That's impressive."

"I have my hammock and try to live off the land. I don't feel the need to attend tourist traps, support the over indulgences of the backpacker lifestyle, or pay taxes into a regime I don't believe in and…"

Max proceeds to rattle off what seems to be his well-rehearsed fuck-the-system speech for a solid five minutes. I look around to see what else is happening in the caravan. Goat is driving and contently singing along to Jon Butler Trio on the stereo, Dancing Water is sitting in the passenger's seat painting smiley faces on her fingernails with a spliff hanging out of her mouth and Blas is passed out while using his mat of dreads—and my shoulder—as a pillow. *Shit, I guess I'm stuck in this conversation.*

The more I hear Max speak, the less impressed I am with his "resourceful" ways of traveling.

"Hold on," I interject. "First off, it's inspiring to hear of your knowledge and capabilities to sustain yourself off jungle plants and free places to hang your hammock…but you can't deny the benefits from taxes and the establishment. I mean, even now, we're driving on a government-paved highway—which was *carved* through a jungle mountain! Someone has to pay for that!"

Max and I continue to debate for longer than I intended on involving myself. My attempts to showcase some appreciation for tourists and taxpayers and the economic spin-off it can provide for locals in a foreign country seems to fall on deaf ears. Max is a smart guy, but is a stereotypical freeloader hippie—complete with unrealistic utopian ideals.

I look around to change the topic. "Hey Goat!" I shout. "Got any road trip music? Maybe some Zeppelin?"

Goat looks up in the rear view mirror, which is covered in various country flag decals from which a dream catcher swings. "You bet there, Just Johnny!"

Blas snaps out of his slumber and lifts his head from my shoulder, leaving a string of saliva. "*Si, musica de* Zeppelin….*sabes, ah,*" he staggers in his Argentinian accent, trying to find the words. "You know *dat* song… *wit* the start like a screaming heroin addict having *sexo*?"

Max and I both turn to stare at Blas who still has his eyes closed.

"That's the first thing I've heard him say in two days," Max says under his breath. "He accidentally ate our entire road trip supply of weed brownies yesterday."

Goat points at Blas in the rearview mirror. "*Immigrant Song*! I got you, ya *Blas*tafarian!" Goat quickly thumbs through his worn iPod, then breaks the silence with the wild wail of Robert Plant. "*Aaahiiiiaaaaahuuuh*!" He howls, singing along. "*We come from the land of the ice and snow, from the midnight sun where the hot springs flow…*" Blas gives a thumbs up, then flips his dreadlocks to the other side of his head and goes back to sleep.

The caravan careens around winding corners through the Costa Rican mountainside set to the sounds of Led Zepplin's *III* album. We're nearing the end of the Braulio Carrilo National Park as we drive down Highway 32 towards the sprawling outskirts of San José. I love Costa Rica, but the capitol city is a dump. Traffic jams fill the city's dirty streets with a car-centric attitude that provides a stark contrast with the nature and eco-tourism mentality permeating the rest of the country. I've never stayed a night in San José unless it was to catch a departing flight. It seems to be a recurring theme for every capital city in Central America—travelers arrive, just to get out as soon as they can.

We barely make it through San José's congestion and extending suburbs when nightfall hits. The highway turns back into a serene drive through the lush tropics—free of any glaring city lights. I check my watch, it's after 7 PM and we still have quite a distance northwest to the Nicaraguan border. Just as I start to question our ability to make customs in time, Goat pulls off onto the side of the road. He flicks a light above his head and tries to read some pen ink messily written inside his sweaty left palm.

"What's up?" I ask.

Goat lifts up his green fedora to find a piece of paper with an address on it. "Got it!" he exclaims. "We're making a pit stop, amigos!"

"Pit stop?" Max asks.

"Yeah," Goat replies. "I've got a friend I haven't seen since I worked on his plantain farm when I was last in Costa Rica, years ago. Thought I'd pay him a visit."

"…Ah, we're already pressed to make the border in time," I say.

Goat shrugs. "All good. I'm sure we can crash at his farm tonight."

"…Does he know we have a caravan full of hippies?" I ask.

Goat's girlfriend, Dancing Water, turns around. "We prefer the term un-conventional free spirits," she says with a wink as she lights a cigarette. I manage to nod instead of rolling my eyes.

Oh man, we're never going to make it. Sean would be beside himself laughing if he knew how right he was…

Goat insists everything will just *work out* as we continue to drive in circles the next two hours looking for his friend's plantain farm along the dark back roads of Costa Rica. I slouch low in my seat and pat Chico on the head. I'm trying my best to settle in with everyone else's attitude of being content to not make any decisions. *Go with the flow John. Just be an un-conventional free spirit—void of any opposing judgment…*

I'm trying my best to settle in with everyone else's attitude of being content to not make any decisions.

I resolve to quit thinking about taking my bag and jumping off to find a public bus to Nicaragua because:

A)   There aren't any people nearby—let alone buses.

B)   It would mean Sean was right and I'd never hear the end of it.

C)   This was starting to turn into quite the interesting adventure.

"Maybe this is it?" Dancing Water asks as we pull down a driveway with no sign of lights, cars, or people around.

"Oh, for sure," Goat responds with full optimism. "I had to walk down this driveway everyday after picking plantains in that field over there."

Max takes off his glasses. "You mean that overgrown field that has a broken sign saying 'Land for Sale—No Trespassing,' Goat?"

"Ah…is that what it says?" Goat says a bit nervously. "I don't speak Spanish."

We pull up to an abandoned farmhouse, complete with broken windows and Spanish swears spray painted on the side. Dancing Water looks at Goat with her fierce brown eyes. "When was the last time you talked with your friend?"

"I guess it's been several years now…"

"Great," Max says shaking his head. "Well, we're miles from anywhere, but that spot over there looks like a fine place to set up my hammock."

"Yeah, sorry team," Goat apologizes. "Looks like we're camping tonight. But I'll cover dinner!"

While Goat heats up some leftover rice and beans over his gas stove, Max, Dancing Water and I throw the shag rug on top of the van before we lay down to watch the stars. We leave Blas to continue sleeping off his weed coma inside the van.

"*Ah j'adore…*" Dancing Water says leaning back. "You can see the Big Dipper *and* the Southern Cross!"

I smile. "There's nothing like looking at the night sky to make you realize you're not at home, eh?" I say as we hear something clamber it's way up the front hood.

"Chico!" we all exclaim as Chico settles his paws into our rooftop cuddle puddle. A shooting star suddenly lights up the night sky. "Whooooah!" we all bellow in delight.

"Okay," Dancing Water laughs. "Who's got a spliff?"

I guess that's a key difference between hippies and your standard traveler: Hippies know how to adapt to bad news and make the best of it with an open heart and attitude (and they'd rather roll a joint than write a bad *Trip Advisor* review). As I lay within the warm surround of the tropical night breeze and my new friends, I feel thankful no one stressed to stick to the plan of getting to Nicaragua in one day—because we wouldn't be here now. I gently close my eyes as the stirring buzz of cicadas rises and falls like a vibrating jungle lullaby. Slowly, I drift away.

Chico stretches his legs across my chest as I open my eyes to the sun extending its light into the morning. I roll over from atop the caravan to see Dancing Water passed out across the windshield with a spliff still in her hands, Max is in his hammock between two nearby trees, Blas' feet are sticking out the back door and I almost knock off a half-eaten papaya from the roof. *Wait, haven't I seen this before...?*

"*Buenos dias,*" Goat says from the side door as he stirs a black pot over his travel stove. "Coffee?"

Two joints, half a papaya and over an hour later we finally hit the road, this time with a shared mug of coffee. Within thirty minutes we pull into a gas station and we all feel the grumble of our empty stomachs. Max turns to me. "You know what? I have been thinking about what you said, and I don't want to come across as some fashionable freeloader."

"Hey Max," I start. "I didn't mean..."

"No." Max interrupts. "Let me cover breakfast John. I want to give back to my tribe."

When everyone returns back to the caravan after a tank fill-up and bathroom stop, Max passes around a plate of cut pineapple with some peanuts on the side.

"That's really thoughtful of you, Max." Dancing Water says as we all dig in for a slice.

"Enjoy guys, my treat," Max replies before we can swallow the first bite. "Just let me know if the pineapple tastes like detergent, there was shampoo *all over* the garbage can." We all slowly stop chewing the overripe *piña* and look around to catch each other's eyes. *Yes, how thoughtful Max...*

We reach the Nicaragua Peñas Blancas border crossing by early afternoon. I push Blas' pillow of dreads off my shoulder. "¡*Amigo, tu passaporte!*" I shout trying to wake him up from his three-day nap. "We're at the border!"

"¡*No tengo ninguna drogas, señor!*" Blas yells as he sits straight up and snaps out of his sleep.

"¿*Que amigo?*" I ask. "Blas, we're at the border."

"We're *een* Colombia?" he asks, wiping sleep out of his eye.

"No *amigo*. We're leaving Costa Rica for Nicaragua."

"Ah, cool. *Pura vida*—I mean, *diacachimba...*" Blas says nodding his head with a stoned smile, switching from Costa Rican to Nicaraguan slang.

The customs line to exit Costa Rica move quickly. I pay for Max's $8 departure fee before he can get into a further argument with a confused border officer. Max's attempt to evade the fee because "there shouldn't be any border lines or cost to traveling our planet" didn't translate well. We hop back into the caravan to cross into Nicaragua. Following the line of cars in front of us, a strange smell quickly comes in through the windows.

"Quick, roll up your windows!" Goat shouts. "I think they're spraying all the vehicles with insecticide!" Just as the last window is rolled up, two men in full body safety suits and long sprayers douse the caravan in a toxic fume. "Shit," Goat coughs. "Thanks for the warning amigos…"

As I leave the Nicaraguan customs check, I'm amazed by how quick the border crossing was. "Wow guys, I've done this border crossing many times and this was by far the fastest."

Sloth Crossing in the Caribbean of Costa Rica.
Photo: Matthew Bottrell

"You spoke too soon, Just Johnny," Goat says, being the last to leave the office. "They won't authorize the van through until we get the permit that says it has been fumigated by the border control."

"I thought we just did that."

"Yes, but we were not given any paper by the Nicaraguan official." Goat shakes his head. "So we have to find him, and all they would tell me is that he is walking around somewhere… with a *blue hat*."

The next four hours our caravan crew plays Where's Waldo looking for a blue hat at the Nicaraguan border crossing. *Nothing*. Further information was denied, as was a sneaky attempt to run the van back through the fumigation area. *Nada*. As the night starts to fall everyone feels deflated. Both Goat and the van are in customs limbo—stamped out of Costa Rica but still not stamped into Nicaragua—because of a piece of paper an official forgot to give us.

The frustrating part is that the border is less than an hour away from San Juan del Sur. All afternoon I have been tempted to simply ditch my new amigos and catch a taxi the rest of the way (I'm the only one in the van that can easily afford spending an extra $25 on a travel day). But something makes me want to finish and close this journey with my fellow hippies—and stubbornly prove Sean wrong.

With the border about to close soon, it is looking like we are about to spend another night in the caravan. We will have to wait until tomorrow morning to talk with the main fumigation official. The moment I agree to myself that I'm going to commit to staying with my new tribe, Goat walks out of the customs office wearing a tired smile. "I think they were finally fed up with me pestering them…but I got all the documents stamped." Goat shakes his head. "Let's get to San Juan."

As the van turns the final hill towards San Juan del Sur, we get a glimpse of its landmark: the colossal Jesus statue, *Cristo de la Misericordia*. He stands, bathed in golden light, with his hand reaching out, surveying the setting sun. *We made it.* It was longer than planned, but hey, the greatest gift of travel is how it always hints at more.

The welcoming sights and colors of San Juan del Sur.

I'm glad I got to share a few days with this caravan crew. As our temporary tribe might have indicated, people stick together while traveling for different reasons: freeloaders to minimize their spending, hippies to avoid decision making and travelers to maximize and share the experience of the journey. The best backpackers know when to comprise all three to make the most of their travel experiences.

John Steinbeck captures it best: "People don't take trips—trips take people." And when you open yourself up to the potential of traveling, you just might find yourself crossing Costa Rica with a bunch of hippies and a dog in a gypsy caravan.

APRIL 2014
SAN JUAN DEL SUR, NICARAGUA

coddiwomple
verb
✦ to travel in a purposeful manner towards a vague destination

STEALING SUNSET SURF

We have been waiting in the water all day.
Everyone sitting quietly on their boards,
    scattered in the sun,
    dotting the ocean
            like freckles on a redhead in the summer.
No waves for this lineup today.
And we are hungry for a ride.
                ¿Hola olas?
                ¿Dónde están?

The wind picks up and wicks the last moisture from my skin,
    leaving a slight grit of sea salt
    that I can taste on my face.
Here we are.
Over a dozen of us,
    sitting in the ocean and *dry*.
Every one of us is facing the fading sun,
    as it begins its attempt to turn
                the Pacific Ocean gold.

I can sense the entire lineup drift further
    into their meditative state,
    staring pensively into the blue expanse where ocean meets sky.

I almost forget my purpose while bobbing in the water,
  when I feel something *change*.
Along the horizon,
  something is changing.
A distant swell ripples differently,
  heightening the sun's reflection within it.
            Something is finally coming in!

Instinctively,
  like a school of fish,
  the entire lineup drops chests to boards
    and starts paddling out,
    away from shore.

            Further crests of water become visible.
            Their tips now outlined in white,
            like the Rocky Mountains emerging from the sea.
            Waves! Olas!
            Gracias Pacha Mama!

            The incoming swell is about to peak.
            Before anyone can sit back and spin their board
            around
            to catch our day's commute,
            a flock of locals swoops in from nowhere,
            and starts snagging *every* wave.
            Thiefs! Banditos!
            Five of them,
            circling around us,
            with ease returning to the front of the lineup
            to reposition,
    unchallenged,
        for another wave.
They ride fully outstretched
  to reach out and almost touch the wave,
  but leave the slightest distance
            as if to prove they don't want to get *too* wet.

Damn locals.
So confident,
  cocky
  and smooth.

They take every wave with a straight face,
   revealing an intrinsic inability to smile.
      So, is this for pleasure?
         Or just a statement of skill and territory?

Not a word is said between the rest of us surfers in the lineup,
   besides a few shared laughs of disbelief.
We all know we are surfing *their* favorite break,
   their natural habitat,
     born to be one with the ocean.
   And we all continue staring
        as the last wave of the set is masterfully ridden.

The crescendo of the swell passes its peak.
The five locals immediately vacate the water
   without looking back,
   already knowing they caught the waves of the day.
And the ocean returns,
   to a flat,
      suspense of still thought.

           Damn pelicans.

And I couldn't be more content
   to have witnessed five birds,
      so beautifully
        steal our sunset surf.

FEBRUARY 2016
PLAYA ESCAMECA,
NICARAGUA

Life's tough when the locals hog the surf lineup.

Walking up to the beach expecting great surf but seeing flat mushy waves as guys come out of the water shouting "Oh man, it was great! You should've been here an hour ago!" is like showing up late to the breakfast buffet and seeing the fruit platter— no strawberries or pineapple left…just soggy melon.

MEANWHILE IN CANADA…

Canmore, Alberta

THE BEST PLACE TO (IMPULSIVELY) PARAGLIDE IN MEXICO

Tequila.

Three or four shots—with a side of calamari.

This is the natural progression following the spontaneous decision to paraglide with a stranger after he lands his parachute on a remote beach in Mexico. The man just nods his head, shrugs his shoulders and takes another long drag from his cigarette. "*Si*, I'll take you. *Vamanos*."

No receipt, no paper work, no helmet…just tequila and the offer of a *cerveza* to the man who will soon hold my life in his hands when we drop from over 5000 feet in the sky. *Mehico: me gustas tu.*

Here are a few photos from my afternoon paraglide over the remote village of Yelapa, Jalisco—quite possibly the most beautiful place to paraglide* in all of Mexico.

*Paragliding, similar to hang gliding but without the horizontal, lay down position. Also not to be confused with parasailing—which is a classic beach town attraction of cruising tourists along the seaside with minimal thrills, no higher than the tops of the looming resorts nearby.

Sitting on the beach of Yelapa (a 40 min boat ride South of Puerto Vallarta along the Pacific coast of Mexico) we notice an incoming paraglider, who we convince to take us for a lift! My sister, Andi, helps out with the parachute prep. To paraglide, you can either jump off from a tall take off or, what we did, use a boat and long line to ascend you into the sky

It's hard to believe we are up almost 5000 feet and still being towed by the boat, barely visible below.

We spend a long five minutes lost in a thick cloud. We can't see anything above or below us—definitely an eerie feeling filled with pure silence.

When we finally emerge from our cloud, the driver shouts "Holy shit! We're still out over the ocean...that's not good." Never quite the reassuring words you want to hear when free flying 5000 feet above the ground.

We regain control after a few minutes diverting the wind currents and safely glide over the fishing village of Yelapa. It is a beautiful carless pueblo town that is a popular day trip for tourists from Puerto Vallarta, especially known for its short hike to the town's waterfall.

The view of Yelapa Bay from El Jardin Hostel and Eco Retreat.

So look out for two sun and wind-burnt expats, come sweeping in to the beach of Yelapa on a parachute. Buy them a beer, throw back a few shots of liquid courage and you just might end up gliding above one of the most breathtaking aerial views in all of Mexico!

¿Por qué no?

CHAPTER 6
Down The Rabbit Hole

"Those who were seen dancing were thought to be insane by those who could not hear the music."
FRIEDRICH NIETZSCHE

Coming of Age by Andie Nicole Palynchuk

Castles in the Air by Andie Nicole Palynchuk

Traveling = Psychedelics

Under The Influence

There's little difference between traveling and doing psychedelics.

They both involve heightened emotions, pushing your comfort zone and circumventing the mundane, while gaining new perspectives on both ordinary and extraordinary situations. It doesn't matter if it's mushrooms, Mexico, peyote, Peru, ayahuasca, Guadalajara, LSD or NYC; they all require opening up to the journey sought. There's a reason why it's called *a trip.*

Whether you are flying solo or with your favorite fellow sightseers, trust is crucial for every experience. You need confidence within yourself to withstand any difficult situations that might arise—and tough times are often inevitable. The challenges that emerge during world travels and ingestion of mind-altering drugs are a part of the process. You can't predict where things might take you; you just have to be ready and willing to commit to the moment until it passes. *It's the journey, not the destination...right?* Once you've overcome that deterrent and put it behind you, you will be all the more primed to benefit from the peak of the experience.

And what an incredible experience it all can be. Like hitting a personal reset button, a good trip can invigorate the senses and revitalize how you interpret life around you:

soaking the golden glow of a sleepy sun in the city,
tasting the colors of coconut curry cooked in the street,
savoring salty skin after an ocean's cool embrace,
the smell of the mountains breathing after a rain,
the simple sounds of life as it works
and functions around you.

Both traveling and psychedelics boost and enhance your awareness. Under their effects, simply walking down the street has the potential to be a life-changing event. It is this enjoyment of the moment that brings depth to the soul of the world—something everyone could use opening up to.

With everything in life, however, balance is essential. The only difference between medicine and poison is the dose. And just like immoderate intake of psychedelic drugs, so too can you travel excessively. If partying is the only focus, you'll miss the invaluable lessons and opportunity around you. If you push too hard to experience too much too soon, you will burn yourself out and loathe the moments you came to love. Without a conscious balance you will wake up broke, depleted of emotion and needing to go home. The perspectives and states of mind that occur under the influence of traveling and psychedelics are too powerful to be taken for granted.

So immerse yourself in a balanced journey,
and don't forget your journal.
Whichever trip you take,
it'll be worth writing down.

MAY 2016
PLAYA ESCAMECA, NICARAGUA

That priceless last conversation
you have with your Mom as she drops
you off at the airport before you fly solo to
Burning Man—which she mainly interprets
as a giant drug-fuelled binge of getting weird
in the desert (…and not saying it *isn't* that):
"John, have a great time. And just,
well…stay away from the…*bad* stuff."
"Yeah Mom…just the *good* stuff."
"…Just the *good* stuff."

The Temple of Transition
at Burning Man 2011

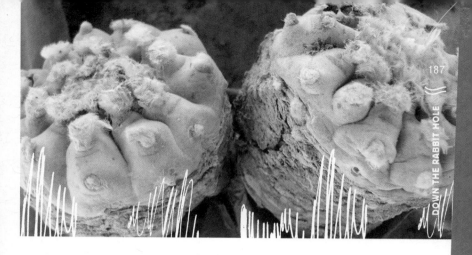

The Knock of Peyote
Unintended Lessons from a Mexican Cactus

"So, who wants to eat some peyote?"

I cough on my watermelon smoothie as I put it back on the restaurant table. Manuel and I briefly look at each other's raised eyebrows before looking back at Jerry as he pulls out a small cactus from his day bag.

"You brought a hallucinogenic cactus on our morning surf trip!?" I blurt out.

Jerry shrugs. "Well, I like to have a backup plan in case the waves suck."

And they did. In an attempt to find better surf than Sayulita's busy and small beach break, our local Guadalajara friend, Manuel, drove us to Punta Mita. We hired a boat to drop us at a nearby point break but the waves were blown out by a strong on shore wind and our hired boat driver didn't come back to get us until an hour after our negotiated time. The result was an exhausting battle with the ocean to not get swept into the sharp coastal rocks decorated with black sea urchins. We normally prefer the repercussive fatigue from *catching* waves versus attempts to *avoid* them.

> Jerry shrugs. "Well, I like to have a backup plan in case the waves suck."

The three of us are sitting in sun-faded, plastic Coca-Cola chairs like discarded wet blankets hung out to dry. Not quite the time or place for trying a strong psychedelic for the first time.

Manual takes another swig of his Pacifico beer. "Amigo," he asks. "*Where* did you buy peyote?"

"Johnny and I bought a few cactus buttons from our Huichol friend, Jose, a few days ago," Jerry says casually pulling out his camping knife and observing the fist-sized plant. "He sells Huichol bracelets on the beach and his dad's a shaman that does ceremonies every full moon."

"Yeah," I say. "The intention is to eat them overnight in the desert with a bit more ritual…not exactly at a family restaurant."

Jerry is a Golden, British Colombia native in his late thirties with green eyes. His shaggy sun-bleached blond hair matches mine, indicating that he too is chasing summer—swapping out his snowboard this season for a surfboard. He puts his knife into the tough outer skin. We all stare at the soft, fleshy green inside as it slowly reveals itself underneath.

"*Que loco,*" Manuel mutters, leaning back in his chair. "*Si,* the indigenous people of the Sierra Madre mountains have long used peyote in their religious practices to speak with the spirits," he pauses to sip his Pacifico beer, "but, this isn't exactly the place I'd want to talk with them." Manuel laughs. "Regardless, I need to drive back to Guadalajara tonight. But do as you please, you crazy Canadians."

Jerry looks over at me. "Come on Johnny, it'll be fun. What else do you have to do on a Sunday in Mexico?" Jerry says, cutting the cactus into sections.

I look away and slurp up the rest of my watermelon smoothie. "Don't make me do this on my own Johnny Boy…" Jerry says, taunting me by licking some of the cactus juice from his finger. "Oh God, that's bitter as hell!" Jerry coughs, spitting on the ground with his face recoiling like he had just sucked a lemon. "Good thing I brought some jam, that is *terrible*!"

"You're really selling this…" I say, rolling my eyes. "You can drop the theatrics. You know I'm too easily guilted into your shenanigans." I pile on a spoonful of strawberry jam on one of the peyote sections sitting on the table. "Cheers amigo," I say to Jerry biting into one of the sections. My cheeks immediately pucker up as my teeth sink into the cactus. It has the texture of an unripened pineapple and sharp bitterness like it's been soaked in battery acid. "Whoa!" I cough. "We're going to need more jam!"

Jerry and I choke down the whole cactus in less than five minutes—skin and all. The only parts not consumed are the short spines on top of the cactus. My lips and mouth feel permanently shriveled from the lingering taste.

"Well…" I say scraping the jar of jam clean with a knife. "I didn't foresee eating a raw cactus today." Jerry and I share a chuckle before sinking into a slightly awkward silence—the kind that often follows the spontaneous consumption of drugs; a calm before the storm as you process what you just did and the potential ramifications of what now lay ahead. *Well, see you later Sunday!*

It has the texture of an unripened pineapple and sharp bitterness like it's been soaked in battery acid.

My experience with hallucinogens is moderate. Like many Canadians, I am a casual weed smoker and have experimented before with mushrooms. A month earlier I also had a light stint with mescaline, the active alkaloid compound found in peyote but dried into a powder—a girlfriend and I had a few finger dips of the mescaline powder and many belly laughs before stumbling into a Mexican carnival. (I believe her words were "Fuck the fair! I'm here for the colors.") Otherwise my horizons had still yet to be fully broadened by the realm and possibility of psychedelics and the many doors they could unlock.

An hour in, I cannot feel a thing. My impatience grows alongside the fatigue in my body from the morning surf and the need for a nap. The span between taking psychedelics and waiting for them to *do something* is always a ticking clock of anticipation. No one wants to stay sober if you take drugs—that's why you take drugs. No one wants to overindulge either, and get booted from your mind and body like the fat German kid getting kicked out of Willy Wonka's factory for eating too much chocolate (although being whisked away by Oompa Loompas as they sing you a song would make an equally hilarious and terrifying bad trip).

Jerry, Manuel and I haven't said a word for a while now. The intensifying midday Mexican heat has slowed time down. We each sit quietly sweating and reflecting in the Punta Mita restaurant. I attempt to force a trip on myself by looking around and trying to digest simple perceptions differently. *Are the ripples and reflection on the water more mesmerizing than before? That tree has a lot of colors in it. Am I thinking more than normal? Teeth are weird…*

Although nothing seems to be happening from the Peyote, just the placebo effect has me observing and thinking differently. It reminds me of the advice I was told when I took mushrooms for the first time: "Dude, forget you took anything. Just let yourself be as you are. Let things come naturally and the drug will integrate itself into *your* life instead of forcing your life into a drug." True that. No one likes the rookie at the party that overanalyzes and keeps asking people "Do I look *high*? Am I acting *high*?!"

"Okay amigos," Manuel says under a stifled yawn, snapping Jerry and I out of our daze. "You guys are as boring as your silly cactus and I need to get back to Guadalajara soon." Manuel finishes the last of his warm beer. "I'll drop you off back in Sayulita."

Let's get weirden. *(Nimbin, Australia)*

"Yeah, definitely." I nod, sitting up in my chair. "Jerry, I think we need to eat more next time or do it properly with Jose and his dad in a formal ceremony." I wave to the waiter. "*¡La cuenta por favor amigo!*"

Our trio leaves Punta Mita with a sunken weight of salty failure on our shoulders. No waves. No trips. No ambition left to waste on this lazy Sunday. I feel the sun radiating off the asphalt as we hit the highway in the peak of the day's heat. Manuel's jeep speeds past a blur of Mexican roadside culture: tin taco stands, feral chickens, pickup trucks overburdened with bananas, sneaky siestas under sombreros, a man fanning his hubcap street grill with a blow dryer… no shortage of visual stimulation in *Mehico*.

Jerry and I get dropped off in the shaded palm tree canopy of our campground in Sayulita. It is definitely siesta o'clock. I see the communal hammock calling my name as it makes a big, lazy smile swaying empty between two palms. Before I can put down my surfboard Jerry interrupts the silence.

"We should probably eat one of your peyote buttons now," he smiles.

"*Ay pinche cabron* Jerry! The only trip I feel like taking is falling asleep!"

"Hey *hombre,* we had one of mine already...fair's fair."

Jerry and I share a lazy Mexican stare down.

"Nothing even happened with the first one," he pleads. "It would be a waste to not continue, man. Just sayin'..."

I put my surfboard down. "Well, we're going to need some more jam."

Nothing seems to bring out best-of-intentioned peer pressure like traveling and illicit substances. We eat the second cactus button even faster than the first. I immediately start to feel a little sick; not from eating raw peyote, but from consuming two jars of poor quality, artificially sweetened Mexican jam. Once the sugar rush dies off, I sense something brewing, like the initial signs of small bubbles when water starts to boil, except the bubbles are a warmth that starts in my stomach and bubbles up into a smile on my face. *Hmm, I think I'm cooking—cooking with cactus.*

"Cool Johnny, thanks. Should be an interesting day," Jerry says quickly, taking off barefoot toward the beach without the hint of a look back. I don't even have time to interject or ask any questions. He's gone. The realization floats into my head that this is going to be one of those solo, fend-for-yourself type of trips. *Should be an interesting day indeed there, Jerry. Thanks.*

To most people, being left alone after just consuming drugs is a mild nightmare—especially on something you've never tried before. No safety blanket of someone on your level to comfort your psyche or even share random giggle fits with. After several years of solo backpacking, I have become well accustomed to independent and introspective journeys, but figure I should seek some type of

Nothing seems to bring out best-of-intentioned peer pressure like traveling and illicit substances.

company. With a superfluous glance in both directions like I am about to cross an invisible street, I stand up from my lawn chair and head into town. *Hmm, these bubbles keep bubbling bigger…*

It starts with a lazy sandal shuffle down the broken Mexican sidewalk and slowly turns into a strut with a smirk. The late afternoon sun is coming down softer and friendlier, feeling more like a warm hug than a burning slap. I can't tell if the town is starting to liven up or if it's just me. My perceptions are opening up to the warmth of colors and external stimulus. Walking gets more absorbing. The beat of my feet and sway of my hands start to sync in with random street sounds around me: birds chirping, palm leaves rustling, a lady sweeping her steps, the nearby waves crashing and a street vendor calling out to sell his ice cream. "*¡Nieve, nieve, nieve!*" My head bounces and nods happily along like a cartoon bandito bobblehead doll on the dash of a Mexican taxi.

Yup, I'm high.

I cruise past Sayulita's town square. With its funky gazebo, pastel-colored steps and enclosed shade of arching palm trees it always entices worldly characters to come and pass time—or joints. A couple Huichol natives work attentively on their beadwork behind their table of crafts to sell to the passing tourists. A local is passed out under a tree with a cheap bottle of tequila sitting exploited by his side. Several dreadlocked backpackers share a lazy jam session with a guitar and broken *djembe* drum—likely letting their travel plans and day's intentions idle like the rest of us. Sayulita can definitely be a traveler's vortex that sucks backpackers in and spits them out months later, broke, hung over and without any other traveling accomplished.

I can't tell if the town is starting to liven up or if it's just me.

Bubble. Bubble. Bubble. My buzz continues to boil, expanding out from my skin. Like most drunk or stoned tourists in Mexico, I get a sudden urge to put my feet in the ocean. Arriving at the main entrance to the beach, I kick off my sandals, seemingly oblivious that the sand has been baking under the sun all day. Instead of intelligently putting my sandals back on, I do the gringo beach shuffle, slowly speeding up my strides to the ocean—each step burning deeper. I hear an imaginary fizzle once my feet reach the cool, salty water. *Stupid gringo.* Looking around I intake my surroundings all at once and get an overload from the mass of people, noise and music from the busy beach bars. *Retreat!*

I continue in the wet sand towards the empty beaches north of town. As I pass the bars and restaurants on my right, the blasting music from each one changes every 20 steps like I'm walking across a radio dial of reggae and Jack Johnson stations. Doesn't matter where you are in the world, if there is a beach, chances are you are within earshot of either Bob Marley or *Banana Pancakes* playing.

Crossing the river and escaping the bustle, my peyote buzz stops escalating and finds a steady groove to permeate within me. No more boiling, just a lid on top to simmer and contain the heat. I stop my sandy strut, look around and take in the tropical surroundings with a content smile. I raise my arms up, tilt my head back and embrace the sun with a skyward stretch like waking up in a giant hotel bed, realizing I have more space to extend into. I breathe in and drink the warmth of the sun. *Aaaahhh.*

At that exact moment I hear a summoning: A steady beat, calling out for celebration—*Drums*! I snap out of my stretch to move swiftly toward the rhythmic sounds coming from further down the beach. Every step I take I get pulled closer to the energy that is building. I pass a last stretch of palm trees to see a clearing on the beach that is overflowing with life: djembes, bongos, hula-hoops, fire spinning, dancing bodies and swirling hips.

Freshly cut peyote.

"Come join us *guapo*." A dreadlocked girl calls out to me as she reaches for my hand. Her tanned skin intensifies the brightness of her smile. "We're celebrating the day and the setting sun!" She leads me into the heart of the gathering. Her hand is soft to the touch but firm in confidence. We pass a waft of marijuana smoke and *paulo santo* incense coming from some guitar players sitting in the sand to our left. Laughing faces pass around a sandy bottle of rum to our right. *Ok. This is where I belong. This is my momentary home base.*

"*Me llamo Johnny.*" I say, slightly smitten.

"Ana," She responds. "I think I've seen you around town, you play guitar at Don Pato's Open Mic, *si*?" Ana says with a different Spanish accent that hints she's not from Mexico. Her smile is so big, it wrinkles her red painted dots that outline her eyes, giving her a further exotic charm. I tell her that the Don Pato rooftop patio is my local haunt for live music and we share a laugh when we both register that we've shared a round of tequila shots, somewhere in the blurred plight of last call.

The conversation doesn't go too far before Ana realizes I'm not exactly sober. I explain the unexpected trip I'm on.

"*Que?* Here? Now? On peyote?? The local people might call you *loco* for not having some sort of ceremony or blessing." Ana says giving the hint that she has a fair amount of experience with peyote and other hallucinogenics (a noticeable theme around Sayulita). Her voice escalates as we near the rumbling drum circle. "Well *Juanito*, ask Peyote to treat you well and she will bring you a good night!"

Ana lets go of my hand with a wink and dances her way into the middle of the drum circle, closing her eyes and raising her arms up over her head to the building beat. Her words linger in my mind and I stare blankly ahead. *Ask Peyote?* Ana said it so simply like it was a person. The thought of ingesting an entity—an entire culture via the peyote cactus—descends on me.

Another girl cries out and joins Ana to dance in the middle of the drumming bodies. "Ay yi yi yo!" More people jump in and it seems Ana has ignited a dance party. Stomping feet, banging drums, open smiles and salty smells of sea breeze and sweat— gypsy life in a nutshell. The sun grows wide and heavy as it sinks closer to the ocean, spraying gold colors out onto the beach like the sky is juicing an orange. The drumming slows and the whole gathering begin to howl like a pack of beach wolves until the sun submerges itself completely into the sea. The drummers kick back in and so does the party. Applause breaks out and people cheer like the ball has dropped at New Year's Eve in Times Square.

A man with brown eyes and dark black beads hanging over his bare chest passes me a joint with a simple nod. "*Feliz dia.*" He says with smoke billowing out of his smile.

"Feliz dia." I respond taking the joint between both of our index fingers then rolling it off his finger and onto my thumb—the classic we-know-how-to-smoke-weed pass. I take a deep inhale as I put it up to my lips. *And happy day to you too Señora Peyote, let's have a good night shall we?*

I can't tell if it is the deep hit of weed or the fact I formally address peyote as a person—but everything changes. My head becomes light and dizzy and my vision turns everything into color that fractals out in complex patterns and shapes. Everything is evolving and blending together as I turn around to try and get the bearings of where I am. There is a pull of intuition calling me to a vacated section of the beach to sit and reflect alone— *or am I alone?* My feet stumble in the sand as I gather myself and

THE EYES ARE THE WINDOWS TO WHERE THE SOUL IS SUPPOSED TO BE.

push my momentum forward with the difficulty of moving a human-sized Jenga tower of teetering marshmallows. *You can do this. Right foot...left...*

Something else starts stirring in me. Similar to the escalating bubbling feeling I had earlier but much more profound. The sensation inside me has the tension of a secret that I can't keep quiet anymore. I need to spill the beans—whatever the *beans* are. There is a presence in front of me, but it's closed off as if a door is between us—and both of us are holding our hand up to knock. I find a spot on the beach away from the music and busy atmosphere and my body crashes down with a quiet thud in the sand. I cross my legs and sit straight like a seated radio antenna ready to receive a signal...and I do.

These are the words I wrote down in my journal that night:

THE KNOCK
APRIL 7th '20

I had to break free for a while.
I had to get _it_ out   And when it knocked,
Consciousness broke loose & burst into colors carrying kaliedoscopes
up into the sky. Purple spirals danced creating winding staircases
lifting up higher & farther.
It was positive. My content was content
But the elevator peaked, the background darkened
    & the falling feeling tricked the mind realizing the stairs
    were an illusion which also led straight down
                                    to the dark depths.
Respect she whispered.
Respect & understanding for the self & surrounding through substance
    can lift awakening or drop madly below.
I smiled.
She had built early trust & nodded.
That was all.
    And I promised to let it out next time she knocked.

In Touch With Yourself by Evgenia Mikhaylova

I open my eyes to the blackness of night, like waking from a familiar dream. The ocean is audible in front of me but only visible with occasional white crests of waves catching the soft moonlight. I am alone on the beach. Looking over my left shoulder, I see a fire, dancing bodies and hear the sounds of the drums—did someone press the pause button on the night? I am less than 60 yards away yet feel a complete disconnect from all the stimulation of the party. My head starts to adjust to everything around me.

Wait, what just happened??

"STEP INSIDE
    YOUR HEAD TO FIND
HIDING FROM WITHIN.
CAUSE YOU CANT CLOSE YOUR EYES
    BUT ONLY
        CLOSE YOUR LIDS
                        — J. Eardy

I get up to my feet with no difficulty walking, seeing or perceiving my surroundings. Besides being a little light-headed I feel a sober lever has been flipped—but I didn't touch the switch. *Was I talking to someone?*

As I make my way back to the gathering, I look up above the swaying palms to the crescent moon with its tips pointing up to the sky. It is smiling down on me like it has just told me a secret. I share a breath with the wind coming off the sea.

Muchas gracias.

I snap out of my daze with the sound of my name: "Johnny!" A shadow shouts as it moves toward me from the fire. "Juanito, I've been looking for you!"

"Ana!" I say recognizing her face as she comes closer.

"Johnny, I think I found a friend of yours!" she laughs pointing to Jerry moving slowly behind her. Jerry gives me a smirk and an eye roll like he has just been through his own knock around by a Mexican cactus. Our eyes meet to share a quick glance of understanding, followed by a laugh.

"We'll talk tomorrow." I say to Jerry as I grab Ana's hand. "Right now, we dance!"

APRIL 2011
SAYULITA, MEXICO

DIZZY AND DAPPER

If there's one strange thing
About this melody
It's gotta be
I've been drinking so long and now
It doesn't even phase me
Shots have got the main theme
With a Jack and Coke to save me
Bacardi for serenity
Chased with lime and grenadine
So shoot a straight shot to feel it
The salt spilt tequila
With lime squeezed to seal it
You reel quick
Dizzy and dapper gone ballistic
What is this?
Hangover fixed
With a six-pack trick?
A tall gin mixed
With salt rims to lick
On the rocks like Barney Rubble
Cause you know we're drinking
   doubles
Think to sink a bit of trouble
          Bartender I
              need my drink!

FEBRUARY 2011
CAYMAN ISLANDS

shenanigan |SHə'nanəgən|
noun
+ silly or high spirited behavior; mischief
+ tricky or questionable practices or
  conduct

*I'm not a fan of a shenanigan at all. I only
enjoy a layered plethora of shenanigan.*

plethora |'pleTHərə|
noun
+ an amount that is much greater than what is necessary

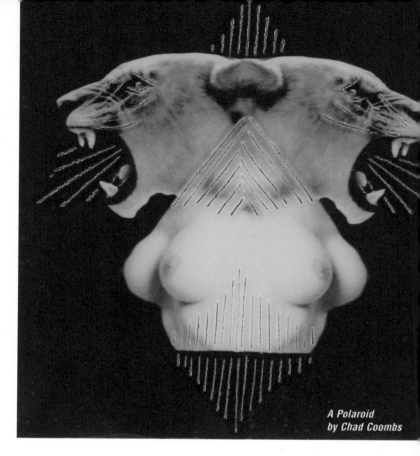

A Polaroid
by Chad Coombs

Cocaine VS LSD

Aussies, Being Set on Fire by a Stripper and its Combined Effects on the Psyche

*C*ocaine is a shitty drug.
The thought keeps repeating itself in my head.
You're NOT doing cocaine this weekend, John...
"Heyooo!" one of the Australian's shouts as he throws another big bag of blow on the kitchen table to a raucous applause. "She's gonna be a *feckin'* wild weekend mates!"
Ah, shit.

Aussies love partying, and they also love drugs (or is that the same thing to them?). When it comes to throwing a bachelor party—or as they say, *bucks party*—you know there is going to be *heaps* of both. Today there is no shortage of booze either: 12 cases of beer, three bottles of red wine, two bottles each of rum and vodka, a big bag of weed, 18-year-old scotch and a cucumber to go with the Hendricks gin. We are only eight people so far—and we have an entire mansion rented on Wollongong Beach. *Ah, shit. This is literally going to be a 48-hour Gong Show...*

I had been living and working in Sydney for several months. It didn't take me long to find a cool crew of young professionals and entrepreneurs that love surfing as much as throwing an epic party. They took me under their wing right away. The more demanding the workweek, the harder we hit the surf and the booze on the weekend. As soon as I found out we were throwing a big bucks party for one of our good friends who is getting married, I tried to research if liver pills were a real thing (hmm, detox to retox?). And now, with the amount of coke around, I know I'm about to drink and smoke even more to try and match the level that things are about to hit. That is until I hear Matty kick through the door...

There's nothing like being saved from the peer pressure of cocaine by dropping acid.

"*Rrright* mates! I've got ten tabs of acid! Who's ready to get *weird*?!"

Matty's exclamation is met with mixed reaction.

"Whoa, Matty," one of the young accountants says as he cracks a beer, "This isn't *Burning Man,* mate."

"Yea," another Sydney local chips in, "I don't plan on playing any bongos while running down the beach naked tonight... well, yet."

I look over at my friend Dezzy and we exchange a smile. He's a fellow musician who stays away from cocaine and also dabbles in psychedelics—with or without naked bongo playing.

"Dezzy and I can help you out there Matty!" I shout.

Dezzy nods. "Yeah mate, we can take a peak down the rabbit hole with ya."

Phew. Nothing like being saved from the peer pressure of cocaine by dropping acid.

"Well," the accountant chips in, picking up and wagging one of the bags of blow over his head. "Why don't we just see who can finish their bag of tricks first!" He jokes with a cheeky smile that also hints at an intent to follow through with his challenge.

Welcome to partying with Aussies: They throw down with the aptitude of a loose cannon on a paper boat; sink or swim, if you're to stay on their level, you're going down with their ship.

And that is how you start a 48-hour social experiment of cocaine versus LSD.

In the world of drugs, cocaine and LSD are almost as far apart as you can get: A social stimulant versus a reclusive psychedelic. Cocaine often extroverts an introvert (to *mingle* and spew everything *on* their mind), whereas a strong hit of acid can introvert an extrovert (to *escape* and spew everything *within* their mind). Coke hits you quick and can come crashing down just as fast. LSD makes for a long journey to commit to—often between six to 12 hours.

It's not just the vast contrast in effects between cocaine and LSD. People that seek to consume them often turn into polar opposite personalities as well:

Night owls versus daytrippers.

Quick fixers versus extended journeyers.

Ego pushers versus ego dismantlers.

Numb-ers versus perceivers.

Dependency versus independency.

But for me, the biggest difference is that unlike cocaine, I've never witnessed someone that just *needs* a hit of acid to wake up, straighten them out or get through a day of work. It just doesn't happen like that. But at least the two sides can always come together and unite over some bass-thumping electronic music.

Matty hands out a small square of blotter paper to Dezzy and me. Imprinted onto the chit of paper I see the smile of Felix the Cat looking back at me. "Cheers mates," Matty says raising his hand then licking the square from his palm. The three of us hold our tongues out like an acid toast to each other then close our mouths letting the paper dissolve as we carry on with the rest of the celebration. Petey, the best man for the wedding, has just shown up with a stack of blue housecoats for each of the 10 guys to wear for the weekend. "*Right* mates," he says passing them out. "It is a bucks party, but if *yer* gunna *buck* it without your

grundies unda these…just keep *yer* damn coat tied *togetha*!" Petey puts another bottle of scotch on the table. "Now it was a *helluva* week in the office, so someone pass me a cigar to go with this scotch and line me up a couple rips to kick off this weekend, *eh*?"

The sun is still shining bright and there are already a few empty cases of beer and an empty bottle of rum in the kitchen. I am starting to feel an extra twinkle from the sun's reflection on the metal appliances and added vibrancy of the colors around me. At this point, I have tried LSD once before. It was in Mexico the year before at a full moon party in the jungle. I remember needing to escape the crowd to climb and jump around on giant rocks in the river. I was looping back for more laps

> **Nature and the simple pleasures of observing and playing like a child had never felt so good or been so captivating.**

around the river rocks like I was doing runs on a ski hill. Nature and the simple pleasures of observing and playing like a child had never felt so good or been so captivating. As my friend once poetically explained it, "Tripping on acid is like being a child… *on acid."*

"Well, looks like Mikey is the first to crack the ice," Petey says, reaching across the table for the bottle of scotch, pausing, then grabbing the gin instead.

"He puked already?" I reply, sipping my can of Foster's.

"Nah," Petey shakes his head, pouring a four-finger shot. "Scotty, the Queensland *bogan,* already landed that *hona'* after shot-gunning a few too many frosty Fosteys. Yea Mikey, the *wanka,* already took off naked running down the beach."

"He at least have his house coat on?"

"Yea," Petey says, adding the tiniest splash of water to his gin. "But it was tied around his *feckin'* head. Have you seen that *cucumba*?"

"Dezzy was drumming with it until it broke after someone slapped it across his face."

"Ah, she'll be 'right. *Gonna* be a *bugga* long weekend Johnny. Care for a cheeky line?"

"Nah, I don't do blow," I say cracking another can of beer. "This acid's picking up though."

"That stuff scares the shit out of me."

"Funny, I was going to say the same about cocaine."

"…Matty, Mikey, Petey, Scotty…Hey Dezzy," I say to him as we sit on the kitchen countertop next to a growing pile of empty cans and bottles. "Why do you guys have to put an 'eee' behind every word and person's name?"

Dezzy shakes his head like the question snapped him out of a vivid daydream. "Ah, what's that *mate*?"

"You know," I clear my throat and step into my best Aussie accent. "*Ay crikey, matey* no *biggie*. Whether you're an *Aussie tradie* or *bikie* on the *pokies,* just grab another *cheeky stubby* from the *eskie* for *brekkie* before we take the *utey* to that *grotty woolies* in *Brizzie wouldja?*"

"*Fair dinkum* mate," Dezzy says. "*S'trewth*. You're picking up Aussie style pretty well yourself there John*neee Eee*. My turn—*eh?*" Dezzy clears his throat and starts up in his exaggerated Canadian accent. "*…oh* yeah *hey*? *Wanna* take '*er* out for a *rip* to *Timmy Ho's* with some *dill Spitz* there *bud*? A*boot* time I cash in my *looonies n' tooonies n'* grab another *double-double* before *Red Deer.*"

"I see you've spent some time in Canada, Dezzy."

"Oh *yah, eh*?"

"Who wants to hear us beat box into this bucket?!" Dezzy and I shout, running around the house. The guys in the kitchen just look at us like we're stoned hippies. "Do they not realize how *cool* this sounds right now?" I say sticking my head back into the bucket and spitting a beat.

"Man, they need to be on *our* level right now…Johnny, hit me with a verse!"

A verse unrehearsed?
  Shit, I'll drop some heat!
Spitting rhymes, with minds tied
  In some LSD…

Dezzy and I continue to drum, beatbox, freestyle and use every pot, pan and spatula to keep a beat. We somehow manage to end sporadically on the same beat before collapsing on the ground in a fit of laughter.

Stoned Riff: A Typical Conversation

"Being stoned and making music…"

"Yeah, the best combination since…"

"…peanut butter and jelly."

"Or maybe peanut butter on apples. With a bit of cinnamon."

"Or maybe just peanut butter on a spoon."

"Maybe just the spoon."

"I could use a good spoon."

"10,000 spoons and all you *neeeeed* is a knife…"

"Well, unless you're the middle spoon in all that spooning. It's gotta feel nice."

"How come no one's written a song about a spatula?"

"Yeah, definitely more efficient than spoons. Way more surface area."

"And none of this romantic spooning business…they're made to flip out.*"

"This is your brain…this is your brain—on *spatula!*"

"I'm feeling pretty *spatched* myself."

"Hmm, I feel like hot butter through a knife."

"Wait, what were we talking about?"

"Yeah, why am I hungry?"

The LSD is pulling me into a new frame of perspective. It's oddly familiar. It feels like the sensation I get when I notice myself falling asleep: My consciousness deepens and settles itself along a new level of brain activity. Except now I don't have to worry about being too aware of the changing alteration and waking myself up; this is one dream I get to be *awake* in.

So here I float.

I'm treading along in the daydream of my inner child.
Enchanted by the most mundane diversions…

I am utterly captivated. My body is frozen in place in preparation for the big impact. As I stare, there it sits: quietly still and perfectly serene amid the endless flow around itself—seemingly unaware how close it is to the edge. It hasn't even turned to face the direction it inescapably drifts. *Is it unaware of its own fate?* I feel the need to call out to Matty and Dezzy, but they have already arrived, noticing the preoccupation in front of me. The three of us share a knowing silence: It is soon about to *hit*. Time slows as we absorb the moment around us. Without moving itself, it shifts closer to its boundary—the wall of fixed restriction that is creating its captivity.

Every slight movement is filled with light, dazzling brighter as it escalates toward the inevitable. The momentum builds behind it as it closes in…and…*oh, a near miss!* I hear Dezzy and Matty breathing faster. None of us can blink. With a shimmering energy around it, it rises slightly for another attempt and gets pulled in like a slow motion magnet directly into its own barrier. It strikes quickly then recoils back in a clockwise rotation, drifting away on its next journey across the abyss. The three of us explode from our suspended stillness in ecstatic jubilation!

"Holy *feeeeckin'* shit *ya trippa's!*" Petey calls from atop the balcony. "Are you guys seriously watching a *feckin' beach ball* float in the swimming pool?!"

"Would you just let us have a fucking *moment* over here?" I shout back.

We turn back to face the ball as it sits atop the backyard pool.

"What a rush," Dezzy says.

Matty puts his arm around the two of us. "Thanks for sharing that with me *mates.*"

"Well," I say shaking myself a bit. "Good luck getting stupid kicks like that from cocaine." We shed our housecoats and jump into the pool, launching the beach ball out onto the grass.

There is a numb energy in the kitchen as I walk in.

Snnnnnnnnnnnnnnnffff. Scotty recoils back in his chair, scratching his nose. "Holy shit mates, I feel so good…I, I can't *feel* my face."

"What a waste," I say as I sit on the floor nearby. I soak the golden warmth of the sun's setting rays as they cascade into the living room window, hitting me in the face. "I feel so good because I can feel *everything.*"

My consciousness deepens and settles itself along a new line of brain activity

I'm back in the kitchen again. Matty and I just finished a trippy Frisbee session on the beach (we may have *stared* at the Frisbee more than we were throwing it) and I am in need of some water. "Hydrate to *de*hydrate there *mate!*" Scotty says, throwing me a three-pack of Powerade. He is still unmoved from his kitchen chair, vodka and numbed expression. I look at the trio of colors vacuum-packed in plastic: red, green and bright blue. They look even more vibrantly artificial than normal. I get a strange unease about the notion of drinking colors to keep my body functioning. *Hmm, later for dinner I'll eat a fabricated triangle with small circles…wait, I'm high, it's called pepperoni pizza.*

I struggle to crack the thick plastic that is sealed around the three plastic Powerade bottles that has another plastic seal around the plastic mouthpiece. I throw the entire package of rubbish onto the floor. It bounces like an impenetrable plastic force field. "Is this really how humans hydrate ourselves in the 21st Century?!" I exclaim in frustration.

"You're on acid dude," Scotty says, clearly not comprehending the psychedelic scope of my realization.

"Yeah, of course I am!" I exclaim. "But it shouldn't take drugs to expose humans to the fact we are obsessed with overconsumption and creations of excess waste!"

Scotty stares at me somewhat stupefied.

Right, add this to the extending list of conversations not *to have between a guy on LSD and a guy coke'd off his face.*

I have escaped into the shaded comfort of a tree in the backyard. Being around other people is too overwhelming right now (or maybe it's just me that's overwhelming). My vision is sputtering strong tracers and I am getting flooded with new perspectives and spurts of creativity that demand solitude to

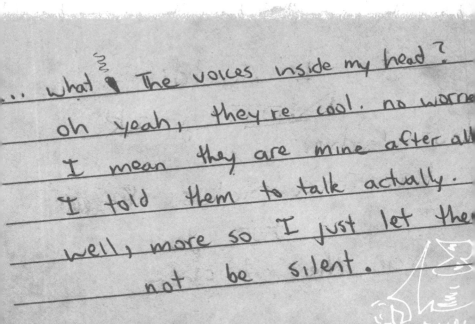

… what ₃ The voices inside my head?
oh yeah, they're cool. no worries
I mean they are mine after all
I told them to talk actually.
well, more so I just let them
not be silent.

process. All I can handle at this moment is being alone in nature, while putting a pen to my journal. *Ok, I'm ready to let loose whatever scribbles or words filter through me and out onto the page.*

"*Oy* Johnny!" I hear Petey shout from the top balcony. "Johnny get in *'ere* mate!"

"Busy!" I shout back, not wanting anything to do with other people as I stir in my own headspace alone outside.

"*Feck me* you are! You *gotta* get back in *'ere* mate, *bloody stat!*" Petey yells back with clear assertion. "The *peelers* are *'ere* mate! The *strippa's!*"

Oh, fuck me. Strippers?

That is not something I feel capable of handling right now.

"Jooooohnaaaay!" I hear the rest of the boys holler from inside the house.

Shit. I gotta go back in there...

Minor contemplations and changes of scenery are always amplified to ridiculous levels on drugs. When I find an environment, style of music or group of people (or lack thereof) that comforts my headspace as I deal with the summit of a trip, it feels devastating and slightly terrifying to leave it. I remember a beautiful day in a Montreal park, enjoying mushrooms with friends, when I was nominated to leave to find water. *Go into a store? Me? Deal with 'regular' people in 'normal' situations??* Utterly. Terrifying.

Minor contemplations and changes of scenery are always amplified to ridiculous levels on drugs.

Right now, peaking on acid and having to deal with the the shit show of a bunch of coked out Aussies in a small space with strippers feels like a dreadful pop-up medical exam on how to pass a kidney stone through my third eye.

This is going to be weird.

As I walk up the stairs to the living room I can already hear the hooting and hollering intensifying over the soundtrack of Buckcherry's *Crazy Bitch*. *I am not on their level right now...I need to find Dezzy and Matty.* The stairs sway back and forth slightly like walking on a rope bridge. I take a deep breath to brace myself for whatever might be coming next.

Two women are buck naked on top of each other on the living room floor. Petey hollers at me with a bottle of scotch in his hand. "Johnny *mate!* You're missing the *show!*" The room smells like sweat, booze and sexual gluttony. Both women are attractive—well, stripper attractive, with too much makeup and fake blonde hair. One looks in her mid 20s and the other early 30s. Mikey throws me a beer and I try to not stand too uncomfortably in the background tripping balls. If only I were drunk—and not trying to process the colors breathing off the wall—I'd be able to fit in with this mess a little easier.

Watching strippers isn't really my thing anyway. It's the same reason I don't casually watch porn with a bunch of guys. It's all pretty awkward. *So the intention is to just stare? Am I supposed to get an erection? What good is it to be turned on with a bunch of dudes?* The only times I have deliberately gone to a strip club was with a group of girls who were totally into it: cheering the strippers on, stoked on the athletic skill involved and feeling empowered by a confident woman in charge—it was a blast. This, right now, just feels like a shallow, male chauvinistic ritual to provoke manliness in the most superficial and expensive way. *But who knows, maybe I'm just over analyzing things…I'm on acid.*

Palms² by J. Early

The women start scissoring and thrusting into each other on the carpet, seemingly trying to make the loudest smacking noises possible. A couple of the guys start howling. *Was I supposed to applaud there?* There is a two second silence as the song from their stereo changes into the next. It lingers *forever.* In that moment the sound of skin slapping and heavy breathing from everyone fills the room. It feels hollow and unsettling. I look over at Dezzy and Matty and they are shifting in their seat; I feel the same: unsure whether to sit or stand as I process the show. *Are these girls enjoying this? Is this business casual for them? What do their mothers think?*

I sip my beer but alcohol doesn't taste right. Nothing in this room will remedy my desire to climb a tree and stare at my hands right now. *I need to quietly escape this…* As I set down my beer to sneak out the backdoor, the older stripper calls out. "*Ay* Lola, '*is* one '*ere* doesn't '*ave* any '*air* on '*is* chest!" Before I realize what's happening, she grabs my hand, pulls me into the circus spotlight and rips off my housecoat as she throws me onto the floor. All the boys start cheering. *What the hell is happening?!*

As I lay there in my board shorts, she straddles me—naked—and sprays a white foam all over my chest. My mind is running way behind the actions taking place. I'm still trying to process why people are staring at me, and why there is a vagina in my face before I realize she's set me on fucking *fire*. Flames shoot out from my stomach as she ignites the foam that she's sprayed on me. My mind races in a million directions, spewing thoughts like the heat rising from my body. *Is this happening right now? Am I supposed to be in pain? This fuzzy carpet feels amazing on my back… wait, that's a vagina on my chest! And…it's putting out the fire??*

Flames shoot out from my stomach as she ignites the foam that she's sprayed on me.

I'm beyond capable of comprehending what's happening. The stripper pins my hands down and starts riding out the flames with pelvic thrusts like some twisted pornographic movie hero. *What is this, Indiana Jones and the Temple of Poon? Why do I smell watermelons? Why do I feel an anatomy lesson is being shoved in my face?* The entire room is filled with loud sounds and dense laughter. Her breasts bounce and quiver in a strobe effect through the fumes rising in front of my vision. The intensity on her face projects visions of a wild cat on attack. The fire is now out but she continues to snake and twist her hips on my chest. I look up at the ceiling as I exhale. *Whoa, there's a weird pattern on the roof…Wait, John! Concentrate! Do something to make it seem like you're enjoying this and not just hallucinating on LSD…or is this a dream?* I slap the stripper's ass with an open palm. The room cheers and applauds. *No, not dreaming John. A very real stripper is just naked on top of you and you may or may not have been on fire. Deal with it.*

As the song fades out, she lightly slaps me across the face. "Well done, *mate*." She stands up and addresses the room. "Give it up for '*im*, he's a good *cunt ay*? Cute fucker too." The group of Aussies starts hooting and hollering as they chant my name. I walk over and grab my beer and slam it back. *Yeah, that tastes better now.* I poke around at my stomach. Besides being a bit red, greasy and smelling like a fruity bonfire, I'm still intact. *I can't say the same for my psyche though…*

"'*Right* mates, that pretty much concludes our time here," the older stripper says, confidently standing naked in front of a room of high men. "And the rest of the payment is cash only."

"Ah Charity," Petey says a bit nervously. "Before you go, can we, ah…"

"Can you do a line off my tits? Yeah, it's extra."

"Get the groom!" The boys chant.

I think this is my time to leave.

I stand in front of the mirror in the bathroom. I'm stuck in mental limbo. I'm not sure if that whole ordeal sobered me up or made me more intoxicated. As I take a deep breath in, the walls of the bathroom take a reassuring breath with me, squeezing in and releasing out. *Thanks bathroom, always a humble space of refuge for us people as we deal with our shit, eh?*

I'm not sure how the next 40 hours are going to surpass the first eight, but it'll be an interesting ride for sure. Partying with Aussies is always an endurance test. Maybe the surf will pick up—it's the only known way I've detached an Aussie from the momentum of a wild party. I already heard one of them shout out that they're nearly finished their mountain of coke; further proof why I stay away from a drug that commands constant additional consumption. But hey, everyone has their individual ways to get their kicks. You just hope everyone can realize the balance needed to keep their habits in check while they soak up a good time.

I currently have no desire to drop another tab of acid; I think I've heightened my experience enough for this weekend's Wollon-Gong Show. But I do find an occasional dabble with psychedelics to have the ability to provide valuable lessons—strongly dependent on setting and user intention. It can be a reset button to appreciate simple perspectives and valuable new insights—like how to avoid cocaine by dropping acid or ways to find gratitude a stripper didn't set your face on fire. *Now, time to get my journal and find that tree to climb.*

= A Clear Conscience is usually the sign of a Bad Memory. =

DECEMBER 2011

WOLLONGONG BEACH, AUSTRALIA

When you wake up and happen to remember most of the drunken house party guitar freestyles about your Aussie neighbor's cat being a drug dealer…you write a song!

♫♪ Salem was a Cat

Mm hmm
Salem was a…cat
Salem was a…

Night creature
Eight laced to feature
Quick on the scene
Cause he's always one to be
    there
With a mean stare stacked
With no slack to spill cheap
    thrills
He's got his curiosity to kill
    Cause he's a cat!

Mm hmm
Salem was a…cat
Salem was a…

Smooth criminal
Mind of subliminal
Messages to catch
Big deals for the minimal
Typical style
To catwalk the streets
Can't cheat
Always landing on his feet
    Cause he's a cat!
    Salem was a…cat

JANUARY 2012
SYDNEY, AUSTRALIA

If I wake up in your house after a night drinking —I'm taking an apple.

I don't care who you are or what your sharing protocol might be; I'm searching your fridge for a glorious red apple. It just makes everything better. A crisp bite into a crusty hangover. A refresh with fresh fruit. Teeth feel cleaner, nothing heavy on the gut and makes for a casual stroll, with apple at hand, to say "Good morning, I slept in your house last night."

So thank you for the place to crash and thank you for the apple—it's a one-two package.

"Strange, these knockoff sunglasses were *way* more expensive than I thought…and it came with a free bag of flour."

WHEN THE AWKWARD GUY AT YOUR HOSTEL UNKNOWINGLY BUYS DRUGS FROM A STREET HAWKER IN NICARAGUA

Look Who's Crazy

Mystery Mushrooms From an Indonesian Road Stand

A roadside warung in Kuta Lombok, Indonesia.

"Are these…mushrooms??" I ask again, looking into a lone plastic cup sitting on the top shelf of a small fridge next to two glass bottles of Coca-Cola. The Indonesian man remains silent, smiling and staring.. A water buffalo lets out a long *moooooo* in the wet pasture behind us. He blinks, and then our awkward staredown resumes. *Hmm. I don't think he speaks any English.*

The two of us are in the middle of nowhere. I had pulled up to a random roadside *warung*, a small Indonesian convenience stand constructed of bamboo. The Indonesian man was selling little more than some fruit, a few packets of crackers, bottled water, a couple of Cokes and some bootleg gasoline in old Absolut Vodka bottles. I was somewhere on the island of Lombok, Indonesia. I had been on my scooter looking for some new surf breaks along the island's southern coast when I had to stop to replenish the sweat escaping from every pore. I can practically swim in this midday tropical humidity. Now that I have found hydration from this man's cheaply bottled Indonesian water, my focus shifts to his cup of mystery.

I hold up the plastic cup filled with black and white stringy fungi and retry my question with body language. "This," I say pointing to the cup, "MUSH-ROOM?" My eyes and tongue flail around, attempting a universal depiction of tripping out.

The man doesn't move from his smiling stare, then he lets out three quick laughs and slowly nods his head. He is a short man with a sweat-stained white tank top plastered over his slight pot-belly and a wispy black moustache that arches up with his motionless smile. A bead of sweat runs down my forehead. We stare at each other in silence. *Ok. He's not really selling me on this.*

"Amigo," I start, accidentally defaulting into Spanish as I often do with a communication barrier of a new language. "These MUSH-ROOMS...they WEAK? Or STRONG??" I emphasis the word with a big flex of my right arm. Mr. Indonesian Smiley-Stare lets the question linger in the humidity. He seems to hardly be breathing. My arm stays flexed and we both stand like statues, staring, waiting for a hopeless hint of clarity.

Ah, I give up. I drop my shoulders and exhale with a shake of the head that says 'I'm done here' and I move to return the cup back to the fridge. As soon as I touch the fridge handle, the Indonesian man sparks into life. He not only responds to my question in fairly competent English, but also inadvertently gives the best basic definition of mushrooms I have ever heard:

"Oh, you know, eat mushroom when you happy...you be *very* happy! Eat mushroom when you sad...you be *very* sad..." The man emphasizes a frown on his face with his index fingers before returning back to his still, staring smile.

Huh. I felt like I was at some gypsy-puppet carnival game, and I needed to put in another coin to get another fungal fortune-reading.

I have been craving a new headspace to experience Asia since I got here.

"Convincing enough! I'll take the whole lot!" I put the whole cup of wild Indonesian fungus on the bamboo ledge as I fish out some *rupiah* to pay. As soon as the money is in the man's hand, I get a foreboding drop in my stomach. *As long as I eat them when I'm happy, right?...Ah, am I happy?*

I quickly shake any self-doubt about the purchase. After all, I have been craving a new headspace to experience Asia since I got here. Alcohol doesn't exactly generate new perceptions like psychedelics (and it's getting difficult to continue drinking the local Indonesian moonshine known as *arak*). Smoking weed in the Muslim islands of Indonesia is a very serious offence and could mean a majorly extended vacation...in prison. Mushrooms in Indonesia, however, flirt that boundary of law and are technically

legal, especially in the tourist bars of the Gili Islands. And what more
can you ask for in a psychedelic experience than the relaxed vibe and
beauty of some of the most pristine beaches in Southeast Asia?

The rest of the morning passes without much thought toward
my mystery cup of 'shrooms. The waves I find are barreling in
nearly triple overhead—to which my mediocre surf skills give a
double *nope!* While cruising back toward Kuta
Lombok with my surf board I stop for lunch at a
small tin shanty for their advertised "Spicy Soop."

I sit down at their only table and an eight year
old girl with a pink bow tie in her hair promptly
comes out to take my order: either spicy soup
with meatballs or spicy soup *without* meatballs.
"With meatballs, *terima kasih,*" I say, thanking
her with a polite bow and trying to make the most
out of the few Indonesian words I know. The girl
giggles and runs off to the next section under
the tin roof (which I assume is her family's living
room) where her mother awaits orders between
making meatballs.

Two young tourists, a guy doubling a girl on
a scooter, pull off the road and park next to my
scooter. They take off their helmets as they come
up to the table. The guy has short dark hair with a
fit, slim build and the girl has a long, blond ponytail
with welcoming blue eyes.

"Best soup on the island," the guy says with a
smile as he sits across from me.

"You mean *soop,*" I quip to a few laughs.

"My name's Justin," he says reaching out for a
handshake. "This is my girlfriend Sarah. We're from
British Colombia, Canada."

"Hey, small world meeting fellow Canadians at
the local Indonesian soup lady!"

The three of us continue to exchange the
customary travel small talk (Where are you from? How long are
you traveling? Where are you going next?...) as they place their
soup order—*with* meatballs. I immediately sense a good vibe from
them both and when I hear that they are actually from a hippie
community on one of the islands off the coast of B.C., I feel the

need to share my morning mushroom purchase story. It perks up their attention like the ears on a dog hearing his food bowl getting filled.

"Eat mushroom when you happy...you be very happy!" Sarah laughs, quoting her favorite part of my story. "That is quite the definition!"

"Well, I'm not feeling very sad today," Justin asserts, raising his eyebrow. "Should we...?" The three of us slowly look up from our newly-arrived steaming soups, mischievous grins building on our faces.

To many people, psychedelics are not a light consideration, especially the people with whom we choose to experience them. But backpacking skews that—considerably. When you tap into your nomadic flow, you open yourself and your psyche up to every opportunity and perception that comes your way—often only trusted on the whim of your gut. And hey, why trip alone?

When you tap into your nomadic flow, you open yourself and your psyche up to every opportunity and perception that comes your way—often only trusted on the whim of your gut.

The three of us remain in a stirred silence. An unspoken agreement is being ratified—signed in raised eyebrows and smiles. Before anyone can say *Bintang Beer,* my entire cup of Indonesian roadside mushrooms is passed around and emptied into all three of our steaming soup bowls. Our meatballs—now floating between black and white mounds of stringy fungi—get decorated in hot sauce and crushed peanuts. We devour the works in under five minutes. *Enak!*

It's interesting how eating a mystery cup of unverified mushrooms in a foreign country with people you just met will change the circumstance of small talk. For the next hour—as we wait for things to kick in—we skip the rest of the introductory 'get to know you' dialogue and go straight into deep, heart-to-heart talks about life, drugs, religion, aliens, inter-dimensional travel and funny cat videos. It was the conversational equivalent to asking a random girl at the bar if she wants a drink, then both of you suddenly clearing the counter top to screw right there on the bar. *Well, that escalated didn't it...*

Over an hour later, the heat of the mid-afternoon sun hits and so does our trip. Justin, Sarah and I find ourselves sprawled out on our sarongs on a vacant beach near town, giggling like childhood

friends. Big fluffy clouds roll in with swirls on top and perfectly flat bottoms like they were fresh out of God's oven. As I stare at them, I become a mini *Super Mario* bopping underneath them with my fist, hearing coins burst out: *Pting, Pting! Whoa, this afternoon is getting fun…*

I start playing with my perception like a psychologist experimenting in a lucid dream. I gaze out and shift my focus from near to far, then to my peripheral vision, with the feeling of controlling a set of binoculars. The bay is surrounded by lush green cliffs that appear to shrink as they wrap to the distant right tip of the bay. I stare out at the smallest part of the cliffs and turn my head slowly to the right to feel them grow in size—the rising sound of a xylophone scale rings out in my mind as I turn: dadadadadadadada! And back down, like I am playing a giant cliff piano. Justin and Sarah catch what I'm doing, follow along, and all three of us start sounding out rising and falling musical scales as we move our heads, staring out into the distance. A captivating minute passes, before we all turn towards each other to share a silent glance and burst into more childish laughter. *The locals must think we're crazy.*

I look down and take a deep breath to break from our giggle fit. I lean my face into my hands. Something inside me is escalating. It percolates up from my belly until I feel the sensation suddenly break free. My body buzzes like the warmth of a thousand bees humming in unison. It would be more pleasant if it didn't feel so unusual and foreign. *This is getting ridiculous…* And as if the mushrooms were responding with a 'you ain't seen nothing yet,' the beach below me starts shifting.

The sand breaks into hexagonal patterns that dance and vibrate around each other, shifting like kaleidoscopes. The deeper I stare, the deeper things displace in its space. I'm intrigued as I feel something tantalizing me, baiting me further. I shake my head to snap myself out of the trance and my vision returns to normal for a split second before I get lost in the designs of the orange sarong I'm sitting on. The fabricated arrangements of the material fade into new shapes that emerge and pop out like a 3D Magic Eye poster. Spirals and spheres blissfully swirl around each other while remaining intertwined as they grow bigger and smaller. I open my palms to see the images and vividness spreading out onto them like spilled paint. Everything is connected. I feel a strange welcoming into this new consciousness that all matter appears to contain. It's dangerously beautiful.

Plight as a Feather by J. Early

Everything I stare at puts my judgment of depth into question as it all starts to exist on a new plane of perception. Both the natural and inanimate objects I stare at, shift and breathe with their own code of shapes and movements. It's like I am pushing an invisible threshold into a new world of processing visible stimuli on a deeper dimension. The world around me is intensifying. A mix of curiosity and fear hits me as things start to escalate beyond a controllable and enjoyable state. I sense an enticing pull to experiment and push further into this new realm before an instinctual jolt shakes me out of the dream.

"Guys, I'm *tripping* out."

A pair of giggles is exchanged from behind me. I have a brief moment of clarity as I look back to see my new friends, Justin and Sarah, smiling and lying contentedly on their backs. The familiarity of our temporary beach camp and strewn-out belongings brings comfort as I try to process what is happening in my head.

"Anyone want to go for a swim?" Sarah asks, without moving from her upward sky gaze.

"Oh, I brought the snorkel gear!" Justin exclaims, "We should hit the ocean!" He sits up straight with determined ambition. *Is he kidding me? Are they not on my level??*

I feel my brief state of clarity loosen as the next wave of the mushroom trip builds up again. A gurgle of my stomach spreads a buzzing sensation back through my limbs, climbing up with a dizzying pull on my head.

"Guys, I think I'm getting too high." I say calmly, focusing my eyes with difficulty.

"You okay John?" Sarah asks, sitting up with ease and putting a comforting hand on my back.

"Yeah, I just think things are hitting me a lot stronger than you two."

Everything I stare at puts my judgment of depth into question as it all starts to exist on a new plane of perception.

I close my eyes and take an extended breath with myself. On the next inhale, I open my eyes to see several dark blobs coming into focus, moving towards me, each one carrying something…I snap back into normal vision as I hear "Mister, Mister! Please!", followed by childish laughter—oh, the local Lombok kids! Everyday they come to sell us their handmade bracelets and guilt tourists into giving them money. *Wow, not what I'm needing right now…*

A wooden board of bracelets gets shoved in my face. "Please, please! Buy from me!" shouts a small boy with a dirty Mickey Mouse shirt.

"No, no, from me! Buy me!" Another girl pleads, holding up her own assortment of colorful bracelets above the boy's. From behind me, a small hand pulls at the back of my tank top. My perceptional intake starts revving. The pull to peer into deeper shapes surfaces again. The ability for me to concentrate and maintain my mental clarity starts unraveling by the second. If I thought staring into the sand was intense and over stimulating, this was definitely surpassing that.

"No, sorry…" I start, trying to make out whose voice is from where and which hand is from whom. Voices feel like friction on my skin. Colors start getting too bright. The Mickey Mouse face floats off the boy's shirt in front of me and gives me a look that says 'Oh shit!' I close my eyes to escape more visuals. There is more laughing from somewhere.

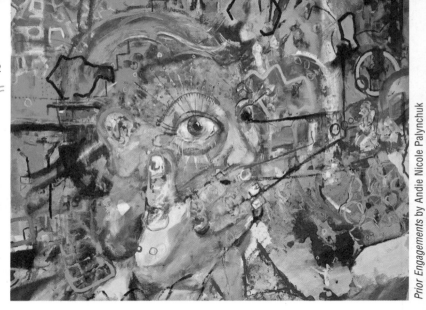

Prior Engagements by Andie Nicole Palynchuk

"I've already bought, like, five bracelets from this guy!' a familiar voice declares. I squint my eyes to see Justin now on his feet and lifting up the boy from in front of me. The kid starts laughing uncontrollably. Justin spins on the beach with the boy over his shoulder. A higher pitch of giggles circles out. Three other kids start inspecting and playing with Justin's snorkel gear sitting to my right side. They start making faces and laughing at each other as they try on the mask—twice the size as their small faces. The intensity of the situation lessens as the mood quickly turns into childish fun. The motor of my mind downshifts into a more neutral state. I look to my left to see Sarah drawing pictures in the sand with one of the girls. A long breath of relief escapes my mouth. *Okay. I'm okay. I can coast through this.*

Voices feel like friction on my skin. Colors start getting too bright.

A disheveled figure shuffles towards us from along the beach. I look up to see an Indonesian man approach me. His clothes are in tatters, barely hanging on to his frail figure. His long black hair is greasy and missing in patches, showing red marks along his scalp. He kneels down in front of me with a grunt, hiding his blistered bare feet in the sand and lets out a communicative moan, flashing the few teeth he has left in his mouth. *Oh boy, what is happening…?*

"Oh, he crazy!" The girl that was drawing with Sarah shouts, jumping up and sitting down next to me. "Don't talk him, he no speak, he just *craaaaazy.*" The last word echoes and lingers in my mind as I focus with all my ability to not get sucked into another trance that I feel is pulling at me from behind my head. The beach starts to spin again.

"Crazy man! Crazy man!" The other kids shout as they come and sit next to me as if to protect me from this homeless island local.

I narrow my eyes to focus on the man open his mouth, as if to speak, but nothing comes out except another awkward groan between his missing teeth. He then cups his fingers together and points them into his mouth.

"Oh…" I begin with mounting difficulty of forming words in my mouth and pushing them out. "He…he's okay. Just…he's just hungry guyssss." I fumble both my words and arms trying to look for some sort of food to give the man. As I look down around me, flashes of vertigo make it difficult to grasp my immediate surroundings.

"Here man, want some crackers?" Justin leans in and gives the man a packet of crackers. The man quickly opens it up and empties it into his mouth. I look at Justin. He seems totally fine; not a hint of the same level of difficulty I'm encountering. As he sits next to me, he puts his hand on my shoulder. "How you doing Johnny?"

"Ah, struggling." I say with my eyes closed. "Too, *phewww*… too many things happening." I push out another long exhale. Something feels toxic.

"Drink some water, man." Justin hands me his water bottle, "We should get out of here and find you some hot tea." I nod as I guzzle down the rest of his water bottle. A small grunt escapes my mouth. The kids sitting next to me stare up like there might be *two* crazy people on the beach now. I don't blame them. I feel the thread of my reality starting to pull and begging to be unraveled—except now it's totally lost the blissful essence of interconnection I'd experienced earlier.

I open my eyes to find the Indonesian man staring right back at me. His eyes are softer now. A silent exchange of understanding is passed and a light moan escapes his mouth along with a few crumbs of crackers, as if to say, *Oh, being crazy isn't so bad.*

A friendly voice rings out from behind me. "*Apa Kabar* everyone! How is everybody today?" I feel a quick slap on my back. "Johnny you no surf today!"

I turn dizzily to my right, "Oh…hey, Deo. Yeah…" I struggle to recognize my local surf friend and try to act like I'm not amidst a terrible mushroom trip. My stomach churns and a prickly buzz reaches across my body. It trickles under my skin with a noxious crawl taking the energy around me and pulling me down like a weight in water. *Too many people…*

"Yeah man, big waves today…" Deo says, unnoticed to my current state. "Oh, you meet our local Lombok Crazy?" Deo chuckles, pointing at the homeless Indonesian man, still sitting in front of us picking at his long, dirty fingernails.

"Oh, he's…yeah, he's okay," I say, wrestling with my words as my head swivels unsurely on my shoulders. My heart starts to beat heavier feeling like it's fighting off an infection. *I need to escape.*

"Yeah, he used to be good friend of mine," Deo says casually. "One day he took too many mushrooms…not been the same since."

My stomach drops. A blanket of fear hits me with a dark realization of Deo's words.

"So…sorry?" I sputter, trying to look up at Deo with my unfixed eyes.

"Yeah, Indonesia has two trippy mushroom," Deo explains blithely. "One happy one for fun and one make you crazy. He took crazy one by accident and had very bad mushroom trip…maybe he still on the same trip. Hard to tell…but…John? John you okay?" Deo squats next to me, taking a drag from his clove cigarette and looks into my eyes for the first time. "Hmm, John you look kinda crazy too…you okay friend?"

This isn't happening. This isn't happening…

Words are known to affect your physical health. The power of a simple string of spoken words not only impacts on and elicits emotion but can immediately make physical changes in your body depending on how those words are perceived and processed. Deo's words hit me like a blow dart to the jugular. Each mention of the word 'crazy' dug into my psyche and sent me down into a worried place that felt like the boundary of sanity was not just visible, but I was passing it on cruise control—with my toothless Indo friend riding shotgun, spitting crackers out of his mouth.

"Mmmuaaa nahh…" I push out from my gut, with a physical difficulty in forming words with my mouth. "Ooh-kay. Yaaa… I'm oh-kay."

Am I okay? Is this happening to me? Have I crossed a point of no return? My thoughts are fairly clear but communicating them appears impossible right now. I feel the sensation taking a grip on me, as if it were ready to settle in to a state of permanence.

"Yeah, Johnny's okay," Justin breaks in, "I think he just needs a cup of tea, right? Let's get you outta here, buddy."

I hear Deo make a clapping noise and shout something in Indonesian to which a scamper of little feet kick up sand and run off. My eyes are closed but I feel the space clear. It lightens the prickly buzz on my skin. Fatigue sets in and the last thing I recall is Deo and Justin talking softly before two sets of arms pick me up, and help me to my feet.

The taste of black tea in my mouth is a bitter and beautiful wakeup. *Wait, was I dreaming? Where am I? How long have I been sitting here?* I look around with a renewed sense of clarity in my vision and perspective but still coated with a foggy confusion. Across from me I see the familiar and comfortable smiles of my new friends, Justin and Sarah. *Wait, we couldn't have only met this morning, did we? Were they ever strangers?*

"How are you feeling John?" Sarah asks with a motherly kindness.

I shrug. "I…I think I'm back," I say with a modest laugh as I comfort my warm cup of tea. "But that was not exactly the easiest roller coaster to endure."

Justin nodded. "Yeah man, you definitely hit a different level than the two of us," he says, picking at some rice on a plate that looks like it's been sitting in front of him for a while. "I mean, we were under the effects, but not as deep as you seemed to go…not sure why."

Sarah puts her arm across Justin's shoulders. "Yeah, we've both had our share of difficult experiences with hallucinogenics," she says with a gentle glance into my tired eyes. "They can teach you so much but can also turn on you somewhat unexpectedly. It can be a tricky balance."

The three of us continued to talk and laugh for what felt like ages in that café. I certainly needed it. I'm not sure what I would have done without their help. It was like we had known each other forever, yet when the sun went down and we parted ways for the night, I would never see them again. Such is the beauty and intensity of meeting people while traveling. In the moment, strangers will be your best friends ready to help you through whatever incident life might throw at you—for better or worse. Then you part ways, let it all go and get ready for the next experience to share with the next person to shake your hand as you eat your meatball *soop*.

I sit in that same café for the rest of the night drinking tea while deep in thought. I struggle to eat a meal of rice and fried *tempeh*. There is a need to let go and move on from all the negative sensations I had dealt with that day. I also contemplate all the positive and beautiful realizations that had lifted me just before it. What duality. What a spectrum of perception that exists out there. *But what exactly had I tapped into that provided such a perceptual experience? Do all hallucinations feel so cognitively tangible?*

As the night went on I reflect on the day like it was a gift. An unexpected gift to cross that line, albeit briefly, to experience the intense difficulty of losing your mind. Being a *crazy*. The capacity of having such lucid and clear thoughts but not being able to express or communicate them was beyond frustrating.

I should find and spend some time with our local Lombok crazy friend. I think I owe him a bowl of meatball soup at the very least...

As I walk back to my guesthouse, leaving my scooter to pick up the next day, I gain a new appreciation for my current state of perception and recognition. A sound mind—what a *blessing*. The air is humid and warm on the skin and there is a light glow within the quiet jungle tonight. The moon displays its fullness after shedding a cloud, brightening the trees and vines to my right. I stop and stare at the large leaves that sway in the breeze and, just for a second, the patterns imprinted on top of them seem to jump out and converge in a breathing assortment of entangled shapes. I feel a flashing temptation summoning me in to look deeper, but I turn my head. A sly smile crosses my face and I continue my walk. The quote of an old poet dips into my mind as I head into the night:

> ## "Some people never go crazy,
> ## what truly horrible lives they must live."
> ### CHARLES BUKOWSKI

MARCH 2012
KUTA LOMBOK, INDONESIA

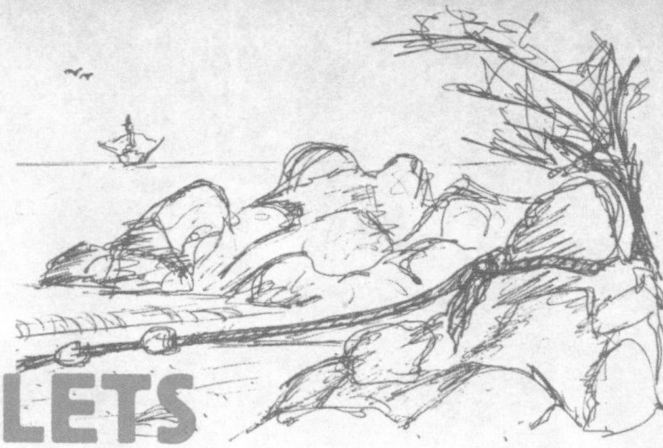

♫ Blue VIOLETS

Loathe the coast caress
Late light for the shedding
The sun's constant state of setting
Loathe the coast caress

Loathe the coast caress
Chasing mesc to meth
Bend to transcend
When laced to race the best
Chased
With a solid taste of silence
Try this
Five hits of blue violets
Licensed through street cents
Not violence
High sense
Is still sought and hand picked
Thrilled quick
When you break to burn like
candlewicks
Loathe the coast caress

Late light for the shedding
The sun's constant state of setting
Loathe the coast caress

Physically speaking
mind tapped for the tweaking
Illogical chaos
Meet your full rhyme and reason
Now please Miss
Flip flat your attack for this
Adapt quick and I'll stick
With your sun-kissed skin
Shining light with a hint
Of lime, tequila and gin
Is your salt from the sea?
Or simply straight off the rim
Because it's hard to know
Where you're not now to begin
When you're stuck in the deep end
You can't confess soft sins
In this mess
So loathe the Coast caress

Late light for the shedding
The sun's constant state of setting

MARCH 2011
SAYULITA, MEXICO

"*Turn On* meant go within to activate your neural and genetic equipment. Become sensitive to the many and various levels of consciousness and the specific triggers that engage them. Drugs were one way to accomplish this end. *Tune In* meant interact harmoniously with the world around you—externalize, materialize, express your new internal perspectives. *Drop Out* suggested an elective, selective, graceful process of detachment from involuntary or unconscious commitments. *Drop Out* meant self-reliance, a discovery of one's singularity, a commitment to mobility, choice, and change. Unhappily my explanations of this sequence of personal development were often misinterpreted to mean 'Get stoned and abandon all constructive activity.'" *Timothy Leary on his infamous counterculture phrase "Turn on, tune in, drop out",* Flashbacks, *1983*

CHAPTER 7

The Peruvian Prescription

"If we try to penetrate the secrets of nature with the means available to us, one finds that behind all recognizable connections, there is something delicate, intangible and inexplicable. The deep respect for these forces which are beyond our ability to comprehend, is my religion."

ALBERT EINSTEIN.

Coca Leaf Readings with Wilma

Fortune Telling from an Andean Healer

Wilma dropping coca leaves during my fortune reading.

" **S** he's ready. Who is going first?"
"It's John's birthday today, he should go."
"John, are you ready to see Wilma?"
Ah, I think I'm going to vomit...

It isn't that I'm really nervous—I mean—I am a little. I'm in a remote mountain town outside of Cusco in Peru, about to talk with a stranger that possibly knows more about me than my friends, and is likely to dig up deep personal issues by intuition while discussing the fate of my life's path—that's a *bit* intense. But I've had my fortune read and talked with genuine healers and psychics before. It's quite an incredible experience if you're open to the concept.

But the tickle in my stomach today isn't nervousness—I'm just ridiculously hung over. Damn Cusco. Going out for a "few birthday shots" makes for a terrible morning when you're drinking at an 11,000-foot elevation. It shouldn't take a psychic to predict that altitude sickness and booze don't mix well.

"Yeah, I can go first," I respond to my friends, who are also here to get their individual coca leaf reading. Our crew has been backpacking Peru for three weeks together. We heard from a friend (who had lived in the Sacred Valley for a vacation of spiritual healing) that Wilma was the best coca leaf reader in the mountains. With only one day left in Cuzco, we decided to find a taxi that could take us to the small mountain town of Huascao, where Wilma practices her traditional Andean medicine and healing.

From my time in Peru, I am aware of the importance of the coca leaf in the Andean culture, but don't exactly know what to expect or how the process for a *reading* works. Internationally the coca plant gets a bad rep because its leaves are the core ingredient in cocaine. Amusingly, nearly all tourists on arrival into Cuzco (especially the older type who would cause an uproar if this medicinal herb or tea were to become legal at home) end up relying on its ability to help with altitude sickness. I've already chewed several handfuls of the stuff this morning. It tastes like a bitter herb and enough of it can leave your tongue slightly numb. *Definitely not a magical hangover cure though.*

I spit the remaining wad of coca leaves out of my mouth as I get escorted by Wilma's helper into a separate hallway, away from the dirt floor courtyard we have been waiting in. There is nothing lavish about the communal housing or poor neighbourhood we are in. No crazy carnival-style billboards advertising mystical palm readings or money back guarantees if you didn't like your fortune. Nothing hokey or contrived here. Just a welcoming smile from the locals between hanging laundry out to dry, chickens running by your feet and a cleansed feeling in the air.

Wilma's helper is wearing a white apron that matches her sparkly white Peruvian top hat that covers the top of her long black

> There is nothing lavish about the communal housing or poor neighbourhood we are in. No crazy carnival-style billboards advertising mystical palm readings or money back guarantees if you didn't like your fortune.

The communal living space where Wilma lives and works.

pony tail—a common style of the local women here (apparently you can tell which village an Andean woman is from by her hat). It's a beautiful look, but feels slightly out of place amidst the tin shacks and street dogs; if she had a tuxedo on to match, I'd expect her to bust into a *Piano Man* cover in a martini bar. She turns to point her hat at me, *"Cuando estas listo, por favor entrar,"* motioning toward beads dangling in the doorway of a dark room. *When you are ready, please enter.* I take a deep breath and try to clear my nausea. *Hold yourself together John…if you vomit on a Peruvian shaman, that's sure to be some bad juju…*

I pass through a curtain of beads to enter a small and simple room with blue walls covered in random cultural and shamanic mementos. Wilma, a short, middle-aged local from a lineage of Andean healers, sits at a table with her eyes closed in meditation. Her wisdom appears to surpass her still youthful face. Coca leaves sit scattered on top of several handmade fabrics. I sit across from Wilma and wait to be addressed. A strong, trusting energy fills the room. As we sit in silence I forget that I had felt ill at all this morning.

"Write down your name, where you are from and your birthday for me, *por favor.*" Wilma says gently but firmly, passing me a paper and pen. I notice Wilma's demeanor has changed from when she initially welcomed us warmly into her community. She still maintains her natural affection, but she has definitely tapped into a more serious focus for the reading. As I write down the requested information, I realize no matter the culture, religion or place in the world, your name, birthdate and location of birth seem to always be key instruments in reading your life's path.

"*También,*" Wilma adds before I finish, "please write your favorite place…that makes you feel safe." I pause and look up. *Interesting…that's a new one.* It initially stumps me until I think of my family cabin on Lake Katepwa where I grew up spending every summer of my youth. *Definitely my happy place.*

Wilma takes my paper and looks it over quickly with little expression. "John, please hold onto these leaves and breathe into them until you are done." She hands me a multi-colored fabric with the coca leaves bundled in the middle. I hold onto them, reflect for several moments and then focus in on my intention for this reading. I take a deep breath and slowly breathe out my intention into the parcel of leaves.

Estoy listo Wilma. I'm ready.

Wilma takes the leaves carefully into her hands, holds them up over the table and bows her head. She starts praying to herself, whispering Spanish lightly under her breath. I can't catch many words, but it sounds like she's asking the spirits of the leaves to give an accurate reading and enable her to decipher their messages clearly.

Wilma lifts her head, gives them a shake, sprinkles four or five leaves from the bundle, and the reading begins.

Wilma's communal healing room.

"You have a very strong energy and ability to connect with others." Wilma says using the pen to examine the leaves and how they fell. "You have more feminine than masculine energy—not a bad thing—but a balanced energy is ideal."

I nod. Sounds about right since I grew up and have always been close with my older sister, Andrea. Wilma continues, "You are like two different people: outgoing and sociable then withdrawn and sensitive. Always very open with your energy…" Wilma pauses to gather her words in English, "but you need to be careful to not open yourself up too much to heavy energy that might come by you." Wilma looks up at me in the eyes to emphasize the last sentence. "Know when to conserve your energy. Listen to yourself more. You make good decisions, you don't need to listen or follow anyone else's lead."

Wilma's words come across with complete sincerity and truthfulness. I'm totally captivated. She sprinkles some more coca leaves on top of the ones that have already fallen and looks at them closely. *What is she seeing in these leaves?* Wilma nods to herself. "You have the ability to heal and are starting to realize some of your psychic abilities." Wilma looks up at me. "John are you planning on working with the ayahuasca medicine?" she asks, referring to the powerful Amazonian psychedelic many people travel to Peru to work with for healing and spiritual purposes.

Wilma's sincere advice is delivered gently, like from a grandmother I'd known but never met.

I nod, both surprised and impressed with her inquiry. "Yes, I leave for the Iquitos jungle in over a week." The realization I am only a couple weeks away from my first ayahuasca ceremony shakes me slightly. *I need to get back on my pre-ceremony diet of no booze, meat or sugar. Last night's cheeky birthday shots can't happen again.*

Wilma picks through the leaves on the table, "You will need to be more determined with your *dieta* and cleansing," she says, practically reading my mind. "Take garlic, honey and lime daily. It will help you purify before you work with the Mother Vine. She will help you finish some of your questions and will serve you well. Ask her for clarity in your purpose."

I nod again, taking in her guidance. "Wilma, I have been experimenting with psychedelics for several years now. Do you feel they are a benefit to me?"

Wilma picks up some of the coca leaves that had already fallen and drops them down again. "John, psychedelics are healthy for you to ground yourself, speak with nature and tap your creativity. You know the respect you need to show them and the power of time and place. Trust yourself." Wilma and I share an agreeing look in each other's eyes.

"So," Wilma starts with a slight smile, "do you want to hear about love in your life?" She asks like it's always the main question people want an answer to.

"Sure, why not?" I laugh. Wilma clears the tablecloth of leaves, adds them to the rest in her other hand and proceeds to sprinkle more coca onto the open fabric. She looks closely.

"You are like honey, all the bees flock to you. Sometimes it is switched and you chase all the pretty flowers…" Wilma pauses. "You are nearing the end of this phase and will start to look for only true partners to spend your life with."

Wilma continues to read the leaves and get into further details and forecasts about my future relationships, family, health and career options. Everything comes across as a credible prediction and sincere advice delivered gently, like from a grandmother I'd known but never met. The whole reading takes less than 30 minutes. Wilma concludes by looking me in the eyes and saying cunningly, "Write your book."

I walk out of the room and back into the open courtyard feeling lighter. A fresh perspective washes over me and I feel the need to sit alone, reflect, and process what was said. My hangover and altitude sickness seemed to have vanished the moment I sat down with Wilma. She is still quite young, but carries the knowledge and aura of many generations of Andean elders and healers.

Like many people, part of me naturally wants to refute the reading as rubbish; nothing more than broad conclusions based on good guesses and quick judgments of character. Can a handful of leaves really *tell* you anything? I, for one, believe they can. Besides my previous experiences with psychic-style readings—which all contained aspects of impossible to fake accuracy—I am becoming conscious of the concealed knowledge located within plants. No

Ancient Incan masonry in Cusco where they precisely cut and shape the stones to fit without mortar. Their techniques were so astonishing it was said they could 'speak with the rocks'.

country I have been to showcases its appreciation for the wisdom of plants more than Peru. Communicating with nature has been imbedded in the Andean culture and their ways of life for millennia.

Wilma is an incredible example of someone that shares her traditions, plant knowledge and, more importantly, her gift to bridge these realms to other cultures. Today's tech-loving society might need to reconnect more than ever with the natural world around us.

JUNE 2015
HUASCAO, PERU

The local women of Cusco sitting with their tourist-friendly goats.

Gettin' High in High Places

Towns with their corresponding height above sea level:[6]

La Rinconada, Peru: 5,100 meters (17,700 feet)
*With a population of over 50,000 people, La Rinconada is the highest city in the world according to *National Geographic Magazine* (2003).

Leadville, Colorado (USA): 3,084 meters (10,152 feet)
*With a population of over 3,000 people, and the nickname 'The Two-Mile-High City' (nearly twice the elevation of Denver), it is the highest city in the United States.

Lake Louise, Alberta (Canada): 1,661 meters (5,449 feet)
*Lake Louise is the highest town in Canada, ranking the country #65 on the world's highest elevation list. Kimberley, British Columbia, known as the "Bavarian City of the Rockies," claims the highest city in Canada title at 1,120 metres (3,670 feet).

Madrid, Spain: 667 meters (2,188 feet)
*Madrid claims the highest major city in the European Union. Kruševo, Macedonia takes the highest city in Europe title at 1,350 metres (4,430 feet) above sea level.

Reykjavik, Iceland: 39 meters (129 feet)
*While the country sits fairly low elevation wise—Iceland is technically the "*highest* country in the world" ...due to their love of sweet Mary Jane. The 2014 World Drug Report by The United Nations rated weed consumption for each country's population.[7] Iceland took the high prize with 18.3% of the country's population reported as using the illegal herb regularly, followed by Zambia (17.7%), and the United States (14.8%). For those curious, Canada made the Top 10 (at 12.2%) and even beat out Jamaica (at 9.8%)

The Fourth Dimension of Machu Picchu

Teachings of a Medicine Man Atop Peru's Wonder of the World

Trying to evade pictures of Machu Picchu in Peru is like trying to avoid seeing a Full Moon Party tank top in Thailand—it's nearly impossible. Throughout my entire two months in South America, I have been consciously looking away from every poster, brochure or menu with the Incan icon so my visit to one of the new Seven Wonders of the World will smack me in the face with all its force. And it *did*.

You feel Machu Picchu before you see it. There's something about the space, the surroundings and its mystifying history that warms the heart while simultaneously sending tingles across your skin. There is power here. A lost magic finally found again. Peaceful energy permeates the rising mountains and it settles into the souls

Standing above the citadel of Machu Picchu with our Peruvian medicine man and teacher, Julian.

that seek it. No wonder a civilization spent generations building their natural sanctuary here.

Machu Picchu is a collection of ancient ruins situated within the Andes Mountains 8,000 feet above sea level. Constructed by the hands of the Incan people in the 1400s, it was later abandoned around the time of the Spanish conquest. Apart from the local people, it was unknown to the world until 1911 when American Historian Hiram Bingham discovered it (or was taken to it by a young local farmer). Further information of this type is in abundance on a standard tour of the ruins—thank goodness I'm currently not involved with a *standard* tour.

> **Machu Picchu is a collection of ancient ruins situated within the Andes Mountains 8,000 feet above sea level.**

Our traveling group of friends is fortunate to have received a contact for a local Incan medicine man, Julian, to be our guide. The first thing he tells us in Spanish is "I'm not going to preach the common concepts or modern understandings of this place. They are often mistaken. I am going to share with you a special place and what it means for my people and to our ancestors—not the American who *discovered* it."

Completely captivated, our group of friends sits listening to Julian on one of the far left terraces overlooking the panorama of the ruins within their prominent mountain perch. The iconic Huayna Picchu Mountain towers over the citadel like the centerpiece of a crown to its inner-laid jewels. It truly is perfect.

I've never felt nature and architecture blending so harmoniously. Julian stands in front of us with his short stature, calm demeanor and brown eyes that hold a lineage of wisdom and understanding. He is wearing a red zip-up and a wide-brimmed beige hat with a rainbow band (the flag of the Cuzco region—*not* gay pride, as many locals are quick to point out).

"Machu Picchu," Julian says in his slow and careful English, "translates from Quechua language for *old and high mountain*. But my ancestors often interpret it as *chewing of the coca leaves*. It is a place to gather, discuss, learn and chew coca." Julian pauses to add some more coca leaves to the wad he already has in his mouth. I also have been chewing coca daily since getting into the high Cusco region; it helps with the altitude sickness while paying respect to the traditional ways of hiking in the area (it is also a nice, very mild stimulant that slightly numbs the tongue—it *is* what cocaine is derived from, after all).

Julian puts his hands together slowly before speaking. "My people believe Machu Picchu has existed for many years longer than westerners conclude. When the Spanish came, this place meant so much to our ancestors that we knew we had to hide the structures and roads, and let it go in order to keep it from destruction." Julian motions at the view behind him. "Many historians often assume this place was for a king or ruler, or even a type of military fortress," he says.

> **"My people call this area the *Navel of the World*, for it brings the rain and life to the continents."**
>
> JULIAN

"This is not true. It was a university—for the people. A place to awaken and connect with nature. These terraces were made for testing new crops and farming methods. It is where clouds are born, rising up from the valley floor. My people call this area the *Navel of the World,* for it brings the rain and life to the continents." Julian points up to the top of the summit that dominates the encircling valley floor (if Machu Picchu is a belly button…it would definitely be an outie*). "Huayna Picchu means *new peak,"* he says. "And it creates a natural antenna that acts as a sender and receiver with the cosmos. Machu Picchu was built in harmony with nature to harness and maximize the energy within the area. That is why standing here we feel such power and connection from the earth."

Goosebumps rise across my arms. Julian speaks with such openness and sound wisdom; it is evident he is sharing the words that have been passed down to him from his ancestors that built this marvel of human achievement (it was the only way the Incan people passed down knowledge—they had no written language).

"How did they build this?" my good friend Rory Chappelle asks. "Isn't it still a mystery how they cut perfectly into such enormous rock and moved it across this mountain without knowledge of the wheel or using big animals or iron tools?"

Julian responds quickly in his relaxed and expressionless bearing. "Machu Picchu was built in the fourth dimension."

The last two words linger as Julian's answer settles into everyone's mind. *Fourth dimension? Is he talking about how it was constructed on a multi-leveled surface or, wait... what?* No one says anything. We simply sit in anticipation for Julian to continue as he carefully picks out several more coca leaves to add into his mouth. He takes a slow breath and continues. "The fourth dimension is a higher resonance and relationship with nature and all it encompasses. My people were able to speak with the plants and the rocks. That is how they knew where to cut perfect lines to create these walls and terraces without

My good friend Rory, barefooting the mountain of Machu Picchu.

mortar or modern technology. It was built in a dream, as a dream. Humans and nature."

Silence again falls on our group. The clouds start to drift up from the valley floor to hide and reveal the structures and mountains in front of us. I slowly raise my hand.

"Julian?" I ask slowly. "So...how does one reach the fourth dimension?"

It was built in a **dream,** as a dream.

Julian pauses, looks down, and then looks back into my eyes thoughtfully. He then finds a simple and perfect answer to such a rhetorical question.

"To live in the fourth dimension…you must open your heart, and *observe*."

The stone stairs that pass the heart of Machu Picchu.

Climbing up the steep Incan stone trail to the top of the actual Machu Picchu Mountain is an additional 2,100 vertical feet (about a 90-minute trek) from the ruins of the citadel. With the afternoon clouds now rolling in, we cannot see anything besides the stone stairs directly in front of us that appear to rise up endlessly. Before we begin, Julian passes a large bag of coca leaves and instructs us to select four of the most complete leaves we can find. At the end of the day—after placing our intentions into these leaves—we are to bury them. This will allow the earth to help manifest our intentions into reality. He also recommends walking barefoot or putting coca leaves in our shoes to keep us grounded on the journey. Julian then asks us to hike in silent meditation as we ascend.

Over halfway up Julian pauses and breaks the silence.

"To live in the fourth dimension… you must open your heart, and *observe*."
JULIAN

"This is the *heart* of Machu Picchu," he says putting his hand over a large boulder of emerald granite. If he hadn't pointed it out, it would have blended in with the rest of the rock from which the stairs are carved. Looking closer, it radiates a subtle dark green polish and shimmer. Julian turns towards us. "This stone is the only one like it for miles around. The reason Machu Picchu feels so clear, calm and welcoming is because the negative energy is directed and filtered into this stone. When you touch the heart of Machu Picchu, give thanks and also ask for its help on your journey—it has a lot of power within it."

As we make it to the summit of the mountain, it becomes obvious the clouds that have rolled in will cover any visibility—we can't see 10 feet in front of us, let alone the view from our 10,000-foot lookout. Regardless of seeing anything (or snapping a new profile picture) everyone can feel the marvel of being atop Machu Picchu Mountain. The presence of a vast open altitude fuses with the words of our medicine man's Incan wisdom. Without speaking, everyone in our group finds a space to sit and take in a moment of reflection. I sit cross-legged on a perch of rocks and close my eyes to meditate on the intentions of my visit. Julian's soft-spoken words ring through my mind: *Just open your heart, and observe.*

The sudden sound of Julian's Peruvian flute gently echoes around us. Peace fills the space. I get a sensation that someone my age was once sitting in this exact position hundreds of years before me—same situation, same questions asked of life. *Why am I here? What is the purpose of my journey?* As Julian's music slowly comes to an end, he whispers to our group "Now, open your eyes." The clouds have parted and we get our first bird's eye view of Machu Picchu below us. It is a perspective that provides an otherworldly notion of inspiration, like God looking down from the heavens upon his first creation of civilization.

"Somebody hug me," a friend blurts out, getting teary-eyed. We all laugh and console each other as we take in the beautiful moment.

I'm fortunate to have had some pretty incredible experiences…but this was pure magic.

My 4 COCA LEAVES / INTENTIONS

- o) FAMILY
- o) GRATITUDE
- o) ENERGY
- o) KNOWLEDGE

The view of the citadel once the clouds cleared from the top of Machu Picchu Mountain.

Our group slowly splits off as everyone starts the trek back down towards the citadel on their own time. I stay back a while. I have too many thoughts and feelings conjured up in the last few hours. I need some solo time to sift through and settle them.

On my way down as I pass the Heart of Machu Picchu, I feel oddly drawn towards it. There is a comforting pull that calls for me to stop and put my hands out. Standing and staring in front of its wall of emerald granite, I take a deep breath. *Well John, if you're going to head into the Amazon in two weeks and start talking with plants and ayahuasca vines—might as well start today by talking to some rocks.*

Just open your heart, and observe…

As I place both my palms onto the dark green stone, I feel the tiniest of shocks like I had dragged my feet across carpet and touched metal. An odd warmth contacts my fingertips. Opening my hands wider, I send an outward burst of gratitude from my heart. *Hey, thank you. And please help me continue forward with this journey.*

An immediate response manifests in my head that narrates as "Hey, help *me!*" A quick laugh gets shared somehow between the rock and I before an image of Earth flashes in my mind. *The Navel of the World, the Heart of Machu Picchu, humans and nature…we all can speak, and the planet is telling you to stop treating her like humans are superior.*

I pull my hands off the wall uttering a whispered, "whoa."

A strange smile crosses my face as if I have just woken up from a lucid dream. I quickly put my hand back onto the rock to see if I can tap into that space again—nothing. Just a rock. I get slightly anxious and look around to see if anyone else is watching my weird interaction with the side of a mountain. No one is in sight. A cheerful satisfaction overtakes me and I start to laugh. The space seems to speak out with a contented, "You're welcome."

I turn around to continue the trek down the ancient Incan pathway with a smile on my face. *Hmm, after I bury these coca leaves I'll have to find Julian to ask him more about this fourth dimension…*

THE CALL OF AYAHUASCA

Jungle Awakenings in the Amazon

He's definitely done hallucinogenics before...that woman is on a spiritual quest...those two are just here to photograph the jungle...that guy is still tripping from the '60s...hmm, I don't think that girl knows what she's gotten herself into...wait, what have I gotten myself into?

Picking out the foreigners from the Peruvian locals on the flight from Lima to Iquitos is easy. Figuring out their reason for visiting the isolated Amazonian city is the interesting part. As it becomes the world's unofficial mecca for psychedelic jungle medicine—predominantly in the form of ayahuasca ceremonies—it is safe to assume most tourists drawn to Iquitos aren't just seeking a standard travel *trip*.

Ayahuasca is an entheogenic* brew made from the DMT*-abundant chacruna leaf and stem of the ayahuasca vine. It also happens to be one of the world's strongest hallucinogenics. *Ayahuasca* is a local Quechua word that translates as *vine of the souls* or *vine of the dead*. The first use of ayahuasca is difficult to pinpoint but many estimates go back as far as 4,000 and 5,000 years ago. Outside of unearthed artifacts and descriptions of ancient ceremonies, much of the evidence is its prevalent use in traditional ceremony in nearly all indigenous cultures across the entire Amazon basin—tribes that have been substantially distant and disconnected for millennia. Because it is so ingrained in the culture here, ayahuasca and its other jungle medicine counterparts are legal in most of South America but banned nearly everywhere else in the world. Internationally, DMT itself is widely illegal but the unprepared individual plants often skirt by legally.

> **Drinking the thick, dark brown jungle tea in ceremony is apparently the Amazonian way to tap into and speak with the spirit world—notably the plant spirits.**

Drinking the thick, dark brown jungle tea in ceremony is apparently the Amazonian way to tap into and speak with the spirit world—notably the plant spirits. They treat the *Mother Vine* as an entity, a teacher. With the right intention and preparation* an individual is said to be able to access higher spiritual dimensions that can produce intense revelations, healings and awakenings to their purpose on earth. Not to be grouped with recreational psychedelics, an experience on ayahuasca (5-8 hours) is reported to be intensified because of the difficulties that can arise during ceremony. Vomiting, nausea, hot/cold flashes and diarrhea are part of the purging process to rid negative energy and release entrenched emotions that build up over the course of one's life. That is why it is regarded as a medicine and has been hailed as a powerful treatment for depression, PTSD, alcoholism and opiate addiction. *Definitely NOT a standard travel trip.*

They say you shouldn't seek ayahuasca—she will call *you*. I've been happy to trust this advice over the last few years as I've become more aware of the jungle medicine. The more I research and hear

*Entheogen: |enˈthēəˌjen, -jən|
noun
+ 'generating the divine within'
+ a chemical substance (typically of plant origin) used in religious, shamanic or spiritual purposes that often induces psychological or physiological changes from non-ordinary states of consciousness.

DMT [*N,N*-Dimethyltryptamine]
+ a psychedelic compound of the tryptamine family
+ structural analog of seratonin, melatonin, psilocybin, 5-MeO-DMT and other psychedelic tryptamines
+ can produce powerful psychedelic experiences including intense visuals, euphoria and hallucinations
+ some scientists believe that small amounts of DMT are produced naturally in humans, plants and all living things; as well as released during birth, death and deep states of dreaming

*La Dieta:

There are many different concepts of how to approach the pre-ceremony diet. The common notion is that for a minimum of a week (and up to a month for best results) an individual taking ayahuasca needs to cleanse themself by avoiding meat, refined sugars, strong spices, alcohol and sex. The day of the ceremony, ayahuasca is only to be drunk on an empty stomach.

about ayahuasca, the more I am invited to one-off ceremonies in Nicaragua, Costa Rica and elsewhere. As interested as I've been, I always decline. It never feels right. I know if I am to ever experience the medicinal teachings of the *Vine of Souls,* as passed down for thousands of years by the tribes and shamans in South America's jungles, I have to go to the source. Now, the further south my travels lead me, the more I feel her pull. Her call to me is the natural calm and confidence that has built up as things feel right the more I acknowledge what is drawing me: *Aya wants to speak with me.*

The short 90-minute flight passes quickly but amazingly we seem to have flown over every possible climate in that time: rocky beaches, dry mountains, lush farmland, arid desert and tropical jungle. The diversity of Peru is astonishing (as is all the clothing and supplies you try to squeeze in your backpack to experience it). Flying over the Amazon for the first time leaves me breathless. It is so immense and dense that it looks like an infinite putting green made out of broccoli tops with the mighty Amazon river as winding like a massive brown snake through the green horizon as far as the eye can see.

Iquitos appears out of nowhere. It is the largest city in the world that cannot be reached by road (its population is 400,000). The only options are to fly in or take the slow boat along the Amazon—not exactly a possibility from Lima. Leaving the airport I'm bombarded by moto-taxi drivers and bustling

The Nile has historically been thought of as the longest river in the world. However, new studies are trying to prove that the Amazon is actually longer. Both rivers have estimates that range between 6,400-7,000 kilometers in length (longer than the 6,371 kilometer radius of Earth). The Amazon does have the biggest flow, however, discharging five times as much water as any other river on the planet.

traffic that makes me feel as though I'm back in Thailand's land of tuk-tuks instead of Peru. Five minutes into my bumpy taxi ride I am reminded that I am in the middle of Iquitos and its ayahuasca tourism boom:

"Want some ayahuasca or San Pedro cactus amigo?" my driver asks me over his shoulder while honking and swerving in and out of his lane. "I know many shaman. You tell me how I help!"

It's a common theme that has emerged in this lucrative new Third World industry: Everyone knows a shaman. And the locals all want a slice of the money pie tourists are now bringing into the area. When dealing with the fusion of spirituality and psychedelic healing, trust is *crucial* to the experience. You have to confide in the shaman who creates the medicine and administers the dose while facilitating the entire ceremony. As anyone who has experimented with hallucinogenics before can attest, set and setting will make or break a trip.

Driving past the main square of Iquitos, Plaza de Armas, there is still a sense of the late 19th Century rubber boom that originally brought foreigners to the area. European-Amazonian-style architecture and terraces showcase the money that was brought by the early rubber barons (along with the exploitation that came with it). Most buildings depict years of age from the tropical habitat but still maintain their original splendor. Among the native people there is a mix of third-generation Asians, European expats and young psychedelic tourists mingling the nearby restaurants. The plaza and street corners are crowded with local

Driving by tuk tuk in the busy streets of Iquitos.

street vendors selling fruit, sweets and jungle crafts. Noise and smog from the moto-taxis fills the air. Iquitos is a living melting pot of cultures. It's difficult to comprehend that this area is actually isolated in the middle of the Amazon.

The plan for my personal ayahuasca journey is to take a two-hour boat ride deep into the jungle and spend a week at Refugio

Altiplano. It's a retreat center that has been facilitating ceremonies with Amazonian plant medicine since 1996 and is highly regarded by my close friends and colleagues in Peru. For $180 a night it includes transportation, a personal jungle cabin, all meals (no dinner on ceremony nights) and four ceremonies within five days. *Straight into the deep end of shamanic wisdom I go…this wasn't a prank call, right Aya?*

My moto-taxi drops me off in front of the Refugio's Iquitos office to catch our boat into the Amazon. I'm not really sure what to expect from the other people that are also drawn to such an experience. Have they done this before? How strictly have they taken the pre-ceremony *dieta?* Are they seeking spiritual awakening? In need of healing? Just looking to get high in the jungle? Why exactly am *I* here?

As I step into the *oficina,* there are several other reserved but smiling faces that greet me. Everyone's eyes meet as if to agree we are all in on a secret that, together, we're about to explore a lot further. My new jungle family consists of a young Italian who is practicing a career in alternative spiritual healing for physical ailments, a couple in

> **Everyone's eyes meet as if to agree we are all in on a secret that, together, we're about to explore a lot further.**

their 40s from New Hampshire who are both clinical psychologists and experienced in psychedelics, and a New Zealander backpacker in his late 20s who has taken ayahuasca several times before. No one feels the need to say too much. There is an unspoken awareness that we'll have enough time for that when we're all alone in the jungle.

In the corner of the room sits a short man quietly observing the room. I soon learn he is not only our boat driver, but also our shaman. Meeting a modern-day medicine woman or shaman is always a bit perplexing. Maybe I've watched too many Hollywood movies or National Geographic documentaries that always define things with over-the-top personas and costumes. But the image in my head of a shaman always results into a man in face paint with a long beard, wearing piercings, beads and a loincloth with strange smoke always hovering and following, shrouding him in mystery. José is none of these things (thankfully). He wears blue jeans, a collared T-shirt and is clean-shaven with short salt and pepper hair that sticks out from his baseball cap. Besides looking like a typical Peruvian local, he could be anyone's dad or uncle. The big

Arriving at the boat launch of Refugio Altiplano, deep into the Amazon.

difference is that Jose grew up in the jungle, built Refugio Altiplano practically by hand and has over 25 years experience growing and brewing ayahuasca and facilitating ceremonies. As Refugio's new owner Kelly Green puts it "He's the *Man*."

The muddy brown water splashes loudly against our boat. As we turn into the main channel of the Amazon River, the other side disappears into a faint green line of treetops. The river is so wide we might as well be on a giant lake. After an hour of passing the occasional village of tin shanties and small houses built on wooden beams over the ever-changing shoreline, José turns off into a random section of unlabeled water passageways. We continue for another hour, switching between large river sections and dense shortcuts where the trees smack the boat on either side. The natural instinct of Jose's jungle navigation is undeniable. Even if I had a map in front of me, my attempt to follow along would look like a child's scribbling on the maze of a coloring book.

"Welcome home!" Kelly shouts as José drives the boat into a final hidden nook. A hand painted Refugio Altiplano sign shines out from the top of the *palapa* boat launch. The retreat center's name is Spanish for *Refuge of the High Plane*, and it becomes evident with several sets of stairs climbing uphill into a jungle sanctuary that is an ideal location for the journey ahead—an engagement with the all knowing Mother Vine, ayahuasca.

Kelly Green leads us through the immense, multi-level wooden structure that serves as kitchen, eating area and communal hangout space. Kelly, a jolly free spirit from Seattle who loves to retell his days of following around The Grateful Dead, is the new owner of Refugio Altiplano. Being a long-time visitor he was distressed when he heard about the founder's death and decided to raise money to buy the property and maintain Refugio's legacy. Kelly pauses and turns to us with his usual cheerful smile. "And this is our little amigo, Martin," he says motioning to a monkey eating a banana on the floor. "Years ago Martin was brought and left here without warning. He's not native to this area so couldn't get reintegrated into the wild. He's friendly, but careful, as he gets worked up *very* easily." As I walk closer, Martin quickly jumps up my arm, climbs on my head and starts whooping and screeching, pulling my hair. "See?" Kelly laughs. "He loves you, John!"

As I'm being led out to my jungle cabin, we pass the *maloca* where the ceremonies will take place. It is an open circular area under a towering *palapa* roof—the temple grounds of the Amazon. I get a slight chill considering what has and what will soon transpire

Standing with my ayahuasca journal in front of the ceremony maloca.

under that beautiful roof. Later tonight we will be summoned to ceremony where we will drink the spirit of the Mother Vine in the silent darkness of the jungle. The thought is both intimidating and comforting. *I'm ready.*

JUNE 2015
AMAZON JUNGLE, PERU

THE 1ST CEREMONY
June 14, 2015

The *maloca* is only lit by candlelight; one in the center of the open room and two by José at his table along the back wall where he sits with a tall glass bottle of ayahuasca. Urias, the ceremonial *maestro*, helps cleanse the air with his *mapachos* of rolled jungle tobacco. The *maestro* is like the shaman's right-hand man who sings *icaros* throughout the night—songs that connect into the spirit world to facilitate and heal during ceremony. The two of them say their prayers and are first to ingest the jungle medicine. One by one José invites us up, gives us a quick read to sense what dose to administer, and pours the thick brown liquid into a small cup. It appears most people are only getting a quarter of a cup. I recall Kelly mentioning that José makes some of the strongest brew in Iquitos and that this last batch has been fermenting in strength for over a month. *Ah…does this maloca have seatbelts?*

José's eyes lock mine across the shadows—I'm up. I step away from my floor mat and pillow (that will soon serve as my psychedelic sanctuary) and sit next to my shaman. He looks me in the eyes, flashes a brief smile and pours about

Our shaman, José, about to begin ceremony

a third of a cup—more than the others, like he senses that I am capable of a stronger dose. I hold the cup to my heart and whisper into it my intention for the first ceremony: to meet the Mother Vine and be open to her intention for me. José and I exchange a quick "Salud" and I throw back the liquid, emptying the cup. *Hey, that's not so bad. People say how terrible it tastes but I kind of enjoyed that… like a nutty smoothie of mild earthy herbs* (it will serve as the last time I ever 'enjoy' the taste and avoid gagging drinking ayahuasca. I soon learn it only gets worse after your first taste). I thank José and return to my mat to sit in meditative anticipation. When José finishes his final blessings to us in the room, he snuffs out the candles with his *shacapa* leaf fan. The room enters into a darkness blacker than I have ever felt. *Well, here we go…*

It starts with a light pull, 10 or 15 minutes in. Like cold hands welcoming the feeling of a growing fire—but this fire is building momentum deep inside my gut and inner self, calling me in. I take an extensive breath into my gut. It stokes embers that burn brightly within, igniting my soul. Urias starts singing a beautiful *icaros* in his native *shapibo,* sounding like the spirit of a Native American elder. It changes the space.

> The room enters into a darkness blacker than I have ever felt.

    Oh, there it goes.

Like a glowing infinite web of warmth, I am plugged into pure unconditional love. Vibrant colors and patterns prelude and shadow various people of importance in my life. I share smiles

June 14 2015

1ST CEREMONY

Dose b/w 1/3 of a cup
* strong steeped brew, made about 1 month ago - strengthens as it ferments.

→ In preparation for anything specifically a ful taste, violent vomiting diarrhea, dark emotions, ...
& yet I was gifted several hours of controlled euphoria
It started with a light pull 5-10 mins in, like the feeling when you feel fire grow & you're staying too close

and belly laughs of both past and pending. I am able to soak up and enjoy their loving embraces. The endearment continues as I connect with the next friend, person or family member in my spiraling web of gratitude.

Ah, such bliss. Is this.

I am in a lucid dream, controlling the depth of my own perception of love and appreciation. I fill the space between visions with bright colors and natural patterns: honeycombs, layered spirals, weaving vines and passing clouds. It's like I'm playing with the energy inside me, equally creating and spectating the visions that are in front of me.

I feel the warm, sultry breath of a feminine energy over my left shoulder. She has a naturally beautiful face made from a mosaic of all my closest female friends and past loves. Ayahuasca, she is flirting with me—and me with her.

Oh, hi. Funny seeing you here… about time you joined the party.

My heart is in the catcher's mitt of further blasts of affection and gratitude. I spend the whole night allocating people in my life to receive and share love like a game of catch. As I sense the pull of Aya's tendrils loosening, I can't help but feel amazement with how beautiful and effortless the ceremony has been: No purging, no fear and no dark emotions or challenges of incorporating such a powerful medicine and psychedelic into my system. I was in preparation for *anything*. And yet I was gifted several hours of controlled euphoria and unconditional gratitude for all the people I love in my life.

> I spend the whole night allocating people in my life to receive and share love like a game of catch.

With a last fleeting message from Mother Aya before we both rest for the night, she answers me, without words, but with uninhibited understanding:

I see who you are and I know what you do. And it is good.
Take tonight as a simple introduction—a first date.
Things will be difficult ahead, as we have much work to do.
But for now, receive this ceremony as an uplifting gift from the spirits
…and we will see you soon.

The smile grows on my face as I put my hands over my heart. I clearly have things I need to release and mend—but well played Mother Vine. You sure know how to break the ice.

THE 2ND CEREMONY
June 15, 2015

Una limpieza por el cuerpo y buena energia por la vida y mi espiritu.
A cleanse for the body and good energy for my life and spirit

I exhale my intention through my breath and into the full cup of Ayahuasca José has poured for me. It's clear he has upped the ante for tonight's ceremony. No one last night had the need to purge, but we all sense it will be different tonight. We're past the get to know you phase with the jungle medicine. José snuffs out the last candle and the room enters its familiar setting of pure darkness—only this time it is a welcoming blanket of comfort.

Things are much more gradual this time. By time the first *icaros* starts, I know I will not be content with a simple and smooth blissful night. I need a *cleaning*. A solid flush out.

About an hour passes in the darkness and even with my fellow psychic warriors getting sick around me, my guts are unmoved. I try to time it appropriately—to not interfere with José and Urias singing their *icaros*—and I stand up in the night. Mentally clear, but obviously into the effect, standing and walking in pitch black to my shaman like a toddler approaching their grandfather. *I'm coming…slowly…*

I sit quietly next to José and he already knows.

"*Más*," he says as a statement more than a question: more.

"*Si, gracias hermano.*"

He pours a third of a cup of his wickedly strong batch and whispers and breathes his protection over it before handing it to me.

"*Salud.*"

"*Salud.*"

Adios…

I'm not sure who smiles first, me or my sister, but once I see those teeth flash between those thin lips, I can't help but smile so contently that we both build up into unspoken, full-hearted laughter. Stuck in the moment.

I love you Andi.

2˚ CEREMONY

'una limpieza por el cuerpo y
buena energia por la vida y mi espiritu
d into my cup of ayahuasca *
* exhaled intention through my breath

DOSE: 1 cup + ¼ cup

Jose snuffed out the last candle
+ we returned back to pure darkness
only this time it was a welcoming
blanket of comfort

This was much more gradual this time.
By time the first icaros started I knew I
would not be content with a simple & smooth
blissful night. I needed a cleaning
A solid flush out.

JUNE 15
2015

Singing continues alongside the constant beat of a rattle shaking.

Ayahuascaaaaaaa...
Medicinaaaaaaaa...

My dad pops into my flowing matrix of color and light.
Yes. Time to show this legend some appreciation.
I get vivid flashes of all his professional and personal accomplishments including his influence as my father. There is still so much for me to learn from him.
Okay Dad, teach me what you know.
Boom.
Ayahuasca turns the world into a small and dense heavy disc visible in front of me. It flattens me with its weight of fatherly knowledge.
Hmm. Maybe I should have started asking this a long time ago...

> **Ayahuasca turns the world into a small and dense heavy disc visible in front of me. It flattens me with its weight of fatherly knowledge.**

Something has tapped into my brain.
It is tinkering around looking for ways to re-program the circuitry, like a full defragmentation of my mental hard drive. I tap my head with my fingers and ask deliberately like Neo as he gets wired into The Matrix: *Make me smarter.*
An outside intuition fires back: *Already working on it.*
I feel the neurons and synapses in my brain start firing and turning on. At the same time I detect a hand sensing along and flushing out my intestines like a soft stroke of a caressing sponge.
Clean it out! I encourage. I know I need to purge out some of life's shit I've taken in over the years. I unconsciously use my left hand to brush the top of my head down past my body, through my belly, like an additional mine sweep to sift negative energy away. *Shed it!*
The tinkering in my brain escalates to a point where I can feel static around my head and my eyes start flickering. Everything suddenly stops and I open my eyes into the darkness with a deep breath and a wry smile as if to say: *I know kung fu.*

There is electricity in the Amazon—and I am not just talking about the occasional flashes from distant electrical storms that light up the *maloca*. There is a full orchestra of electric energy with the crickets, birds, monkeys and toads vibrating the jungle.

I tap into this underlying snapping and crackling like becoming aware of the communication of a TV's lost channel of white noise—but right now it is the source of more than 10% of the planet's biodiversity. And they are speaking to each other; call and answer. That is part of the code I've cracked with my ambient-sensitive ears. Singling out one set of the hundreds of sounds around, I can hear the space and mood of their communication. Everything is able to find its place and timing within this Amazon soundtrack.

I realize my legs are shaking, smacking together instinctively in participation.

I am here too.

We are here.

My finger stretches out and pokes some sort of soft welcoming artifact.

Is this a pillow? Mattress?

I can no longer place my exact whereabouts or *whatabouts* is near me.

Hmm, this thing is squishy but slightly firm…

My finger can't let go. It is connected.

Can you be so connected to a cushion? Sure. We're supporting each other.

Speaking of which. Thank you mattress for having my back. Oh. Ha! Holy shit, I'm high.

I might be several hours late to the purge party, but I could feel it build all night. I reach out for my bucket and let out sounds and toxicity from deep within me. I have had my fair experience of vomiting in various states, but this is *different*. I can sense the discharge of things that have been hidden away for years. Tremendous relief frees itself from places I didn't know existed.

Both willingly and unconsciously I am feeding the purge and ridding myself of all varieties of negativity encountered in my life: countless nights drinking cheap booze for pointless gains in social

circles—purge. The scores of assumptions I've jumped to without
the information needed for a proper decision—purge. False
judgments and projections made onto others—purge. *Get. It. Out.*

I can even hear the smiles and silent cheering from the
others in the room of my first purge of the night: *About time John!
Lighten yourself!*

The ayahuasca is filtering right through my whole body. All the
shitty fast food, chemical additives and animal waste products—
big purge.

That inherent intention opens up a new door and floods out
in an awareness of all the farmed animals I've ever consumed.
Suddenly I am transformed into the head space of a caged pig:
*Where am I? Why are they doing this to me? Is this really all life has
to offer? Hey! I have love to give people!* Purge.

Then comes a sea of Styrofoam. It engulfs me with all that
I have discarded over my life. Shiny, fake, sparkling white and
bunching together with that same sound like Styrofoam nails on
chalkboard as if to say: *Yeah, you threw me out, but I'm not gone. I'm
still somewhere trying to break down, slowly. You're welcome.* Purge.

I look down into my bucket as a lightening flash lights the
space for a moment's glance at the thin layer of dark bile in the
bottom. I have never seen anything like it in my life—let alone
something that has just come *out of me.* There isn't much physical
mass to it but has the weight of years of accumulated darkness and
toxicity from both mental and physical realms.

Instantly the image of my bucket's contents turns into the
polluted rivers and waterways that Chinese fishermen are floating
on in Asia right now—purge.

Get. It. Out.

When José relights the center candle, signifying the slow
close to the ceremony, I am still in full discussion with Mother
Ayahuasca. Everyone else is coming to and ready to head back to
their jungle cabins to sleep and reflect but I'm clearly staying the
night in this *maloca.*

The onset of dawn brings faint yellow light to the jungle. I find
myself staring up into the seemingly endless rafters and ladders of
this immense *maloca* roof. *Oh, the stories this roof could tell...*

It is about 6:30 AM, over 10 hours since the start of ceremony and I am still in a fairly heavy trance lying on my mat. I manage to get up and put on my rubber boots; I'm ready for a good tooth brushing. Walking back into the jungle I see a giant hawk staring at me from atop the perch of the highest tree in the area. I stop to exchange a short moment with him and then he quickly flies off—like he had been waiting to confirm my safe departure back home to my jungle hut.

Laying in my cabin bed, I could only have had an hour of sleep when something wakes me with an apparent message of importance. I roll on my back and answer by opening my heart to a profound sensation and vision.

There is a wide black and white circle. Encompassing it, I have a full awareness and physical sense of a completely secured grip—the kind I've had on difficult sections of rock climbing, where I'm ascending and keeping myself up with only tiny hand placements and near impossible holds, creating a desire to give up until a final reach finds a holy grail of grips. From it I can easily support myself, enabling relief, comfort and balance with both hands full and secure. It brings reassurance I can let everything else relax because I have locked myself into a position of attainment until I'm ready to move forward—*THAT* sensation. But here, lying on my back, I am holding my life—all life—in an atom. It is simultaneously as small as a particle and as big as the universe. Either way, my grip on it is unchanged. And it is *pure bliss.*

> But here, lying on my back, I am holding my life—all life—in an atom.

I am receiving a transparent lesson that encourages and reassures me:

I'VE GOT THIS.

The message is black and white.
Connection with the World.
Oneness with God.
Attainment of being God.
Control and comfort within me and all that is life.
I've got this.

HOW TO MAKE AYAHUASCA

After our second ceremony, I was fortunate enough to help make our next batch of ayahuasca on our day off between ceremonies—a tradition that has been passed down for thousands of years by the people of the Amazon.

Refugio Altiplano's head shaman, José, showing off a four- to five-year-old ayahuasca vine (usually one to two inches thick), ideal for a ceremonial brew. José says he uses sky ayahuasca (calm and uplifting) instead of storm ayahuasca (electric intensity).

Our ceremony maestro, Urias, holding up the other ingredient for ayahuasca, the chacruna leaf.

The simple looking chacruna leaf is actually full of the psychedelic tryptamine DMT. However, eating or smoking chacruna alone will not cause any effect— only when brewed traditionally with ayahuasca does the DMT get released in a usable form. When I asked José how his ancestors knew to mix these two plants out of all the biodiversity of the Amazon to make ayahuasca, he looked at me and laughed "The plants told us!"

After stripping the bark off the vines (to remove the bitter taste…still tastes terrible though) the locals layer the vine and chacruna leaves into what José calls a "big five-layer aya sandwich."

After José does a ceremonial jungle tobacco blessing over the ayahuasca and chacruna, they add drinkable water to the top of the cauldron. It is then left to boil over a wood fire for eight hours and simmer overnight. The next day we remove the leaves and vines and boil another three to six hours.

One cauldron makes three to four bottles of ayahuasca—more than enough to last twelve people for more than four ceremonies.

Photos: Kathryn Lively

Monkey Love

Senior Martin had one mode:
go bananas.

He would climb all over you,
pull your hair, scream and fuss and
grab any loose clothing or limb to
scare any of the guests away from his
grasp of fury.

Halfway through my ayahuasca
retreat something changed.

I sat down with him with an
open heart, because all he ended up
needing was a little love.

La Medicina

Ayahuasca is not your standard (millennia-year-old) medicine—
but still needs to be treated as such. I asked our shaman,
José, what he thought of the recent popularity and westernized
consumption of the Amazonian vine. He explained to me that if
you want to "get real work done" with ayahuasca, a minimum
of three to four ceremonies is needed under the guidance and
counsel of an experienced shaman. Just like you can't expect to
take one antibiotic pill to rid yourself of an illness, a succession
of well-intended ceremonies is essential to receive the full
capacity of the medicine.

THE 3RD CEREMONY
June 17, 2015

Enseña claridad por mi proposidad.
Teach me clarity for my purpose

Across the candlelight José pours ¾ of a cup. After breathing into it my intention and exchanging a *"salud,"* I down the thick brew in a single gulp and almost spew on the spot. *Whoa, this is definitely getting worse.* It's like drinking Mr. Peanut's vomit after he ate a rotten tree stump full of fermented mud. Sitting back on my floor mat I quickly throw a small mint in my mouth. *Sorry Aya, just a little sugar to get this damn taste out.*

There is a thick, healthy green vine.
The Mother Vine.
And she is growing inside me.
Flourishing from the crown of my head,
through my spine, around all my chakras
and down through my feet.
Strengthening.
Strengthening love
and all I know I am, with a tight hug.
Complete contentment.
Aya is smiling.

The moon is gone and the jungle is completely dark. I feel our *maestro* Urias come close to me. He is sensing my energy to determine with which *icaros* to sing and heal. They say on a good dose of ayahuasca your eyes are ultra sensitive to UV light so you can see the spirits that are already there. In the pitch black of that *maloca*, I see him. Urias is sitting cross-legged and glowing like a gentle moonlight shimmer over still water.
    I sit up to match him.
    Urias begins his intention-filled breathing ending with an exhaled whistle to prepare himself and fend away darkness. He then begins singing in his native tongue that pierces through me and echoes in the room like the cry of the loon. Hearing a shaman

June 17 2015

3ʳᵈ CEREMONY

'Enseña claridad por mi propósidad
[Breathed in Breathed out]

Dose   3/4 cup   ('fuerte')
* it is absolutly getting worse & worse
(like Kelly said)
with every ceremony
* enjoy the taste your first time cause
it'll never taste as 'good'.

The shaman Jose assures me he gave me a 'fuerte' dose Much more than the others But the night was not strong or overwhelming but astandingly clear.

THE PERUVIAN PRESCRIPTION

from two feet away sing in his jungle tongue of *shapibo* to help you
is nothing short of mesmerizing.

His chorus suddenly sends me into the wingspan of the great
condor of Peru, soaring confidently over Colca Canyon. Watching
out over all within the distance. With a slight tip of a wing I can
turn gracefully within the deep blue sky.

It is beautiful.

It is so beautiful I could vomit. And I almost do.

I share a chuckle at the thought of having someone
sing their heart out to you, sitting on a mat in complete
darkness and responding in an abrasive purge of puke. Urias would
never even break his song. Priceless. But after all, it's what he
does. He's a healer. *Note to self: make sure the bucket is upside right.
Vomiting into an upside down bucket in darkness isn't good for anyone.*

**It is so beautiful
I could vomit.
And I almost do.**

My ears are turning on.
Starting with a slight hum then moving into more of a pulse.
Like a sweeping sonar sound open and searching for foreign
    outside signals.
Fellow conveyors of messages.

Other senders and receivers waiting to converse.
Connections are clicking.
Ok, here we go.
My brain is on and plugged in.
My mind is a freshly-charged super computer
ready to process, create and interact with
  everything.
The sounds of processing: deep, content
  breaths.
Followed by whatever sound a smile makes.

Followed by whatever sound a smile makes.

A brief moment interrupts the darkness of night. The floorboards creak to announce the presence of someone in the center of the *maloca*. A flint sparks to light the candle and it immediately brings life and depth to the great rooftop overhead I've been staring blankly into.

It has been four hours since the start of ceremony. Lying on my back I'm stuck in a peripheral gaze to the dark corners that reach endlessly into the top of the rafters. Two eyes suddenly appear. Or is it two fireflies…no, definitely not insects. They move in perfect synchronization of bright green eyes like that of a bat, yet they flutter around and behind the highest beams like a butterfly. If it can't be a bat or firefly or bird or anything…what is it??

A soft but confident voice, with my own narrative, answers pleasingly in my head:

We don't show often…but just keeping an eye on everyone.

Ah, the Great Spirits.

It is such a simple and assuring presence I have no reason to question it. Like wise elders, and even our shaman José, they don't speak out often. Their presence is sometimes all the comfort the moment needs.

Whether I actually begin a conversation with a mystical spirit or simply begin to talk to myself—it doesn't matter. When an intuitive acknowledgement of your life's purpose comes your way, it's best to be open to the message.

I could hear my fellow ayahuasca takers began to stir as we all start to come around at the end of ceremony. Behind my mattress I reach for the round wooden feel of my *kalimba* instrument (a Peruvian thumb piano with two extra holes to create a beautiful *wah* reverb effect) I brought to ceremony. *Let's dedicate this to all the good spirits in the maloca tonight.* I take a deep breath and prepare to break the several hours of silence. Gently thumbing across the tune keys it fills a delicate and mystical melody in the air. I can feel the surprise and delight in the room to the beautiful shift in ambiance. I let the final chord linger as my thumb opens and closes the *wah* hole for a magical reverb effect. The room shares a slow out-breath of sound reflection.

A long five minutes passes. No one moves or says a thing. Just the flicker of our single candle sending shadows dancing to the rafter tops with the soundtrack of an alive Amazon around us. Through the sounds of crickets, birds and the occasional monkey, a low vibrating hum, like an airplane, creeps in. Only it sounds and feels much more natural...and what and where is an airplane flying this deep in the Amazon? Wait, is it *in* the *maloca*?

It comes in louder with a rotating vibrating swirl to it, like it is some sort of energetic cloud going from north to south then somehow starting back north again. A second one starts humming with more of a buzzing, flapping sound. Only this one is behind me—which is interesting because I'm lying down...

My Peruvian Kalimba

My eyes are open but nothing is moving besides the candlelight —more alive now than ever. It should be more startling, but it's okay. It has a warm, confiding presence to it that warms the room. Just as I start smiling in comfort, something hits two feet to the right of where I lay. It has a strong enough impact to vibrate a chord on the *kalimba* sitting on my chest.

A familiar voice narrates again in my head.

Beautiful. Thank you.

THE 4TH CEREMONY
June 18, 2016

*My fourth ceremony was the only ceremony about which I didn't journal about directly after. For weeks following it, I wanted to keep it out of my psyche—simply forget it existed.

It's hard to be considerate of the most terrifying night of your life.

But time is an incredible healer.

Not only have I been able to reflect on the happenings of my fourth ceremony but I've recognized it as a tremendous lesson from which everything within me has grown stronger.

I'm writing and sharing my story because, to me, to not disclose the experience from my fourth ceremony would be wrong.

It would be false marketing of an ancient medicine to not discuss the intense lessons and ways it teaches and heals.

I guess José was right all along. Sometimes the most profound teachings of Ayahuasca can take the longest to realize and manifest into your consciousness.

I'm lying on my mat in the *maloca.*

We're halfway through ceremony and the effects of the ayahuasca in my system is now easily recognizable and comfortable. I'm a little sad my flight back to Lima is tomorrow and I'm not staying the full retreat with the rest of the group who are doing seven ceremonies within 12 days. Ayahuasca has brought nothing but incredible love, insight and healing into my life over this past week.

Visions of patterned colors and worldly gratitude fill the space in front of me. As familiar as it has become it never gets old. I'm sitting cross-legged, meditating on tonight's intention: *Establish the gift to help and heal others and clear away negativity.* I've always believed we all hold the capacity to heal one another—especially ourselves. The last thirty minutes I've been blasting out good intentions— physically feeling it manifest from my heart chakra—to aid the injuries and mental difficulties of those in my life. (Between breaks to laugh aloud, get lost in mesmerizing visions and fly like a Peruvian condor of course.)

I get a sudden vision of worms and squirming parasites flash into my mind. It lingers uncomfortably. I almost laugh to myself. *Hey, that was actually an unpleasant vision. I haven't really had many of those yet...* It flashes again—this time in a stark red color. Then again with the vision of crabs, octopus and insects scavenging around. I shift on my mat trying to bring back the beautiful colors and peaceful shapes I had been accustomed to in ceremony. The color red bursts through my attempts with quick hit of heavy anxiety and hostility. I sit up straight, fully awake and conscious that something is happening. Tension fills the space around me. I feel something approach with such intensity and magnitude it's like standing in the middle of the highway as two giant speeding semis pass by me. Flashes of red ring loudly throughout my psyche like a D-Day alarm has been triggered. *What the hell is happening?!*

There is a menacing presence that rises above my right shoulder. It's feels detrimental by design. I put up the strongest mental and physical barrier I can as the words "¡*Afuera, afuera!*" escape my mouth: *Out, away!* Along with the presence, visions of scavenging creatures and flares of red form a weight of intense discomfort. I begin to get flashes of pain and negativity from other peoples lives as if they've been directed at me: depression, abuse, greed, physical ailments, anger…The realization hits me that that this might be the response to tonight's intention of wanting to help and heal others. *If carrying the pain of the world is the burden true healers have to deal with…I take back my request! This is WAY too much for me.*

The words of Wilma, my coca leaf reader and medicine woman, enter my mind as I struggle to not get crushed by the force of it all. "You have a very strong energy…but you need to be careful to not open yourself up to heavy energy you might encounter." Her words echo like foreshadow. Something has definitely come by—but I will NOT be an open window for ill opportunity. I sit fervent to rid all evil intentions from myself and the space around me. *Afuera, afuera! You are not welcome by me, by the maloca or anyone else that is good at heart. Afuera!* The jungle outside has come alive: crickets chirping, birds tweeting, monkeys howling…all in unison. They too are conscious of the brewing trouble and ready to help stand ground.

The jungle outside has come alive: crickets chirping, birds tweeting, monkeys howling… all in unison.

The ferocity becomes difficult to bear. I hear José stirring across the room aware there has been a shift in the *maloca*.

"José," I call out and hear him quickly walk over in the darkness. "José, *Ayúdame.*" *Help me.*

"*Sí.*" He answers. Without hesitating he begins reciting Spanish words while placing his thumbs on my forehead wrapping his middle fingers around the crown of my head. On specific words he puts pressure on my head and then suddenly walks away.

José you're leaving me?! I really need help getting through this and it's…oh, it's…GONE.

It was gone. Out and away. The most immense relief of pressure and stress I've ever experienced. Like suffering the mental and physical terror of an underwater nightmare and I finally surfaced clear-headed and able to breathe again. I am back to myself—alone—sitting on my mat in the night of the *maloca;* free of any visions, colors or negative sensations. José was back on the other side of the room already halfway through singing another *icaros.*

What the hell just happened?

I know my first three ceremonies were blissfully conflict-free but Ayahuasca, if you had something to teach me, you didn't need to rip off my training wheels and spit them back in my face as you boot me off the side of a cliff.

But José, you really are a mystical healing shaman…

The rest of the night passes with beautiful colors and visions of love and gratitude I had become used to with ayahuasca. If any inclinations of the same negativity would creep up, I would simply whisper *"afuera"* and become a rock of impenetrable good intention. Whether tonight was a lesson, a test, a bad dream or none or all of the above, the mother vine seemed pleased and gifted me with a sensation of riding an endless wave— a perfect barrel that never moved. As pleasant as things have turned out I'm still completely shaken up; my psyche needs rest.

After the ceremony I sit down with José and share a mapacho jungle cigarette with him. I break the silence *"¿Que pasado esta noche?"* What happened tonight?

José chuckles then responds *"Una buena ceremonia"* and takes another drag of smoke.

A good ceremony? It's just that simple? Just another casual day at work for a shaman: battling people's demons, purifying space and changing lives…

> **"There is no coming to consciousness without pain. People will do anything, no matter how absurd, in order to avoid facing their own Soul. One does not become enlightened by imagining figures of light, but by making the darkness conscious."**
>
> CARL JUNG

The weeks following my first Ayahuasca experiences in the Amazon I was convinced it would also be the last of my jungle vine drinking. I had my experience, had my cleanse, had my blissful revelations along with getting the shit (almost literary) scared out of me...*been there, done that.*

As the year passes, the more I travel and work around Central America the more I continue to get invites for random one-off ceremonies. "Not a chance" is my natural reaction. I have stood by the notion that it is sacred medicine— from the Amazon—and should only be consumed in formal ritual near the source. I also don't need to risk any intense repeats of my fourth ceremony without the guide of José or another shaman I truly trust. It's not exactly a "Hey, wanna drink ayahuasca at my house on Friday?" kind of gathering— and never should be. But things began to shift and once again I got the call from Ayahuasca to converge into her realm of symbiotic teachings.

Bocas del Toro, Panama

I'm currently sitting in limbo on the dock of my friend's house in Panama. After finishing my work for the season I'm at a crossroads of where in the world my next move should be. The main objective is to find a familiar space to write and compile the book you now have now in your hands...Colombia? Guatemala? Costa Rica?

Opening an email from my good friend Gabby (founder of Momentom Collective Circus Arts), I unconsciously type yes before I fully process that she's just asked me to join an ayahuasca ceremony in Nicaragua in three weeks. Surprised by my own gut reaction, I read the email again—nothing changes. It feels right. I quickly try to question my intuition: *what if I don't trust our shaman?* A pulse shoots out from my heart chakra—*You ARE the shaman.* Oh, all right then.

The next email I read is from another friend asking me to take care of his home in Nicaragua while he's away for the next six weeks. *Propitious omens indeed…* I keep nodding along to the realization that Aya is calling me back. Like the implicit warmth still shared after accidentally stepping on your dog's tail, there is an understanding that Aya wants to make amends from our difficult last ceremony together. *What's past is behind us now. Besides, we've got other work to do now…*

APRIL 2016
BOCAS DEL TORO, PANAMA

THE 5TH CEREMONY
May 7th 2016

It begins with the awareness that my eyes are becoming ultra sensitive to light.
> Sensations are rising.
> Good thing it is pitch black.

Buddhas.
Smiling and content Thai Buddha statues.
Often arising in golden rows
   aligned in a warm three-dimensional space,
               sitting in meditation as they weave in and out
                       of the forefront of my mind.
This is a good omen.
A sign of trusting peace and tranquility.
Aya wants to make sure I am not scared but open to the wisdom
                               of unconditional love.
                   This is going to be a good ceremony.

We are three or four songs of *icaros* in.
Things are light and pleasant.
I get a feeling that this might not be a very intense ceremony.
       …and then Vinod, our shaman lights up the candles again.
       He is offering a communal second round of ayahuasca.

   I trusted Vinod immediately upon meeting him. He has been working with ayahuasca for over 20 years and echoes the Peruvian shamanism practices that have been passed down to him. I go up third in our group of ten people—a lot more people and energy

Kundalini And The Tree of 12 Fruits
courtesy of the artist Myztico Campo

than I was used to previously in the Amazon. Vinod pours a full shot glass of the dark and murky brown jungle *medicina*. He whispers his own prayers over the cup and passes it to me with a "*Salud.*"

I carefully speak my intention into the cup, raise it to my head and down it.

Our entire circle goes back for a second cup.

Listamos.

Fewer than 10 minutes after the candles are snuffed out—and our blackness of night is resumed—I feel the real pull. Vividly familiar like it was yesterday. It's hard to believe I'm not back in the *maloca* right now. The pull strengthens. True work is about to begin.

I'm going to need to lie down for this one...

A fourth-dimensional space is opening up before me.
It is moving and flowing like a river—constantly evolving.
It branches out in a matrix of cross sections,
    like a grid work of construction beams and crane towers
        efficiently working and moving.
I have found myself in some sort of master plan.
        A spiritual blueprint.
It is neither written nor definitive.
    Simply evolving
        in the moment.
And here I exist.
We exist.
Everything together.
    Growing.
        For the better.

Hands of spiritual angels weave through my body.
        Plucking and playing,
    tweaking and refining
        as they scoop blockages from my stomach and spine.

Everything is so surreal—yet comfortable.
I've been here before and we both know it.
But there is just so much going on, I feel the need to say something within my dream:

...wow, ah...so, who's in charge here?

Shh, we're working.
Well yes, I can see that...
We don't speak your language either. So quit using your words so much.
Got it.
Breathe. Relax. Be open to it. We're in this together.
                    Working.
                    We're working.
                            We'reking
                                    We're. King.
                                            with Aya.

The evolving nature of life is cascading around in front of me.
Animals, plants and interconnected shapes are flowing freely
                    as if being painted by brushstroke in bright colors.
A thick black outline of a jaguar head
            filled with abstract shapes of red, blue and yellow
            weaves itself across a dark canvas leaving behind a
            thriving vine of life.
Bears, wolves and pumas surge and fuse forward
            followed by deer, rabbits and small mammals
                    in a comet's tail containing nature's food chain.
Everything arises and fades
            like slow expanding fireworks glowing in the night sky.
    All I can—and need to do—is look up in amazement
    and appreciation
                    ...and let out a few "Oohs...and aahs..."

I have *awoken*
            but am still in this dream...

Because
                We're here.
                                Because
                                            Why not?

Names.
I need to get better at names.
Not just people.

Names of plants and birds and animals.
Recognition of life.
Titles to identify and resonate that
I know who and what is around me
and it is appreciated.

Hey Aya,
I know you're busy working your plant medicine on me
and all right now,
but can you help a writer out and fuel me with something creative
to write about?

Just write something and make it stick.

What's that supposed to mean?

Make it... STICK.

¿Que?

STICK.

Hmm.

The Three Adhesives of Experience
Stuck,
Sticky,
and Stick.

All applicable to events.
But only *one* of these words
is what you'll require to change your life.

It's never good to be *stuck* in circumstance.
Nor is it good to be in a really *sticky* situation.
But,
if a real moving experience can *stick;*
well, that's what changes lives.

Finding a valuable lesson in an unlikely event
that will affix itself,
embed into,

and remain with you
—for the better,
well, you should stick with that.

The appearance of smiling golden Buddhas floats back into the front of my mind's eye. There have been some heavy thoughts that have arisen tonight and this recurring imagery brings both comfort and contentment as I release all negativity that emerges or passes by. Each breath helps to shine the statues in a brighter gold. I soak myself within their unconstrained peace.

I begin to think about religion. Christianity comes to mind. As it does, so do the images of the bloodied body of Jesus Christ crucified on a cross: crown of thorns, whips of torment, an apostles betrayal, pain and humiliation... all adorning paintings and statues that line the walls of churches dedicated to discussions of sin, wickedness and repentance to avoid the infinity of purgatory or the depths of hell.

Who can pray and be mindful in this environment?

I turn that page in my mind to return to the silent smiles of meditating Buddhas, all surrounding shrines of happiness, nature and serenity. *Ah, my kind of place.*

But let's consider the options:

Meditations for a content happiness sought
through lack of thought.
VS.
Prayers for a forgiveness of sin sought
through deliberate thought.

The practice of praying for an internal divinity—the God within me feels more profound and real than praying for an external divinity—a God outside of me.

We are all divine.
We are all holders of light.
We are all God.

Evolution has been a reoccurring theme within many of my ayahuasca experiences but the concept is grounding itself in my trip tonight. As the visuals come back there is also a presence with it that demonstrates that this next part of my current journey will be more interactive-based than a colorful illustration for viewing pleasure only.

I am sucked back into the matrix of life and its inter-dimensional blueprint of evolution. It has a natural push and flow of creativity embedded in it. Aya sends me into the framework of Mother Nature and her art of evolution. I get a flash of simultaneously having and working through every good idea I've ever come up with in my life. *Good ideas evolve. Evolution involves good ideas.* It's uplifting while overwhelming—yet doesn't even touch the expansion in front of me: this immense universe of creativity that has been initiated to produce life on our planet. It reaches into me as a concise collective. Within this collective is a higher consciousness, and we are feeling each other out. No words, just concepts of thought. We know we have met many times in many ways, but this is different. This evolving collective is at a crossroads within itself, trying to choose a side—and looking within me to help find intention; intention of our strange and sprawling human species.

> **I am sucked back into the matrix of life and its inter-dimensional blueprint of evolution.**

You have been evolving further outside of our collective.
This ego of your species…it is destructive.
Can we trust this period of rapid evolution for humans to evolve with us?
With nature's consciousness?

I get blasted with several sensations of reality. Potential actualities get sampled in a mix of visions. A twisted human species totally disconnected from nature, plugging into gadgets that feed egos in a polluted environment. It feels dark and detached. Next I experience a warm and loving tribe of people that have shifted into a balance of farming and cooperating with nature. It feels like home.

I find the courage to rise from my mat and walk to the bathroom.

Wow, the lighting in here is spectacular.
The light breeze coming in from the open window is making it a battle for these candles to stay alive. Or maybe the candles are just

exuberantly at work, trying to light this big, dark space with such
little wicks and even shorter attention spans.

> *Some light over there!*
> *Bah!*
> *Flicker over here…*
> *Shoo shadow!*
> *Feel my illumination!*
> *Hey, what's in that corner?*
> *Flicker, flicker, flicker.*

I look at my face in the mirror.
Whoa.
There's that *thing* I am, staring back at me…
  But is that *me*?
I begin to look at myself
  with a strange new perspective and interpretation;
  like when you stare at one word so long it becomes oddly foreign:
  You're only used to looking at it superficially
    because it's always within the same predetermined context.
Not now.
My face turns into a hieroglyphic of a thousand people
              —a thousand faces to interpret.
I have tapped into the ability to step outside
  of the reference I have created
        to connect my face with the person I've labeled *me*.
My features are flowing and changing
    with how I perceive them as an outsider.
I've also lost the allusion for what is *normal* or *good*.
                Everything in front of me just *is*.
Is that a big nose or a small nose?
  Are those marks on the skin normal?
    How many millions of others have exact ears like that?

As I zoom out of the tapestry of faces in front of me,
    I get a comforting notion to think, *who cares?*
                It all just is.

I look down to turn on the faucet and look back up to me—my face.
Oh hey, I know that smile…that's me!
Looking good there amigo.

The water comes out of the tap in a stream of abundance.
I look hard, but can't really *see* the water from the flow.
It's just a fluid wave of particles that bends and blurs the sink
    behind it.
The candles flicker to take a closer look as well.
I turn off the tap, but a flow is still there.
It carries over and onto my hands like a river of transparency,
            warping and wavering my open palms and fingertips.
I look back up into the mirror, which has turned into a shimmering
    Impressionist painting of my
reflecting self.

Hmm.
Neat trick there, Aya.

"Ayahuasca is not a drug in the
Western sense, something you
take to get rid of something.
Properly used, it opens up parts
of yourself that you usually
have no access to. The parts
of the brain that hold emotional
memories come together with
those parts that modulate insight
and awareness, so you see past
experiences in a new way."
DR. GABOR MATÉ

The 5 Recurring Teachings of Ayahuasca

The wisdom from the mother vine can be difficult to translate
just as it can be painfully obvious. My personal experiences,
as well as those described by others from a succession of
well-intentioned ceremonies, seem to draw on the same five
themes. These are my interpretations of the Five Recurring
Teachings of Ayahuasca:

Abundance of love
You will see it, you will feel it and you will be moved by the
unrealized sources of love and gratitude in your life.

Loss of ego
You will reflect in a new light and realize the absurdity of living
an artificial life to fuel your ego.

Appreciation for nature
The natural world around you will open up and speak to you,
calling you back to your true roots.

Dealing with your demons
Whether it's dealing with past trauma, acknowledging pain and
suffering or ridding yourself of negativity, you will have to find
ways to bring light to your darkness.

Connectedness with the whole
The realization that a greater collective on a spiritual level
doesn't just exist but that you are a part of it. Contributing to
it just might change your life.

CHAPTER 8
Travel
X Love

All you need is love...
bum badadadum
(Bocas del Toro, Panama)

Travel.
So full of charm
      the ultimate seducer
Has me saying yes
      before I know
      what I'll incur

*Distant love on the
Playa of Burning Man
2011, Nevada Desert.*

TRAVEL
Relationships
When Things Get More *Real* Than Real Life

Romantic relationships are different when you're traveling. Most couples don't realize it until they do it. What's the fastest way to determine if things are going to work out in the long run? Spend a month on a trip together. And I'm not talking about a quick vacation, glitzy holiday or preplanned all-inclusive voyage. That's not traveling, that's just fun. I mean put on a backpack, fly to a developing country, take local transportation and stay in cheap accommodation with the only plan being to have the time of your life as you both get comfortable being uncomfortable. You will grow and learn more about each other this way than you ever could in "real life."

A couple in Paris.

I often find myself defending travel relationships—likely because that is how I've dated or formed connections with most of the individuals in my life. People often assume a relationship that starts and ends on the road doesn't mean as much because it is shorter-lived and not within the frame of what is considered normal at home. It *is* hard to keep a girlfriend when the longest you've stayed in one place is four months in 10 years. But time is simply irrelevant in a relationship, or even friendship, when you're both backpacking—it's more like a vortex. Experiences are constantly blasted your way and accumulate so quickly (in such an intense range of highs and lows) that even a week of traveling can equate to months of being together at home.

I've even used math for those that insist you can't really *know* someone until the fourth date or third month or whatever nonsensical measurement people might use.

...even a week of traveling can equate to months of being together at home.

Seducing the locals in Santorini, Greece.

Ok, let's say you're dating someone at home. You're both working full-time jobs but manage to still see each other 2-3 times a week outside of other friends and commitments (which is pretty good in today's busy lifestyle). Whether it's dinner and a movie, clubbing on Saturday night or Netflix 'n Chill, we're likely talking 3-4 hours per hangout, 2-3 times a week. So if you're not living together, you're lucky to get more than 10-12 hours a week with your significant other.

Compare that to *24 hours a day* of traveling and living with the same person *every day*: packing and moving each morning, debating itineraries, negotiating with the locals, eating out or cooking every meal together, dealing with theft, getting sick and constantly adapting plans and budgets while sharing some of the most magical moments of your life together. Needless to say, the long travel days and daily decision-making constantly push the boundaries of your comfort zones. I like to think you get to know someone a *lot* more while traveling than you do sitting in silence staring at a movie screen together or by how well you both agree on what channel to watch.

"The Weather is Here, Wish You Were Beautiful"
JIMMY BUFFET, *COCONUT TELEGRAPH* ALBUM (1981)

At home, you go on a date when you feel like it and have time to look good. Then, you'll go home when you're tired, sick or need a break from the person. Traveling together doesn't quite offer that luxury. *Not feeling so fresh? Sorry, no showers on this 14-hour night train to Bangkok. You normally dress up on a date? High heels and makeup don't really work in the jungles of Costa Rica. You're a picky eater? Well, neither of us can read this Burmese menu so I guess we'll eat whatever they bring us. It's Day 17 and we've run out of things to talk about? Perfect, we'll learn to enjoy silence together.* And when someone gets sick (it *will* happen), you'll have to stick even closer together to get through it—especially if no one else speaks English in the village you're passing through.

When you travel with someone you get to see the real version of them. All of it. You get to witness the bliss on their face when they have life-changing experiences while also sharing any possible burdens and emotions that emerge alongside it. Within days, you uncover sides of people that otherwise might have taken months or years to surface. Traveling creates that strange—and often uncomfortable—change within an ordinary relationship that allows people to experience more *real life* than real life.

We put incredible amounts of time and money into our relationships. My thought? The most efficient and effective investment might simply be a backpack and plane ticket.

APRIL 2016
BOCAS DEL TORO, PANAMA

It's interesting how language can shape a culture.

To say 'I love you' in Spanish they say *'te quiero'* which means 'I want you.'

A possible explanation for the possessive passion of the Spanish

...and maybe a more accurate definition for today's modern romance.

"Travelling is like flirting with life. It's like saying, I would stay and love you, but I have to go; this is my station."

LISA ST. AUBIN DE TERAN

TRAVELING
~ I LOVE YOU. ~

BUT SOON I WILL HAVE TO
CHEAT ON YOU

AND FINALLY
FIND A GIRLFRIEND.

SAYULITA GYPSY

I met a gypsy girl waking from the sun
She had a smile that could capture anyone
But behind that smile was a little something more than truth
  Cause she's a Gypsy Girl
  With nothing left to lose

She'd wear her feathers and than wrap you in her hands
She'd spin her magic while dancing in the sand
With pupils high and wide, she's not just laughing cause of you
  Cause's she's a Gypsy Girl
  And she's taking you with her too

And she'd sing...
Oh Sayulita
Oh Sayulita ahora
Sin Sayulita de nada
  Cause she's a Gypsy Girl
  With nothing left to lose

Señorita Sayulita con fuego
Volverse loco de bailar con el pueblo
Ahorita estoy fumado, tocando el cielo
  Esa Señorita Gitana
      de Mexico

Y ella cantar...
Oh Sayulita ahora
Sin Sayulita de nada
Oh Sayulita siempre
  Esa Señorita Gitana de Mexico

APRIL 2011
SAYULITA, MEXICO

"There are so few young Uruguayans, sex is rare and exotic. You sleep with a Uruguayan girl... it's like pandas."
JUAN FROM URUGUAY, WHILE WE COUCH-SURFED IN SANTA CRUZ, CALIFORNIA

Blind Date

I'll read you
With my eyes closed
Like Braille
Just fingertips
Across your chest
To this limited sense

I'll read you
In the dark
With the only glow
From the fire we start
With our bodies' flint
And this moment's kindling
For two lips to spark

I'll read you
From front to back
Introduction
Climax
And soft fade to black
Your plot exposed
And story told
To reread again
With eyes still closed.

FEBRUARY 2016
PLAYA MADERAS, NICARAGUA

Ancient Balinese porn?
(Ubud, Indonesia)

Watching the Temple Burn with 50,000 people in silence will leave a strong impression. Burning Man 2011

OPEN FIRE

Her love
is the warmth
of the perfect temperature tea
I can't put down
because I've been waiting
    too long
to put my lips to it

Her love
is the familiarity
of my favorite song
I had yet to hear
because I knew the words
were waiting for her melody

Her love
is the expansion of my arms
as I finally look up
and notice the clouds moving
ready to embrace
something greater than me

Her love
is the necessity

of the morning shine of the sun
to start anew
because it's easy to forget
that all storms will pass

~The difficult reality is that~

Her love
is also an open fire
that burns strong
illuminating the dark
and although I see and feel it
it is not directed at me
but simply needed and shared
for all in sight

Her love
is not *my* love
but simply
love

And that
I have finally accepted

The End of Shallow Fruit

It might have taken more years than I care to admit.
But this is what I've learned.
If you want to attract and be with
        an incredible, beautiful partner
        —a real keeper, a 10/10—
You have to drop picking up the easy pickings.
No more low-hanging fruit.
It's often ripe for the taking,
        it can be hard to pass.
But give it up.

If you want someone worthy of a second date…
Quit going after one-night stands.
It's a sacrifice to better yourself
        from superficial distraction.
Convenience thrives on impermanence.
And a full belly
        doesn't always mean
                a satisfied appetite.

Grow up and aim higher.
Deserve more.
People can tell if you are used to swimming shallow.
Pretending to tread when you can stand.
Dive into the deep end
                and work harder.
Take the risk.
Put yourself out there.

The output often matches the input.
Drop the easy put out and put the effort in
        for quality over discounted quantity.
Nothing sweet ripens in one night.
So forget the easy pickings.
Reach for the higher branch
        and end the pursuit of shallow fruit.
The person you deserve
                is worth the climb.

FEBRUARY 2016
SAN JUAN DEL SUR, NICARAGUA

"What a wonderful thought it is
that some of the best days of our
lives haven't even happened yet..."
ANON

♫ THE REWRITE

Your face leads another direction
Soft place with full inflections
         Laid out in the fledging daylight
I'm sitting still from your beating heart
Thrilled quick then it falls apart
         And trails flat in this melody
         Kept to fade into memory
I look down just to look away
A light pull with the feel to fray
         Made soft thin silk for a while

This relapse leads straight through sunlight
With your one last look and than the rewrite

Your face still holds affection
But displaced for new directions
         Laid full in the sea of sunlight
I'm sitting still from your beating heart
Not sure when the ends to start
         Can we hold off this remedy
         Made soft thin silk for a while

This relapse leads straight through sunlight
With your one last laugh before the rewrite

OCTOBER 2011
SASKATCHEWAN, CANADA

An unexpected attribute of a traveler: getting good at saying goodbye. Give someone a hug and a smile like you'll never see them again but also with the comfort that you'll see them tomorrow—and you might!

She is beloved
because she
should *be loved.*

OUTRO?
"...I THINK I'M GOING TO STAY."
The Closing Quest of the Traveler

The older you get as a traveler,
    the more it is
    about finding that vibe,
        your vibe.
Finding where you want to be.
Accompanied by the people
    you want to see
    in your tribe,
    as you all strive to live
        The Life.

No more
    do-all-I-can-do
    in a month travel.
No more
    see all the sights,
    or party all the nights
        away
    to say,
I'm a *stupid.young.backpacker.*
Not that that wasn't fun,
    or I would have done it
        any other way.
But hey,
I'm over "same-same but different."
I'm ready to slow down
    catch my full stride
        in life
        and be.

So
where do I find myself
    as I find. Myself.
Through the people,

    the work,
        the lifestyle...
And become content
    to the extent I say:
Yup.
I'm changing my flight.
I can't leave this tonight.
The way I fit in,
    the way everything feels
        right.
I don't need to roam
    for a while.
    This. Is. Home.
        For a while.
The style and feel might change,
    will change,
    or at least rearrange
to which I can turn back into being
    sporadic and nomadic.
But right now
    things click.

I've found my place
    and it's a space filled
    with people
    that all share the same
        present quest
    to live the best
and put our current
    travels to rest.
        To be here now.
    And for that,
    I am blessed.

APRIL 2016
PUERTO VIEJO, COSTA RICA

I've been home over a week now and the culture shock is too intense. I thought I could readjust quickly to the vast social differences in Canada from Central America but it has been such a struggle: shaking hands with white guys...it's just too difficult. You're going in for the grab? The pound? The snap? The back pat? The bro hug? The firm deal maker? What?? I'm always lost in the muck of it.

Oh Latin America, how I miss your universal slap/pound.

Easy. Clean. Cool.

Extraño a mis hermanos en Centroamérica.

Thanks again for the airport pickup Dad...but please don't out-hippy me in public again. I have a gypsy image to uphold.

Goodbyes are inevitable.
Heading home is tough.
It's interesting to see how you've taken shape
as you complete the circle of your travels.

But starting a new chapter shouldn't change your book.
The one thing you don't need to say goodbye to is
being a traveler.

I'm not just talking about planning the next trip away from home.
But also finding your journey *within* home.
Be a local tourist.
Enjoy your backyard and hometown
with the fresh eyes you just set upon the rest of the world.
Keep your cravings to explore
Find new boundaries to push for
And always adjust your perspectives for more.
Arriving home to fall back into static familiarity
is a waste of a good journey.
And traveling is in your head
as much as it's under your feet.

Never stop being a traveler.
And always live a life worth journaling.

END NOTES

1   Cheers: some help translating from http://matadornetwork.com/nights/
     how-to-say-cheers-in-50-languages.
2   The 2016 publication on global light pollution: http://advances.
     sciencemag.org/content/2/6/e1600377.
3   84.7 million tourists visited France in 2013 according to the United
     Nations World Tourism Organization.
4   Mexico tops the 2014 OECD list with their ability to work, on average,
     2,228 hours a year. The average American worker puts in 1,780 hours
     and average Canadian worker clocks 1,704 annually.
5   https://en.wikipedia.org/wiki/List_of_most_expensive_cities_for_
     expatriate_employees
6   Source for the highest altitude towns and cities in the world:
     https://en.wikipedia.org/wiki/List_of_highest_towns_by_country.
7   Source for the highest marijuana consumption by country:
     http://www.unodc.org/documents/wdr2014/Cannabis_2014_web.pdf.

The end of all exploring
will be to arrive where you started
              and know the place
                        for the first time.
                   T.S. ELIOT

(San Juan del Sur,
Nicaragua)

PERMISSIONS

Thank you to the following photographers for their respective image on the front cover: Brent McAdam [*The Saskatoon Bessborough*], www.beyondblighty.com [*San Juan del Sur statue*], Raymond Ostertag [*Tikal temple*], Onderwijsgek [*mushrooms*] and George Hodan [*compass*].

The LH 95 stellar nursery in the Large Magellanic Cloud of the Milky Way (pg. 8) courtesy of NASA, ESA, and the Hubble Heritage Team and taken from the public domain.

Songkran photo of the statue of Luang Pho Phra Sai in Nongkhai Thailand (pg. 22), © Thanagon Karaket | Dreamstime.com.

The spraying Japanese toilet photo (pg. 51) is a Wikimedia Commons image from the user Chris 73 and is freely available at //commons.wikimedia.org/wiki/File:JapaneseToiletBidet.jpg under the creative commons cc-by-sa 3.0 license.

All Eckhart Tolle quotes used with permission by the author and publishers: Namaste Publishing, New World Library and Penguin, USA.

Ellen Bass' quote used with permission from the author. Taken from *The Courage to Heal: A Guide for Women Survivors of Child Sexual Abuse*, published by HarperCollins and co-authored by Ellen Bass and Laura Davis.

Excerpt from *Neither Here Nor There* by Bill Bryson. Copyright © 1992 by Perennial, an Imprint of HarperCollins Publishers. Used with permission by the author and publishers.

Albert Camus quote reproduced by permission of Penguin Books Ltd. Taken from *The Outsider* by Albert Camus, translated by Joseph Laredo (Penguin Modern Classics, 2013). Translation copyright © Joseph Laredo, 1982.

Charles Bukowski quote used under the fair use terms by HarperCollins Publishers LLC.

Timothy Leary excerpt taken from his autobiography *Flashbacks* (1983), and used with permission from Penguin Publishing Group.

Albert Einstein quote used with permission from the Albert Einstein Archives. The quote was recorded in the diary of Count Harry Kessler (*The Diary of a Cosmopolitan*, 1971) from a dinner conversation with German critic Alfred Kerr on June 14th, 1927 after Kerr asked if Einstein was a deeply religious man.

Dr. Gabor Maté quote used with permission by the author.

Excerpt from "Little Gidding" from FOUR QUARTETS by T.S. Eliot. Copyright 1936 by Houghton Mifflin Harcourt Publishing Company; Copyright © renewed 1964 by T.S. Eliot. Copyright 1940, 1942 by T.S. Eliot; Copyright © renewed 1968, 1970 by Esme Valerie Eliot. Reprinted by permission of Houghton Mifflin Harcourt Publishing Company. All rights reserved.

Every reasonable effort has been made to contact the copyright holders, but if there are any errors, omissions or quotes that do not fall under fair use, the publisher will be pleased to insert the appropriate acknowledgement in any subsequent printing of this publication.

GIVING BACK

I am thrilled to share proceeds of this book with *The Integral Heart Family* foundation to give back to the children, communities and future minds of rural Central America.

The Integral Heart Family

Stability is a key aspect in providing a solution to the wrath of poverty in Guatemala. Through the education center, *The Integral Heart Foundation* provides educational scholarships for 60 students to receive a compelling education and break out of a vicious cycle of generational poverty.

At the center they receive three healthy meals every day. After school, they participate in the following after school programs: Critical-Thinking, English, Spanish, History, Psychology, Homework Study, Art, and of course, Playtime!

But most important to their success, they are given love, individual attention and dependable adults in their life who they can count on. They have someone who they can show their grades who will say, "I'm proud of you."

Guatemala has some of the warmest and most open people I've ever met.

Our older students, when graduated, will have gone through our teacher training course to pass on their wisdom to younger students—Guatemalans solving the problems of Guatemala.

For more information or to help this great cause check out www.integralheartfamily.org.

Since its inception in 2011 the IHF family food program has provided over 2500 nutrition baskets to our sponsored families. In the first six months since the school opened in March of 2016 *The Integral Heart Foundation* has provided over 8400 meals to its students. Each copy sold of *Tales of the Modern Nomad*, will provide a full meal to one student.

INDEX

The travel journals that created this book.

ABOUT THE AUTHOR

JOHN EARLY is based out of his hometown Saskatoon, Saskatchewan. However, his world travels (like his writing and projects in life) always define new territory. Some of the roles John has taken on include emcee for major music festivals, national tour manager for Nintendo, social host on cruise ships in the Caribbean, touring on the 2010 Olympic Torch Relay across Canada and managing adventure travel tours in Asia and Central America. From Bangkok to Zapopan, a journal and his lactose-intolerant guitar, Norma, have always been at hand. John's formal education consists of a Bachelor of Commerce in Marketing and Management at the University of Saskatchewan and ESC Rouen, France. Since then, it has been John's decade of globe-trotting and the people he's encountered through which he has found his real education and reason to smile in life. This is his first book.

Follow John on Instagram @johntearly

WHERE IN THE WORLD ...
The places between these pages